Chronicles of King Arthur

THE LADY OF THE LAKE
TELLETH ARTHVR OF THE
SWORD EXCALIBVR

Chronicles of
King Arthur

Andrea Hopkins

BCA

LONDON   NEW YORK   SYDNEY   TORONTO

Conceived, edited and designed by Collins & Brown Limited

Editors: Sarah Hoggett and Juliet Gardiner
Picture Research: Philippa Lewis
Art Director: Roger Bristow
Designed by: David Fordham

Filmset by: Goodfellow & Egan, Cambridge
Reproduction by: Daylight, Singapore
Printed and bound in Italy

CONTENTS

INTRODUCTION 6

PART 1 ARTHUR AND MERLIN 11

PART 2 THE KNIGHTS OF THE ROUND TABLE 51
SIR GAWAIN AND THE GREEN KNIGHT 52
THE FIRST TALE OF SIR LANCELOT 69
TRISTAN AND ISOLDE 81
THE SECOND TALE OF SIR LANCELOT 99
THE QUEST OF THE HOLY GRAIL 115

PART 3 THE FALL OF KING ARTHUR 145

LIST OF PRINCIPAL CHARACTERS 190

GLOSSARY 191

PICTURE CREDITS 192

INTRODUCTION

THE LEGEND OF KING ARTHUR as we know it today was all written down in the High Middle Ages; by the 1240s it was complete, although it went on being retold well into the sixteenth century and in later Arthurian revivals. It purports to record the history of a British king who, in the fifth or sixth century, successfully managed to unify the disintegrating tribal kingdoms of Roman Britain and resist the Saxon invasion. During this time of peace and stability, King Arthur is supposed to have created a court of international renown for its military prowess and aristocratic culture. Is the legend true? We will probably never know for certain. Charlemagne, hero of another group of medieval romances (the *Matter of France*), was a real person whose life is amply recorded in historical documents. This is not so with Arthur.

The sources are scarce, and where they exist they cannot be taken as statements of fact; some are obviously contaminated with legendary material, and some are intended more as moral lessons than as records of historical fact. This is the case with the only surviving near contemporary account of British history, the *De excidio Britanniae* ('On the Ruin of Britain') by St Gildas. The point of this narrative was to demonstrate that the Saxons had been permitted by God to ruin Britain as a punishment for the sins of the British, and especially for the shortcomings of five of the petty kings whom Gildas names. Gildas seems to have written his book in about AD 545. In common with other historians, he reports that a British high king had invited a large number of Saxon mercenaries to settle in Britain in order to support him against internal strife, and that these troops subsequently mutinied and overran the lands of their former overlords. This king is clearly the character whom later historians call Vortigern.

The Welsh poetic tradition may have some bearing on the historical status of King Arthur, although it is now impossible to say exactly what or how much. Some of the Welsh poetry that survives is undoubtedly ancient, but it was not written down until many centuries after it was composed and surviving manuscripts are even later than that. At any stage in its long transmission, a poet or scribe may have added an interesting remark about King Arthur. For instance, there is a series of Welsh poems called the *Gododdin*, which records a battle fought at Catterick in Yorkshire where a British force was overwhelmed and killed by Saxons after a heroic resistance. A number of British warriors are celebrated in it, and one is compared with Arthur: 'he glutted black ravens on the rampart of the stronghold even though he was no Arthur.' This poem was originally composed in about AD 600, and if the reference to Arthur is genuine it shows that he was already famous, and specifically famous for killing large numbers of his enemies. Interestingly this tradition is also recorded in a text known as the *Historia Brittonum* by one Nennius. It was written shortly after AD 800, but it contains older material. Nennius seems to have compiled his text indiscriminately from many different sources.

Two more 'historical' mentions of Arthur occur in the *Annals of Wales*, an anonymous Latin chronicle compiled between about AD 960 and AD 980 from a number of older sources. Some of the material in this history is certainly very old. The years are numbered 1 to 533; year 1 is probably AD 445. The entries relating to Arthur are:

> *Year 72: the Battle of Badon in which Arthur bore the cross of Our Lord Jesus Christ on his shoulders for three days and nights, and the Britons were the victors.*
> *Year 93: the strife of Camlann in which Arthur and Medraut [Mordred] perished; and there was plague in Britain and Ireland.*

Although the *Annals* is notoriously unreliable about dates, everyone else named in it was a real person; but without other reliable records, this is not convincing evidence for the existence of Arthur and Mordred.

A small amount of archaeological evidence supports the story told so sparingly in the histories. There are signs that after the first raids and revolts by the Saxons, a British resistance did arise under organized leadership. Excavations in the 1960s and 1970s at Cadbury, originally an Iron Age hill fort, showed that it had been substantially refortified in the fifth century, and that it had enclosed and supported a court of quite impressive size. At that time, no similar refortifications of early sites had been investigated, and it was suggested that this could have been Camelot. This adds credence to the concept of a period of respite for the British against the slow advance of Saxon conquest, and it is also supported by another piece of historical evidence which may have a bearing on the possible identity of the real King Arthur.

All the fragmentary references so far refer to a story of heroic resistance to the Saxons. But in Geoffrey of Monmouth's *History of the Kings of Britain*, that part of the story is just a prelude to what follows, and although Geoffrey is not at all reliable as a historical source himself, he must have drawn on some source for his story of Arthur's continental campaigns. It so happens that reasonably reliable records have survived which tell of a British king who led an army into Gaul on behalf of the fragmenting Roman Empire to combat the invading forces of the Visigothic King Euric in AD 468. This king is known in the sources as Riothamus, a latinization of the British word Rigotamos, meaning 'high king'. This is clearly his title rather than his name, and it is tempting to speculate that his personal name might have been Arthur. Arthur is itself a British version of the Roman name Artorius.

Riothamus advanced with his army into Burgundy; he was subsequently betrayed by a deputy who made a pact with the Visigoths and, after a disastrous battle in which most of his army was killed, he escaped with a few trusted men and disappeared from the records.

Interestingly, the direction in which he was going when he escaped was towards a small town in Burgundy called Avallon. This took place between AD 468 and AD 470, during the reign of the Eastern Emperor Leo I. Geoffrey's only reference to a date for Arthur's war in Burgundy against Lucius Hiberius is that it happened in the reign of the Emperor Leo.

Not only did Geoffrey have access to some form of this story and repeat these features in his version of it, but a separate though not historical source also associates King Arthur with a campaign in Gaul. This is the Breton *Legend of St Goeznovius*, written by a person called William in 1019. This suggests that a separate tradition existed which identified the king known to history as Riothamus with Arthur, and that Geoffrey had access to some source material about him which is now lost. Arthur/ Riothamus could have been the king who united the British against the Saxons and refortified various strongholds in the west, before crossing to Gaul and fighting against the Visigoths for Rome. But unless a dramatic and conclusive piece of new evidence turns up somewhere, we will never know for certain.

King Arthur features in a number of surviving Welsh poems and prose stories and is known to have been mentioned in more that have not survived. It is clear that a whole complex of stories about Arthur and his knights and their deeds had grown up sometime between AD 600 and AD 1100, but because of the great difficulty of dating the material, as mentioned earlier, this development cannot be exactly traced. Much of what the poems and stories have to tell is radically different from the 'historical' fragments examined above, and also different from the account given by Geoffrey of Monmouth. But it is crucial to an appreciation of medieval Arthurian literature; most of the great medieval romances were based, however distantly, on the old Celtic tales and, although their authors recast the tales in the glittering clothes of contemporary courtly culture, the aura of mystery, magic, prodigy and peril, the otherworldly strangeness of Celtic myth can often be glimpsed as a shadowy form beneath that brilliant surface.

There is good evidence that 'British' stories about King Arthur were in circulation before Geoffrey of Monmouth immortalized him in *History of the Kings of Britain*. William of Malmesbury wrote *De gestis regum Anglorum* ('Deeds of the English Kings') in 1125, ten years before Geoffrey's book. He repeats the testimony of Nennius that Arthur helped Aurelius Ambrosius to repel the Saxons.

Most fascinating and mysterious of all, though, is the Arthurian relief carved into the archivolt over the north door of Modena Cathedral in Italy. The carving shows a moated castle in which a lady is being held prisoner by a man. All the characters are identified by names carved above them; these two are 'Winlogee' and 'Mardoc'. To the left of the castle a man called 'Burmaltus', who is armed with an axe or hammer, defends it against three mounted knights, two of whom are named as 'Isdernus' and 'Artus de Bretania'. To the right of the castle, a knight named 'Carrado' is riding out of the gate to attack another knight, 'Galvagin', behind whom ride 'Galvariun' and 'Che'. The carving is early twelfth century, probably between 1120 and 1140, but even if it is contemporary with or later than Geoffrey of Monmouth (1136), it clearly contains characters and an incident which do not appear in the *History of the Kings of Britain*, and must have been based on some other Arthurian source.

Geoffrey of Monmouth's book *History of the Kings of Britain* was written by about 1136. His aim was to trace the lineal descent of British kings from the legendary founder of Britain, Brut, the grandson of Aeneas of Troy. Most medieval historians accepted Geoffrey of Monmouth's account as genuine, though a few were healthily sceptical. Geoffrey's book filled a great gap in available knowledge about the past of the British, and filled it in a most acceptable way—with a past that was glorious, full of heroic endeavour and martial prowess. His book was an immediate success; it is clear that it was being copied within a very short time of its completion, and today well over 200 manuscripts are known, a huge number for a medieval work.

We know that Arthur was already famous before Geoffrey wrote his book; he was known through the orally transmitted popular tales of the Bretons and Welsh. Without Geoffrey of Monmouth, King Arthur might have remained a figure in oral culture, unsophisticated, popular, half-mythical—and he might have survived into the present as a shadowy figure whose story was transmitted in a garbled form through ballads and folk tales, like that of Robin Hood. Geoffrey of Monmouth gave King Arthur respectability, making him legitimate source material for the educated and sophisticated romancers, with the result that half of the finest masterpieces of medieval vernacular literature are Arthurian romances.

Medieval romances first appeared during what is now known as the 'twelfth-century renaissance'—when Europe was seething with new ideas, particularly in religion, theology and philosophy. These widespread intellectual developments paralleled the new emphasis on individual aspirations and achievement which we see in the romances.

Most romances took their stories from three central cycles of subject matter: the *Matter of France*, the *Matter of Rome* and the *Matter of Britain*, most popular and often retold of all, the stories of King Arthur and his knights.

By the final quarter of the twelfth century, the new literary mode in France had already found a master who would never be surpassed—Chrétien de Troyes. Two of his five surviving poems, *Lancelot* and *Perceval*, were possibly the most influential romances written in the Middle Ages. *Lancelot* introduced the character of Sir Lancelot and the subject of his long love affair with Queen Guinevere; subsequently his story became absolutely central to the Arthurian cycle. *Perceval* was the first surviving written version of the Grail legend and, though Chrétien did not live to finish it, the fragment that he wrote was continued by four other poets and inspired all subsequent versions until the *Queste del Saint Graal*. In particular, a group of brilliant young German poets, most of whom were *ministeriales*—unfree knights bound to the service of their lords—translated his work into German.

It was a small step from writing several complementary tales, all set in the framework of King Arthur's court and referring to the same characters and stories, to collecting them into a coherent sequence, a cycle. The first poet to do this seriously was Robert de Boron, in the early years of the thirteenth century, who began a very detailed elaboration of the history of the Holy Grail in his trilogy of poems, *Joseph d'Arimathie*, *Merlin* and *Perceval*. Of these only the first and a fragment of the second have survived, but soon after they were written they were adapted into prose by an anonymous writer; and this in turn gave rise to the huge sequence of prose romances now known as the Vulgate Cycle. This great collection was complete before 1240. It included the Vulgate *Merlin*, telling of Arthur's conception, birth and upbringing, his coming to the throne, securing his kingdom, founding the Round Table and early adventures, the prose *Lancelot*, a massive work covering most of the central years of Arthur's reign; *La Queste del Saint Graal* and the *Mort le roi Artu*, recounting the quest for the Holy Grail and the downfall of the Round Table and the 'death' of the king. These romances are not by same author, but they were certainly adapted from their originals by a group of writers who knew what they were doing and intended to make a coherent cycle.

In England, as might be expected, Arthurian romance was very popular. Over half the surviving English romances are about individual knights and their adventures; of these, by far the most popular hero is Sir Gawain. By contrast Sir Lancelot, the supreme hero of French romance, features in only one surviving poem, the Scottish *Lancelot of the Laik*. Not until Sir Thomas Malory did anyone try either to translate the Vulgate Cycle or to compile their own coherent sequence of Arthurian romances; and Malory did it, he explained, because in his time (1450s-1460s) many gentlemen were no longer able to read French.

Malory cut out a great deal of long rambling material from his French sources and cunningly incorporated new material from English sources. It seems likely that this was done over a period of years, and in separate books, though clearly he had conceived of the whole cycle from the beginning.

Chronicles of King Arthur is a retelling of the great medieval story-cycle known as the *Matter of Britain*. It presents for the first time the most powerful and dramatic episodes of the story in the voices of their original medieval authors. The principal sources of this book are the prose Vulgate Cycle (*Merlin*, *Lancelot*, *La Queste del Saint Graal*, *Mort Artu*) and the *Morte Darthur* of Sir Thomas Malory; but it also incorporates some of the most brilliant and moving stories and scenes from many other poems and tales, in which the voices of their authors can be heard each in his own style, from the wit and precision of Chrétien de Troyes to the stark dignity of Malory.

Author's Note

Wherever possible I have used the original text, printed in italics, with the source indicated in the margin each time there is a change of author. Unitalicised text is my own and is either a close paraphrase, in which I have condensed the material, or a linking passage summarising the story. Most of the sources used—the poems of Chrétien de Troyes, the *Tristan* of Gottfried von Strassburg, the Middle English *Sir Gawain and the Green Knight*, the Old French *Mort Artu* and *Lancelot*—are available in good English translations, though many are dauntingly long. But some, such as the Vulgate *Merlin*, or the Middle English *Morte Arthur*, are translated here for the first time.

ARTHVR AND
THE STRANGE
MANTLE

PART I
ARTHUR & MERLIN

THIS FIRST PART OF THE CYCLE is mainly concerned with Arthur himself – it tells of his conception, his birth and upbringing, the marvel of the Sword in the Stone, his wars to secure the throne and against the Saxons, his marriage to Guinevere and founding of the Fellowship of the Round Table, the sword Excalibur, the tale of Sir Balin, the beguiling of Merlin by the damsel Nimue, the plot to kill Arthur by his half-sister Morgan le Fay.

The begetting of Arthur, cunningly engineered by Merlin, is recounted in some detail by Geoffrey of Monmouth in his *History of the Kings of Britain*, so I have used that as my source for this section. For the episode of the Sword in the Stone I used the Old French Vulgate *Merlin*, *Suite de Merlin* and Malory's *Morte Darthur*; for Arthur's encounter with King Pellinore and the acquisition of Excalibur Malory's account is supplemented by the more detailed *Suite de Merlin*, but I have relied exclusively on Malory for the moving tale of the doomed knight Sir Balin, the Knight with the Two Swords. Here Malory anticipates the Quest of the Holy Grail by giving the history of the Dolorous Stroke, which maims the Fisher King and lays his country to waste until he can be healed by the Grail Knight in years to come; it also anticipates the destruction of the Round Table in civil war, through the fatal conflict of Sir Balin and his brother Sir Balan.

THE BEGETTING OF ARTHUR

D URING THE REIGN of King Uther Pendragon there was a powerful duke named Gorlois of Cornwall. One Easter, King Uther invited all the lords and nobles of his kingdom to a feast in London, bidding them bring their wives and daughters too.

Among the others came Gorlois Duke of Cornwall with his wife Igraine, whose beauty surpassed that of all the other women in Britain. When the king observed her there among the other ladies he became suddenly inflamed with passion and, ignoring all the others, he focused his whole attention on her. He plied her with dishes of food, and to her he sent his own personal attendants, with wine in golden goblets. He smiled at her and flirted with her all the time. When her husband observed this, he was very angry and he left the court at once without taking leave … Then Uther too became angry and ordered him to return to the court so that he could exact reparation for the insult. When it became obvious that Gorlois was not coming, Uther was consumed with rage and swore that he would devastate Gorlois's lands and people unless Gorlois made a full apology at once.

The king gathered a huge army together without delay and set off for the province of Cornwall, where he burned down both cities and castles. But Gorlois was not eager to engage the king in battle, because his own army was very much smaller. For that reason he chose to fortify his castles until he could get help from Ireland. And since he was more anxious for his wife than for himself, he placed her in the castle of Tintagel on the sea coast, which was the best defended refuge he had. He himself entered the castle of Dimilioc. When this was reported to the king, he went to the castle where Gorlois was, laid siege to it, and cut off all access to it.

At length, when several days had passed, the king found his love for Igraine was much on his mind and he called Sir Ulfin Ridcaradoch, a fellow-warrior and an old friend, and revealed what was upsetting him in these words: 'I am burning up with love for Igraine, and in my opinion if I cannot have her I shall be in mortal danger. Advise me how I can satisfy my desire, or I shall die.'

'What use would advice be?' answered Sir Ulfin, 'since no force can enable us to get near her where she is in the fortress of Tintagel? For it is built by the sea, which encloses it on all sides, and there is no other way in, except that offered by a narrow rock path. Three men at arms could hold it against you, even if you took your stand

Geoffrey of Monmouth, *The History of the Kings of Britain.*

Leaving the court without first asking the king's permission was an act of open insubordination, a challenge to the king's authority, which could not go unpunished.

BELOW: *King Uther Pendragon enjoying the favours of Lady Igraine from Geoffrey of Monmouth's* History of the Kings of Britain.

TINTAGEL

Tintagel, Cornwall.

THE RUINS OF TINTAGEL CASTLE are among the most romantic in Europe, perched high up on a rocky promontory off the north coast of Cornwall. According to Geoffrey of Monmouth, this was where King Arthur was conceived. Evidently Geoffrey was familiar with the site of Tintagel Castle, for he describes it accurately as surrounded on all sides by the sea and accessible only via a narrow spit of rock, which could be successfully defended against an army by three men at arms.

The point of the story is that Tintagel is utterly inaccessible and can only be penetrated by guile. At the time Geoffrey was writing (in the 1130s) the promontory was connected to the mainland by a high rocky ridge; this has since crumbled away and today has been replaced by a wooden bridge and stairs. But the present castle did not exist; it was begun not earlier than 1141 by Reginald Earl of Cornwall.

There were other ruins on the promontory, but they were not visible in the twelfth century. Covered by soil, they were excavated in the 1930s, when they were interpreted as the remains of a Celtic monastic community. However, pottery fragments found at the site were identified as imported pieces from the eastern Mediterranean, dating from the fifth and sixth centuries. It has since been suggested that a chieftain's stronghold would have been a more appropriate setting for these high-quality wares than a monastery. Geoffrey may have been recording a local tradition with some basis in fact.

with the whole kingdom of Britain to help you. But if only the prophet Merlin would agree to help, I really think that by his counsel you could achieve your desire.'

Believing this, the king ordered Merlin to be summoned without delay … When Merlin discovered the agony the king was suffering for the sake of Igraine, he was moved by so great a passion. ❧ Merlin said to him, 'Sir, I know everything that is in your heart; and if you will swear to do as I say by your faith as annointed king, you shall have your desire.' The king swore

❧ Sir Thomas Malory, *Morte Darthur.*

by the four Evangelists. 'Sir', said Merlin, 'this is my desire: the first night that you lie with Igraine you will beget a child on her and, when it is born, it must be delivered up to me, to bring up as I shall see fit.'

'Whatever you want, I agree,' said the king.

'Make ready,' said Merlin, 'for tonight you shall lie with Igraine in the castle of Tintagel, and you shall be exactly like her husband the duke. Sir Ulfin will be like Sir Brastias, and I will be like Sir Jordans, the duke's companion. Make sure that you do not speak much to her or to her men, but say you are ill and go straight to bed.'

So King Uther and Sir Ulfin and Merlin took certain drugs and changed themselves into the likeness of Duke Gorlois and his men, and set off for Tintagel. Duke Gorlois saw the king leave his camp and came out to harass the king's host while he was gone; and in the battle that followed he was slain, even before Uther arrived at Tintagel. Meanwhile, Uther was admitted to the castle, because everyone thought he was the duke.

᷏ *The king remained the whole night with Igraine and restored himself by making love to her. That night she conceived Arthur, the most renowned of men, who afterwards became famous for his outstanding bravery.*

᷏ *So, after the death of the duke, King Uther lay with Igraine more than three hours. Before daybreak, Merlin came to the king and bade him make ready, and so he kissed the lady Igraine and departed in all haste. But when the lady heard tell of the duke her husband and how by report he was dead before ever King Uther came to her, then she marvelled who it might be that lay with her in the likeness of her lord. So she mourned privily and held her peace.*

After Uther's victory over Gorlois, his barons advised him to marry Igraine so as to make peace with her, and he was very happy to do so. After nine months, Igraine gave birth to a baby boy, and Merlin came to remind Uther of his promise. Uther gave up the baby to Merlin, to bring up as he saw fit; and Merlin took the baby to a good knight named Sir Ector, to be nourished and taught as one of his own children.

THE SWORD IN THE STONE

AFTER UTHER'S DEATH several years later, all the powerful nobles of the realm fought one another for the throne, till at last Merlin advised the Archbishop of Canterbury to call all the lords together in London at Christmastime so that Christ on the feast of his birth might show them by some miracle who should be king.

᷏ *The day before Christmas all the clergy and all the nobles of rank assembled together in London just as Merlin had instructed them ... they all went to hear divine service on Christmas Day ... and there were so*

Side notes:

᷏ Geoffrey of Monmouth, *The History of the Kings of Britain.*

᷏ Sir Thomas Malory, *Morte Darthur.*

᷏ Anon, Vulgate *Merlin.*

many people that they had to stand outside the church in the square. And there appeared in front of the church a stone, and no one knew what kind of stone it was. In the midst of this stone was set an anvil of iron a foot high, and through this anvil a sword had been thrust right into the stone. And when those who were outside the church saw this, they said it was a great marvel and they ran and told the archbishop. When he heard it, he came to the stone and knelt down before it. There he read the letters of gold inscribed in the stone: 'Whoso pulleth out this sword from this stone and anvil is true-born king of all England.' The archbishop told the people what the letters said. Then … they began to ask one another who should try to draw out the sword first …

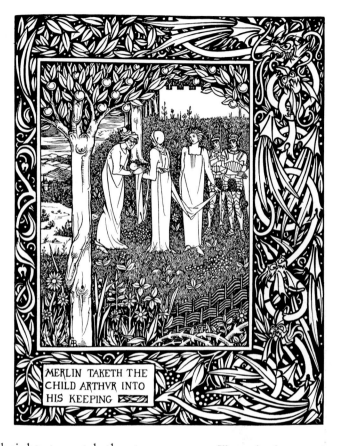

MERLIN TAKETH THE CHILD ARTHVR INTO HIS KEEPING

and to quarrel with one another. The archbishop came and rebuked them sternly. He then chose 250 of the noblest knights who were there and let them make the attempt; but none of them was able to draw out the sword. And, when they had all tried, he ordered others to try, but no one among them could even move it. Then the archbishop charged ten knights to watch the stone and it was proclaimed that there should be a great tourney on New Year's Day when any man who wished might try to draw the sword.

On New Year's Day all the barons went to mass and then to their hostels to dine, and after they had eaten all the knights came together before the town to joust. All the townspeople ran to watch, and the ten knights guarding the stone left their posts to see the mêlée.

Sir Ector had had his eldest son Kay knighted at All Saints. When the mêlée had begun Sir Kay called his brother Arthur to him and said, 'Go to my hostel and find my sword.'

Though untaught, the boy was valiant and courteous, and he replied, 'Willingly, Sir.' He came to the hostel to search for his brother's sword or another, but everyone had gone to watch the jousting, so he could not get in and he began to weep with anger. Then he passed by the front of the church where the stone was, and he saw the sword. He thought that if he could have it, he could take it to his brother. So he got down from his horse, took the sword by the hilt, drew it out and carefully stowed it in his coat.

His brother, who was waiting for him before the town, came to meet him and asked for his sword. Arthur said that he could not find it, but that he had brought another, and drew it out from under his coat. Kay asked

ABOVE: *Illustration by Aubrey Beardsley.*

Anon, Suite de Merlin.

15

ABOVE: *Arthur draws the sword from the stone, from a rare medieval illustration.*

✤ Sir Thomas Malory, *Morte Darthur.*

RIGHT: *Arthur depicted as a mighty ruler: the crowns represent his thirty kingdoms. From* The Chronicle of Peter Langcroft.

him where he had got it, and Arthur told him that it was the sword from the stone. Kay took it, put it under the flap of his coat and went to look for his father. When he found him, he said, 'Sir, I must be the king; for see, the sword from the stone!'

When Ector saw it he was astonished and asked where Kay had got it from. Kay said he had taken it out of the stone. When Ector heard his son say this, he did not believe him and said he knew he was lying. Then they went to the church together, with the other boy behind them. On seeing the stone from which the sword had been drawn, Ector said, 'Kay, do not lie to me. How did you pull out this sword? For if you are lying to me, I shall never love you again.'

Then Kay replied as if he were ashamed, and said, 'Sir, I will not lie to you any more. Arthur my brother brought me the sword, and I do not know how he had it.' …

Ector looked behind him and saw Arthur and said, 'Fair son, come here, take the sword and put it back where you took it from.' And Arthur took the sword and replaced it in the anvil, and the iron closed over it just as it had before. 'How did you get this sword?' said Ector to Arthur.

✤ 'Sir, I will tell you. When I came home for my brother's sword, I found nobody at home and so I thought my brother Kay should not be swordless, and I came here eagerly and pulled out the sword without pains.'

'Now,' said Sir Ector, 'I understand you must be king of this land.'

'Why me?' said Arthur, 'for what cause?'

'Sir,' said Sir Ector, 'because God wills it so, for no man should have drawn out this sword unless he were the true-born king of this land. Now let me see whether you can pull it out again.'

'That is no mastery,' said Arthur.

Sir Ector tried to pull out the sword and failed. 'Now you try,' said Sir Ector to Sir Kay. And Kay pulled at the sword with all his strength, but it would not stir. 'Now you shall try,' said Sir Ector to Arthur.

'Willingly,' said Arthur, and pulled it out easily. And there and then Sir Ector knelt down to the earth, and Sir Kay. 'Alas,' said Arthur, 'my own dear father and brother, why do you kneel to me?'

'Nay, my lord Arthur, it is not so. I was never your father nor of your blood, but I know now that you are of higher blood than I thought. Sir,' said Sir Ector, 'will you be my good and gracious lord when you are king?'

'I should be much to blame otherwise,' said Arthur, 'for you are the man in the world that I am most beholden to, and my good lady and mother your wife, who has fostered and kept me as well as her own son. And if ever

GEOFFREY OF MONMOUTH

GEOFFREY OF MONMOUTH was a prominent clergyman who lived in Oxford from 1129, when he signed his name to the foundation charter of Oseney Abbey, until 1152, when he was consecrated Bishop of St Asaph in Wales. In late 1153 he witnessed the Treaty of Westminster between King Stephen and Henry of Anjou; Welsh chronicles record that he died in 1155.

Geoffrey tells us that he had a friend called Walter the Archdeacon of Oxford, who was 'most learned in all branches of history', and who gave him 'a certain very ancient book written in the British tongue' which was his principal source for the *History of the Kings of Britain*. This book no longer exists, and some scholars doubt that it ever did. Geoffrey may have used the term 'book' loosely to refer to disparate source material, including Welsh histories and genealogies and oral legends about King Arthur that he heard from his friend Walter.

Geoffrey wrote a powerful piece of propaganda. His chief aim was to restore the reputation of the conquered British, usually at the expense of the Romans. Geoffrey is immensely, sometimes embarrassingly pro-British; he pretends that the Roman conquest of Britain did not happen, and he has his fictional British king Belinus sack Rome itself, some hundreds of years before King Arthur's time.

A large part of the legend had already taken shape in Geoffrey's work — the mysterious prophet and magician Merlin; Arthur's conception and birth; his marriage to Guinevere; his sword Excalibur; his four great knights, Sir Gawain, Sir Bedivere the Cupbearer, Sir Kay the Seneschal and Sir Cador of Cornwall; his betrayal by Mordred; their final battle at Camlann; and his disappearance, mortally wounded, to the Isle of Avalon. Geoffrey gathered much of this material from legends and stories that were already circulating widely in Britain and abroad, but to this he added a lot of pseudo-historical material about wars and treaties and battles, polishing his Celtic source material with overtones of courtly manners and chivalry. The result was one of the most influential books in the history of European literature and one which became widely accepted as a genuine account of King Arthur's life.

Seneschal: the steward in charge of a great medieval household. This was the most important of a number of household offices such as marshal, butler, cupbearer, etc., which in a king's household would be held by great nobles.

it be God's will that I be king as you say, desire of me what I can do for you, and I shall not fail you, God forbid I should fail you.'

'Sir,' said Sir Ector, 'I will ask no more of you but that you will make my son, Sir Kay your foster brother, seneschal of all your lands.'

'That shall be done, and more,' said Arthur, 'by the faith of my body, no man shall ever have that office but he, while he and I live.'

They went to the archbishop and explained how the sword had been achieved. All the barons and knights met together again on Twelfth Night and they all tried to draw the sword, but no one could remove it from the stone except Arthur. The lords were very angry about this and said that they would not accept for their king a mere boy who was not of noble blood. So they put off the decision until Candlemas, but nothing changed; no one but Arthur could draw the sword. Once more they delayed until Easter, and then again until Pentecost. At Pentecost, before all the lords and all the common people, Arthur pulled out the sword from the stone once more, and all the people cried out: 'We will have Arthur for our king! Let there be no more delay — we see it is God's will that he shall be our king, and if anyone tries to prevent it we will kill him!' They all begged Arthur's forgiveness for delaying him so long. Arthur was knighted by the best man present, and then the archbishop crowned him king, and he swore to be a true king and to uphold justice all the days of his life.

EXCALIBUR

MANY KINGS AND LORDS could not agree to acknowledge Arthur as king over all of them. King Lot of Orkney, King Uriens of Gore, King Nentres of Garlot, the king of Scotland, the king with the hundred knights, the king of Carados and others all made war against Arthur and fought long and hard to overcome him. Arthur made an alliance with King Ban of Benwick and King Bors of Gaul and, after several years of fighting, he managed to subdue the whole country to his rule, including Scotland and Wales.

After he had returned to Caerleon, Queen Morgawse of Orkney, King Lot's wife, came to visit him, pretending to be a messenger from her husband, but really spying on him.

Because she was a very beautiful lady, the king cast great love unto her, and desired to lie by her; so they were agreed, and he begot Mordred upon her. And she was his sister on his mother's side. She stayed a month and then departed, but all this time King Arthur did not know that she was his sister.

Not long afterwards, King Arthur heard that King Pellinore, the knight of the fountain was challenging all comers to joust with him and had already wounded or killed several good knights. King Arthur armed himself in his finest armour and rode to meet the knight. 'Why do you prevent knights from riding along this road unless they fight with you? I advise you to stop this custom,' said Arthur.

'I shall do as I please,' replied the knight,' and if anyone doesn't like my custom, let him try to change it.'

'I will change it,' said Arthur, and they got ready to joust. They broke three spears against their armour, and then Arthur was unhorsed, so they continued to fight on foot. They fought long, till their armour was hacked to

BELOW: *The Coronation of King Arthur. A woodcut from Guiron le Courtois.*

ABOVE: *Arthur in bed with Queen Morgause, the wife of King Lot, and, unknown to Arthur, his own half-sister.*

pieces and the ground all stained with blood. In the end, King Pellinore had wrested Arthur to the ground, had pulled off his helmet and was about to strike off his head, when Merlin appeared and said:

'Knight, hold your hand, for if you slay that knight you will put this realm into great danger.'

'Why, who is he?' said the knight.

'It is King Arthur,' replied Merlin.

Then the knight would have slain King Arthur for dread of his wrath, and heaved up his sword; but at that Merlin cast an enchantment on the knight, so that he fell to the earth in a great sleep. Then Merlin took up King Arthur, and rode on the knight's horse.

'Alas!' said Arthur, 'what have you done, Merlin? Have you slain this knight by your crafts? There lived not a more worshipful knight than he was; I would gladly lose a year's income to have him alive.'

'Don't worry,' said Merlin, 'he is better off than you; he is only asleep and will awake in three hours ...' Right so he and the king departed, and went to a hermit who was a good man and a great healer. The hermit cleaned all Arthur's wounds and gave him good salves. The king was there three days and, when his wounds were healing so well that he could ride, they departed.

And as they rode, Arthur said, 'I have no sword.'

⁓ 'Cease to trouble,' said Merlin. 'I know of only one good sword in this whole land; it is in a lake inhabited by faeries. If you are able to gain this sword, it will last you through to the end.'

'Ah, fair Merlin,' said the king, 'can you obtain this sword for me?'

'I can only tell you where it is,' replied Merlin ... They rode close by the sea, then Merlin turned left towards a mountain, and thus they came to a lake. 'How does the water look to you?' asked Merlin.

'It looks extremely deep,' replied Arthur, 'and as if no man could enter it without perishing.'

'You speak correctly,' said Merlin. 'No man has entered it without the permission of the faeries and not died as a consequence. Yet know that in this lake is the good sword of which I told you.'

'In this lake?' said the king, 'and how may it be achieved?'

'That you will see soon enough,' answered Merlin, 'if God wills it.' While they were speaking in this manner, they looked into the centre of the lake and saw a sword appear from beneath the waters, held aloft by a hand and arm clad in white samite. 'There you can see,' said Merlin, 'the sword of which I told you, the same sword that you will carry.'

As he spoke they saw a damsel coming towards them over the surface of the water. 'What damsel is that?' said Arthur.

'That is the Lady of the Lake,' said Merlin. 'Within the lake is a rock, and inside it is the fairest palace on earth, and richly furnished; and this damsel will come to you soon. You should speak fair to her, so that she will give you the sword.'

And straight away the damsel came to King Arthur, and greeted him, and he her. 'Damsel,' said Arthur, 'what sword is that, that yonder arm holds above the water? I wish it were mine, for I have no sword.'

'Sir Arthur, King,' said the damsel, 'that sword is mine, and it is called Excalibur, which is to say, Cut-steel. And if you will give me a gift when I ask it of you, you shall have it.'

'By my faith,' said Arthur, 'I will give you whatever gift you may ask.'

'Well,' said the damsel, 'go into that barge, and row your-

⁓ Anon, *Suite de Merlin*.

BELOW: *Arthur receives the sword from the Lady of the Lake. An engraving by Daniel Maclise.*

21

EXCALIBUR AND OTHER MAGICAL SWORDS

EXCALIBUR IS THE NAME of Arthur's sword. Some authors, including Malory, are confused on this point, but Excalibur is not in fact the sword that Arthur miraculously drew out of the stone, which signified to everyone that he was the true king. That sword was broken in two during his combat with King Pellinore. Excalibur is the sword he was later given by the Lady of the Lake; a sword of destiny, which can be wielded only by the king.

Part of the confusion arises because there are several magical swords in the cycle of stories, and some of them play important parts in the structure of the narrative. The Sword in the Stone can only be drawn by the true king, and is thus instrumental in bringing Arthur to his throne. Excalibur symbolizes the well-being of

the kingdom and the qualities of the Round Table fellowship; the Lady instructs Arthur carefully to return it when his life is done. One of the most poignant and mysterious scenes in the whole cycle is that in which Sir Bedivere, at first disobeying the dying king's instructions, finally returns the sword to its mysterious owner.

Another magical sword appears, magically bound to the side of the Damsel of the Lake; the fated knight Balin draws it, thus becoming the Knight with the Two Swords. Merlin takes this sword after Balin's death and prophecies that one day it will be wielded by Sir Galahad, the knight destined to achieve the Holy Grail.

Illustration by Aubrey Beardsley.

self to the sword, and take it and the scabbard with you; I will ask for my gift when I see my time.'

So Arthur and Merlin dismounted and tied their horses to two trees, and they went into the barge, and when they came to the sword that the hand held up, Sir Arthur ❧ *took it up by the hilt, and the hand and arm went under the water.*

And they came back to land, but the damsel was nowhere to be seen, and they rode on.

❧ Malory refers to Arthur as 'Sir' because he is adventuring as a knight rather than ruling as a king.

And Sir Arthur looked at the sword and he liked it passing well.

'Which do you like better,' said Merlin, 'the sword, or the scabbard?'

'I like the sword better,' answered Arthur.

'You are the more unwise,' said Merlin, 'for the scabbard is worth ten of the sword; for while you have the scabbard upon you, you shall never lose a drop of blood, however sorely wounded you may be, and therefore keep the scabbard always with you.'. . .

So they came to Caerleon, of which his knights were passing glad. And when they heard of his adventures, they marvelled that he would hazard his person in this way, alone. But all men of worship said that it was merry to be under such a chieftain, that would put his person in adventure as other poor knights did.

BALIN, OR THE KNIGHT WITH THE
TWO SWORDS

BEFORE LONG, a messenger came to Caerleon from King Rience of North Wales, with a message for King Arthur. And the message was this: that King Rience had vanquished eleven kings, and had made them cut off their beards, which he had used to trim his mantle. There was now space left for a twelfth beard, and King Rience demanded Arthur's beard to fill it, or else he would invade the country, burning and slaying all in his path, and take by force both beard and head. King Arthur replied that this was a shameful and villainous message for one king to send to another, and that although his beard was as yet too scant to make a good trimming for a mantle, he defied King Rience to come and fetch it for himself. Then he made ready for war.

While he was busy with the preparations, there arrived a damsel who had come from the Lady of the Lake. The damsel was girt with a noble sword, and she said: 'This sword gives me great sorrow and annoyance, but it cannot be taken from me except by a knight who is an outstanding warrior, who is without villainy or treachery.

BELOW: *The knight Balin successfully draws the sword from its scabbard. Woodcut from a late 16th-century edition of* Morte Darthur.

THE LADY OF THE LAKE

A CURSORY GLANCE at any collected version of the Arthurian legends quickly shows that there is not one Lady of the Lake, but several. The first Lady of the Lake to appear in the sequence (*Suite de Merlin*) is the one who gives the sword Excalibur to Arthur, and asks him in return to grant her whatever she requests. Subsequently this lady is rudely decapitated by Sir Balin, the Knight with the Two Swords, after she requests his head from Arthur. This lady is therefore unlikely to be the same one as the lady who appears in later tales.

Then there is the Lady of the Lake who kidnapped Sir Lancelot as a small child and brought him up with her in her magical underwater kingdom, instructing him in all the skills and obligations of knighthood (*Prose Lancelot*). This is the same lady mentioned by Chrétien de Troyes as the faery who had brought Lancelot up and given him a magic ring.

Thirdly, there is the Lady of the Lake, variously named as Niniane, Viviane or Nimue, who beguiles and enchants Merlin (*Vulgate Merlin*, *Suite de Merlin*, etc.). Having sealed the living Merlin in his tomb, this lady takes over some of his functions as magical protector, and immediately hastens off to save King Arthur from the evil plots of his sister Morgan le Fay.

Finally there is a group of ladies who collect the dying Arthur after the Battle of Camlann and sail away with him to the Isle of Avalon.

These reflect confused and jumbled versions of a number of Celtic tale elements. It is not surprising that these disparate elements fail to make up one consistent character.

'The Damsel of the Lake called Nimue the Enchantress'. Painting by the Victorian artist, Frank Cadogan Cowper.

Arthur promised that he and all his knights would try to draw the sword; and all the best and bravest knights of the court made the attempt one by one, but none succeeded. At last there came a poorly dressed knight, called Balin. At the first touch of his hand it left the scabbard and when he saw the sword, it pleased him greatly.

'Truly,' said the damsel, 'this is a passing good knight, the best that ever I found ... Now, gentle knight, give me the sword again.'

'Not so,' said Balin, 'for I will keep this sword, unless it is taken from me by force.'

LEFT: *A damsel at King Arthur's Court, French pre-1500 by the Master of the* Roman de la Rose.

'You are not wise to keep the sword,' said the damsel, 'for with that sword you will slay the best friend you have and the man you love most in the world, and the sword shall be your destruction.'

And Balin said, 'I will take the adventure that God will ordain for me, but you shall not have the sword, by the faith of my body.'

Then the damsel went away, grieving and lamenting. Balin took leave of the king, who was sorry to see him go, and promised to be better friends with him thereafter.

While Balin was preparing for his departure, the Lady of the Lake herself arrived at the court. She came on horseback, richly arrayed, and saluted King Arthur. She asked of him the gift that he had promised her when she gave him the sword Excalibur. 'Truly I did promise you a gift,' said King Arthur. 'Ask what you want, and I will give it to you, if it lies within my power.'

And the lady said, 'I want the head of the knight that won the sword, or else the head of the damsel that brought it; for he slew my brother, a good knight and true, and she caused my father's death.'

'I cannot grant either of their heads with honour,' replied King Arthur. 'Ask for something else and you shall have it.'

'I do not require anything else,' replied the Lady of the Lake.

Just then Balin caught sight of the lady; she had slain his mother and he had been searching for her for three years. When he learned that she had asked for his head, he went straight up to her and said, 'You evil creature! You would have my head, and therefore you shall lose yours!' And with one stroke of his sword, he smote off her head in the presence of King Arthur.

'For shame! What have you done?' cried the king. 'You have shamed me for ever, for I was beholden to this lady, and she came here under my safe-conduct; I shall never forgive you for this.'

'Sir,' said Balin, 'she was an evil enchantress who had destroyed many good knights, and she caused my mother to be burned to death by her lies and treachery.'

'Even so,' answered King Arthur, 'you should have forborne to pursue your quarrel with her here in my court. Get out of my sight.'

Balin took up the lady's head and rode out of the court. He gave the head to his squire and told him to take it to his home in Northumberland, so that his family and friends should know that their enemy was dead. 'What will you do, sir?' asked the squire.

'I shall ride as fast as I can to King Rience and do my best to kill him,' said Balin. 'If I can succeed, perhaps King Arthur will forgive me.' And he rode forth.

With Merlin's advice and the help of his brother Balan, Balin managed to capture King Rience as he rode out one night to visit his mistress. Balin and Balan escorted King Rience to Arthur's court *and there delivered him to the porters, and charged them with him; and they two returned to the forest in the dawning of the day.*

King Arthur came then to King Rience and said, 'Sir king, you are welcome: by what adventure came you hither?'

'Sir,' said King Rience, 'I came hither by a hard adventure.'

'Who won you?' said King Arthur.

'Sir,' said the king, 'the knight with the two swords and his brother, which are two marvellous knights of prowess.'

'I know them not,' said Arthur, 'but I am much beholden to them.'

'Ah,' said Merlin, 'I shall tell you: it is Balin who achieved the sword, and Balan his brother, a good knight.'

Then Merlin warned King Arthur that King Rience's brother Nero would soon attack him with a huge army, and advised him to prepare for battle.

The next day Nero was in the field with an army of ten battalions, with many more people than Arthur had. Arthur and his knights fought heroically and did marvellous deeds that day, and Arthur himself slew twenty knights and maimed forty. Balin and Balan appeared on King Arthur's side and fought so well that all men wondered at them, whether they were angels from heaven or demons from hell. Nero's army was worsted in battle; but then came his ally King Lot of Orkney, who had lately been one of Arthur's knights, and fought on Nero's side. King Lot was a good king and a great knight, but he opposed King Arthur because the king had lain with his wife, Queen Morgawse, and got her with child. King Lot fought wondrously that day and it was hard to know which army would win the field; but then came King Pellinore, and he smote a mighty stroke on King Lot as he fought, and cleaved through his helmet and head right down to the eyebrows. And all the host of Orkney fled because their king had been killed, and King Arthur won the day. There were slain at that battle twelve kings on the side of King Lot and Nero, and all were buried with great ceremony the next day.

BELOW: *An early 16th-century woodcut of knights in battle.*

THE DOLOROUS STROKE

IT CHANCED ON THE DAY AFTER the funeral of the twelve kings that King Arthur felt somewhat ill, and was resting in a pavilion in a meadow. He looked out of his pavilion and saw a knight pass by making loud lamentations. He asked the knight what ailed him but the knight would not answer him and rode on. Then Balin came to visit him, and King Arthur greeted him and made him heartily welcome. And King Arthur asked Balin to fetch back the lamenting knight; and Balin said that he would.

He rode more than a pace, and found the knight with a damsel in the forest, and said, 'Sir knight, you must come with me unto King Arthur, for to tell him of your sorrow.'

'That I will not,' said the knight, 'for it will harm me greatly, and do you no good.'

'Sir,' said Balin, 'I pray you make ready, for you must go with me, or else I must fight with you and bring you by force, and I would be loth to do that.'

'Will you be my warrant,' said the knight, 'if I go with you?'

'Yes,' said Balin, 'or I will die for it.'

So the knight left the damsel and came back with Balin to King Arthur but, just as they reached his pavilion *there came one invisible, and smote the knight through the body with a spear. 'Alas,' said the knight, 'I am slain under your safe conduct by a knight called Garlon; therefore take my horse that is better than yours, and ride to the damsel, and follow the quest that I was pursuing as she will lead you, and revenge my death when you can.'*

'That shall I do,' said Balin, and he departed from this knight with great sorrow .... And King Arthur buried the dead knight with all honour.

Sir Balin and the damsel rode on, and met no adventure for three or four days, and then one night they stayed with a rich and gentle man. As they sat at supper, Balin heard someone moaning wretchedly, and asked his host what the trouble was. 'I will tell you,' said his host. 'Lately I was jousting with a knight who is brother to King Pelles. I smote him down twice, and he promised to requite me on my best friend; and then he wounded my son, who can never be healed until he has some of that knight's blood. But the knight always rides invisible and I do not know his name.'

'I can tell you his name,' replied Balin, 'it is Garlon. He has killed a knight that was under my protection, and I would rather meet him than have all the gold in the kingdom.'

'Well,' said his host, 'I know that King Pelles his brother is holding a great feast in twenty days, to which all knights must bring their wife or paramour; and that knight, your enemy and mine, will be there.'

'Then I promise you,' said Balin, 'some of his blood to heal your son.'

In the morning, Balin and the damsel and his host rode towards King Pelles's castle, and they reached it on the day of the feast. Balin was well received; his armour was taken from him and he was given comfortable robes to wear. He refused to leave off his sword, saying it was the custom of his country always to wear it. At dinner Balin asked his neighbour if he could see a knight named Garlon anywhere, and the knight pointed out to him a big, strong, black-faced man. Then Balin wondered to himself what he should do:

RIGHT: *Knights and their ladies at court. From a Flemish late 15th-century Arthurian romance.*

ll temps que
se preu hercu
lles et theseus
retnerent en
grece Et es
toit iuge du puple disrael
vng nomme Jair qui fut
le iii apres Josue alorsfut
regnant en sirie vng tres
puissant roy nome diodicia

qui tenoit soubz luy et sa
seigneurie la pluspart de
perse de mede et mezopota
me et ny auoit pour lors
roy es parties orientalles
dont il ne fust craint et re
doubte plus que nul aultre
Et tant que par sa force et
par sa grant cheualerie qu
estoit en luy il auoit conqs

SIR THOMAS MALORY

P.C. FIELD has now established that the author of *Morte Darthur* was Sir Thomas Malory of Newbold Revel in Warwickshire. Three Thomas Malorys of approximately the right time and place were known to have existed, and this one was always the most likely candidate; but scholars and lovers of literature everywhere were reluctant to accept that it could have been this man who created the greatest masterpiece of English Arthurian romance, because the few facts that are preserved about his life show him to have been a violent criminal who spent long stretches of time in prison.

Thomas Malory of Newbold Revel was probably born in about 1415 into a family of minor country gentry, small landowners who served as justices of the peace, and were sometimes elected to parliament. Malory's father John died in 1433 and Malory inherited from him a small but comfortable estate. In about 1440 he was knighted. In 1443 he and his brother-in-law Eustace Burnaby were charged with an armed robbery in Northamptonshire. This charge, however, was not proven, and Malory was not even brought to trial.

In 1445 Malory was elected Member of Parliament for Warwickshire and married Elizabeth Walsh. In 1450 he became Member of Parliament for Wareham in Dorset, having been put forward by the Duke of York. Malory was violently opposed to his patron's enemy the Duke of Buckingham; he was accused of trying to ambush the duke on 4 January 1450 with twenty-six men, intending to assassinate him. He was not convicted, but further charges were brought against him in 1450 of theft, rape and extortion. A pattern of aggression towards the Duke of Buckingham begins to emerge as in the following year Malory was accused of cattle-rustling and deer-poaching from the duke's park at Caludon in Wiltshire. This time he was convicted and was imprisoned in July 1451. However, he managed to escape and succeeded in breaking into Combe Abbey twice in two days, stealing various treasures and money. He was soon recaptured and spent the best part of the next ten years in prison. Released on bail for a brief period in 1454, Malory took the opportunity to commit another robbery in Essex and was promptly thrown back into prison.

In 1462 a general pardon was issued by the new Yorkist monarch Edward IV, who had deposed Henry VI in 1461. At this point Malory was certainly a Yorkist, for he joined Edward's army when it besieged Lancastrian strongholds that winter. However in 1468 he was named as one of fifteen people who were specifically excluded from another general pardon issued by King Edward IV. Malory had apparently changed sides again; and it was at this time, during his last confinement, that he wrote his masterpiece.

'If I slay him here, I shall not escape, but if I leave him now, perhaps I shall never meet with him again with such a chance, and he will do more harm if he lives.'

Just then Garlon espied that Balin beheld him, and he came and smote Balin on the face with the back of his hand, and said, 'Knight, why are you staring at me? Eat your meat and do what you came for.'

'Very well,' answered Balin, 'that is not the first harm you have done me, so I will indeed do what I came for.' And he rose up fiercely and cleaved his head to the shoulders. 'Give me the truncheon,' ❧ said Balin to his

❧ Truncheon: the broken-off shaft of the spear.

lady, 'wherewith he slew your knight.' And she gave him the truncheon, for she carried it always with her. And with it Balin smote him through the body, and said openly, 'With that truncheon you have slain a good knight, and now it is sticking in your body.' And Balin called his host unto him, saying, 'Now you may fetch enough blood to heal your son.'

But with that all the knights rose from the table to set upon Balin, and King Pelles himself rose up fiercely and said, 'Knight, have you slain my brother? You shall die for it before you depart.'

'Well,' said Balin, 'kill me yourself.'

'Yes,' said King Pelles, 'there shall no man have ado with you but myself, for the love of my brother.' Then King Pelles caught in his hand a grim weapon and smote eagerly at Balin; but Balin put the sword between his head and the stroke, and with the force his sword burst asunder. And when Balin was weaponless he ran into a chamber to seek a weapon, and so from chamber to chamber, but no weapon could he find, and always King Pelles ran after him.

And at last he entered a chamber that was marvellously well and richly prepared, with a bed covered in cloth of gold the richest that could be imagined, and someone lying in it, and nearby stood a table of pure gold with four pillars of silver that held up the table and upon the table stood a marvellous spear strangely wrought. And when Balin saw that spear, he grasped it in his hand and turned to face King Pelles, and smote him passing sore with that spear, so that he fell down in a swoon. And at that stroke the castle roof and walls broke and fell to the earth, and Balin fell down and could stir neither foot nor hand. And so the greater part of the castle, that had fallen down through the Dolorous Stroke, lay upon Pelles and Balin three days.

Then Merlin came and took up Balin, and got him a good horse, for his was dead, and bade him ride out of the country. 'I would have my damsel,' said Balin.

'Lo,' said Merlin, 'where she lies dead.'

And King Pelles lay sorely wounded for many years, and could never be healed until Galahad the high prince healed him in the Quest of the Holy Grail. For in that place was part of the blood of Our Lord Jesus Christ, which Joseph of Arimathea brought into this land, and he himself lay in that rich bed. And the spear was the same spear with which Longius smote Our Lord to the heart. And King Pelles was closely akin to Joseph and was the most worshipful man that lived in those days... Then departed Balin from Merlin and so he rode further through the fair countries and cities, and found the people dead, slain on every side.

BELOW: *Queen Guinevere from Malory's* Morte Darthur, *1529.*

ABOVE: *Joseph of Arimathea catching the blood of Christ in a cup used at the Last Supper. This, according to Robert de Boron, became the Holy Grail.*

And all that were alive cried, 'O Balin, you have caused great damage in these countries, for by the Dolorous Stroke you gave to King Pelles, three countries are destroyed, and doubt not but that vengeance will fall on you at last.'

Balin rode on for eight days without adventure. At last he came to a strange country. *Then he saw an old hoar gentleman coming towards him, who said, 'Balin le Savage, you are passing your bounds to come this way, therefore turn back and it will be the better for you.' And he vanished.*

Then Balin heard a horn blow, as if it were for the death of a beast. 'That blast,' said Balin, 'is blown for me, for I am the prize and yet I am not dead.'

Soon he was met by many knights and ladies who welcomed him with cheerful faces and led him to a castle. The lady of the castle greeted Balin and told him that he must joust with a knight near by who guarded the road against all comers. 'That is an unhappy custom,' said Balin.

'You have only to joust against one knight,' said the lady.

Balin sighed and said, 'My horse is weary, but my heart is not; I would gladly go where my death waits for me.'

Then a knight came to Balin and said, 'Sir, it seems to me that your shield is not good. Allow me to lend you a bigger shield.' So Balin took the shield which was unknown and left his own, and rode to the island where the knight was.

On the road he met a damsel, who cried out, 'O knight Balin, why have you left your shield? Alas, you have put yourself in great danger, for by your shield you would have been known.'

'I am sorry,' said Balin, 'that ever I came into this country; but I cannot now with honour turn back, and I shall accept whatever adventure will come to me.'

Then he saw come riding out of a castle a knight, and his horse trapped all in red, and himself in the same colour. When this knight in red beheld Balin, he thought it might be his brother, because of his two swords, but because he did not recognize the shield he decided that it could not be he. And so they lowered their spears and came marvellously fast together, and they smote each other in the shields, and they each bore down horse and man so that they both lay stunned. But Balin was sorely bruised by the fall of his horse, for he was travel-weary. Then Balan attacked Balin and Balin defended himself, and they both fought until their breath failed.

Then Balin looked up to the castle and saw the tower stand full of ladies. So they went to battle again, and wounded one another terribly, and all the place where they fought was red with their blood. And by that time each of them had smitten the other seven great wounds … and their hauberks came apart so that they were naked on every side. At last Balan, the younger brother, withdrew him a little and laid him down. Then said Balin le Savage, 'What knight are you? For now or never have I fought a knight that could match me.'

'My name,' said he, 'is Balan, brother to the good knight Balin.'

'Alas,' said Balin, 'that ever I should see this day!' and he fell back in a swoon. Then Balan crawled on all fours and drew off the helm of his brother, but he could not recognize his face, it was so hewn and bloody. But when Balin awoke he said, 'O Balan, my brother, you have slain me and I you, wherefore all the world shall speak of us both.'

'Alas,' said Balan, 'that ever I saw this day, for through mishap I did not know you, for I saw well your two swords, but because you had another shield I thought you must be another knight.' …

Just then came the lady of the castle and her people to them, and heard them say that they had come from the same mother's womb, and now would both lie in the same tomb. Balan prayed the lady that she would bury them together in the place where they had fought.

THE FISHER KING AND THE DOLOROUS STROKE

Of ALL THE ENTICING LEGENDS brought into the growing cycle of Arthurian stories, the tale of the Fisher King and the Dolorous Stroke, perhaps more than any other, gives the impression of being imperfectly understood fragments of some earlier and greater whole. This sense of a mystical story somewhere just beyond our reach has led to some fanciful 'reconstructive' work, and inspired, among other things, T.S. Eliot's *The Waste Land.* In fact, as several scholars have pointed out, stories tend to accumulate rather than disintegrate, and that same process is observable here.

Chrétien de Troyes introduced these motifs to the Arthurian cycle in *Perceval*, his final and unfinished poem. Here the innocent and ignorant hero visits the Grail castle, ruled over by a maimed king. Chrétien rather playfully informs us that he became known as the Fisher King because he had taken up fishing as a pastime after his wound prevented him from riding. This king is suffering from a wound which will never heal unless Perceval asks the crucial question. Perceval, whose most recent piece of advice on proper knightly behaviour was an injunction not to be nosy, keeps quiet when he sees the mysterious Grail procession, maidens and the feeding of the king. The Grail Quest ensues.

Chrétien's poem was later continued (at great length) and completed, and quickly adapted into German in the extraordinary *Parzifal* by Wolfram von Eschenbach, but even before that the Grail story was woven into a complicated cycle by Robert de Boron. It was de Boron's Christianized version of events which was adopted and made standard by later romance writers.

The *Suite de Merlin*, and subsequently Malory, popularized the story of the Dolorous Stroke, which maimed the king and laid waste three countries. They thus provided a history for the mysterious never-healing wound of the Fisher King and a reason for the Grail Quest itself, linking together the early part of the cycle and the later.

And she, weeping, agreed to do so. All the ladies and gentlemen wept for pity. Soon Balan died, and Balin died the midnight following, and so they were both buried, and the lady raised a tomb over their bodies.

In the morning came Merlin, and he caused to be written on the tomb in letters of gold: 'Here lies Balin le Savage that was the knight with the two swords, and he that smote the Dolorous Stroke, and here too lies his brother Balan, each slain by the other unknowing.'

And after Balin was dead, Merlin took his sword, and set a new pommel to it. And he bade a knight that was by him to handle the sword, and he tried, but he could not lift it. And Merlin laughed.

'Why do you laugh?' said the knight.

'For this cause,' said Merlin, 'no man shall ever handle this sword but the best knight in the world, and that shall be Sir Lancelot or else Galahad his son, and Lancelot with this sword shall slay the man that he loves best in the world, and that shall be Sir Gawain.' And he had all this written in the pommel of the sword, and then he set the sword into a marble stone, standing upright as big as a mill stone, and the stone floated above the water. After many years, it floated down to Camelot, on the same day that Galahad came there and achieved the sword. Thus ends the tale of Balin and Balan, two brothers from Northumberland, and good knights.

THE ROUND TABLE

Soon after the tragic deaths of Balin and Balan, Merlin returned to the court. At that time there was peace in the land, for King Arthur had overcome all those who opposed him. Arthur rejoiced at Merlin's coming and made great joy of him. And Arthur told Merlin that his barons wished him to marry, and asked for his advice. 'Is there a lady who pleases you more than any other?' said Merlin. Arthur replied that Guinevere, the daughter of King Leodegraunce, was the woman he wished to marry. Then Merlin said, 'If you do not already love her, I would advise you to take another, for her beauty is so great that it may cause the destruction of everything you possess.' But Arthur would have no one but Guinevere. So Merlin and Arthur journeyed to Cameliard to ask for her hand in marriage; and King Leodegraunce was overjoyed to ally himself with the high king, ❧ and granted his wish at once.

Arthur announced his betrothal to Guinevere and for their wedding feast gathered together all the noblest and bravest knights in that realm and all the neighbouring realms.

❧ *Because of these noble barons that Arthur had, each one of whom strove to be the best, and none of whom would think himself a lesser man than the others, Arthur made the Round Table, of which so many stories are told in Britain. This table was fashioned so that every knight and vassal had an*

❧ High king: King Pellinore, King Uriens, King Leodegraunce and others each ruled their own small territory, but Arthur was high king over the whole country.

❧ Wace, *Le Roman de Brut.*

34

THE ROUND TABLE

ON THE WEST WALL of the Great Hall of Winchester Castle hangs a huge round wooden disk, eighteen feet in diameter and weighing $1^1/_4$ tonnes. No one knows how long it has been hanging there. It is first mentioned in John Hardyng's *Chronicle* (1464) where he describes the founding of the Round Table at Winchester and goes on to remark that the actual Table 'hangeth there yet' — implying that it had already been hanging there for a long time. The painting of King Arthur and the names of his principal knights which now decorate the table are much later than this, and we know that the original painting was made in 1516 at the command of the young King Henry VIII. (What we can see now is a crudely restored and repainted version done in 1789.) A contemporary letter records that the table was redecorated because the names of the knights had crumbled away with age and were no longer legible.

When archaeologists examined the disk, they found that it had been made as a real table. Later the legs were removed and it was decorated and hung on the wall. Later still it was reinforced with planks, and a band of iron was clamped all the way round the rim, which had been damaged by wet rot. Closer examina-tion showed that the table was full of holes, which had been plugged up with wine corks before the 1789 repainting. The holes were mostly concentrated near the face of King Arthur and the centre of the rose. The angle of the holes showed clearly that the table had been shot at while hanging on the wall — almost certainly by Cromwellian soldiers in 1645.

The table was X-rayed, showing that there had been no painting underneath the 1516 one. This was a puzzle. Literary references implied that the table had a design on it; and why would anyone hang a blank eighteen-foot wooden disk as a wall decoration? But, when the Victorian iron clasp was removed from the rim, it was found to be studded with many small iron tacks, exactly as if they had once held in place a painted cloth or leather covering.

Dendrochronological dating gave a felling date for the table's timbers of about 1250-1255. What could this tell us about its history? The Great Hall was completed in 1235, and for the next thirty years it was furnished and decorated under the personal supervision of King Henry III. He could have placed the table in the Great Hall during the 1260s. Or King Edward I, a great Arthurian enthusiast, may have ordered the table for a spectacular international festivity.

equal place; when they sat down to eat they were served equally, and no man could boast that he was in a higher place than his peers. No one was considered a stranger there; no one was treated any more or less courteously because he was a Scot, a Breton, a Frank, a Norman, an Angevin, a Fleming, a Burgundian or a Loherin. Men came from every part of Christendom and beyond to join the Fellowship of the Round Table.

🙦 *When the priests had done, Merlin addressed the knights and said, 'It is fitting that you now pay homage to King Arthur, so that he will maintain and honour you as highly as he may through all his reign.' They replied that they would do so at once, and when they arose from their seats and went towards the king to do him homage, Merlin discovered on each seat the name of him who had sat there* in letters of gold.

Just before the wedding, King Arthur knighted Sir Gawain and Sir Tor, the son of King Pellinore. Sir Tor and King Pellinore were both seated at the Round Table and were greatly honoured by the king. And Gawain was angry at this, because King Pellinore had slain his own father, King Lot, in battle. But he held his peace, meaning to take his revenge later. Then everyone sat down to the wedding feast, but two places were empty.

🙦 *What is the cause,' said King Arthur, 'that there be two places void in the sieges?'*

'Sir,' said Merlin, 'there shall no man sit in those places but they that be of most worship. But in the Siege Perilous 🙦 *there shall no man sit therein but one, and if there be any so hardy to do it he shall be destroyed, and he that shall sit there shall have no fellow.'*

🙦 Anon, *Suite de Merlin.*

🙦 Sir Thomas Malory, *Morte Darthur.*

🙦 Siege Perilous: an enchanted seat which burns to ashes anyone who sits in it except for its predestined occupant.

THE BEGUILING OF MERLIN

🙦

KING PELLINORE had brought with him to the court of King Arthur at Camelot a very fair damsel named Nimue, who was one of the damsels of the lake. And after a short time *Merlin fell in a dotage on the damsel … and would let her have no rest but always he would be with her. And ever she made Merlin good cheer till she had learned of him all manner of things that she desired; and he was assotted on her, that he might not be from her. So in time he told King Arthur that he should not dure long, but for all his crafts he should be put in the earth living, and so he told the king many things that should befall, but he warned the king to keep well his sword and scabbard, for they should be stolen from him by the woman he most trusted.*

'Ah,' said King Arthur, 'since you know your fate, provide against it, and put away that misadventure by your crafts.'

RIGHT: *Merlin and Nimue by the pre-Raphaelite artist, Edward Burne-Jones.*

36

MERLIN

MERLIN IS FIRST MENTIONED by Geoffrey of Monmouth, to whom he was at least as important as Arthur. Geoffrey wrote two independent works, the *Prophetae Merlini*, which he later incorporated into his *Historia regum Britanniae*, and the more detailed *Vita Merlini*, in c. 1150. Merlin, or Myrddin, also features in Welsh medieval poems, some of which are narrated by him. None of the surviving texts predates Geoffrey, but they clearly reflect a long-standing oral tradition.

Though later romances tended to emphasize Merlin's skills as a magician, Geoffrey saw him as a seer, whose prophetic vision helped him to influence events.

In the 1190s Robert de Boron wrote his *Merlin*, of which unfortunately only the opening survives. His Merlin works hard for Arthur and his knights to fulfil a specifically Christian and mystical purpose; and this is taken up in the later prose *Vulgate Merlin* and *Suite de Merlin*. The *Suite de Merlin* was the first to introduce the later tradition that he became infatuated with a damsel of the lake, whom he taught his magical skills and who then used them to bury him alive.

⚜ Anon, *Suite de Merlin.*

⚜ There is no English equivalent of the Old French *preudomme*. It implies noble birth, but much more besides — integrity, justice, valour, courtesy, generosity and all the qualities that go to make up a man of solid and proven worth.

⚜ 'No,' said Merlin, 'it cannot be.' And within a little while the damsel of the lake departed, and Merlin went with her wheresoever she went.

One day they were riding through the Forest Perillous … Merlin said to the damsel, 'Damsel, among these rocks I can show you a most beautiful little chamber that I know of, all chiselled out.'

'That would indeed be a marvel,' said the damsel, 'if there is among these rocks a beautiful and well-appointed room, where no one ever comes except devils and wild beasts.'

'Well,' said Merlin, 'not a hundred years ago there lived in this country a king called Assen, a noble man ⚜ and a good knight, who had an excellent and valiant knight for his son, named Anasteu. He loved the daughter of a poor knight with a greater love than mortal man has ever felt for a *woman. When King Assen learned that his son had cast his love so basely, he was very angry ... and said, "If you do not stop seeing her I shall have her killed." ... When the knight heard this he hid the damsel where his father could not find her. He had often hunted in this forest and he knew this little valley well, so he came here, with his best-loved companions and household officers, and he had hewn from the natural rock a beautiful hall and chamber. And when it was done ... he fetched his lover here ... and here they remained all their lives, and enjoyed great happiness and joy together as long as they lived. They both died on the same day and were buried together in the same tomb. Their bodies are there yet ...'*

When the damsel heard this she was very pleased because she thought she would now place Merlin there if it could be done ... and she said to Merlin: 'Truly, Merlin, these lovers you tell me of behaved most faithfully, for they left the world and everyone they knew to live joyfully together.'

And Merlin informed her: 'So have I done, madam, for I have left for your sake the company of King Arthur and the most noble men in the kingdom of Logres, nor have I been any the better for it.'

And she replied, '... I should very much like to see the chamber you told me about that the two lovers made, and you and I shall stay there tonight, for certainly I love the place the better for the faithful love they kept.'

Then Merlin was very pleased and he took servants with torches and followed the path, and they came at length to a narrow iron door, which he opened, and they went inside. *There they found a gorgeously decorated room ... And he led her through another narrow door ... and showed the damsel a beautiful tomb, covered with red samite gorgeously embroidered and worked with gold. And the damsel lifted up the cloth and saw the stone which lay over the tomb, which was of scarlet marble. And she said: 'Could a man's hand lift this stone?'*

'No indeed,' replied Merlin, 'though I could do it; but nevertheless I do not advise you to see the bodies, for no corpse that has lain so long in the ground is other than ugly and horrible.'

'Even so,' she said, 'I want the stone to be raised.'

'Very well,' he replied, and he took it at once by the heaviest end and lifted it up ...

The damsel looked in, and saw the bodies of the two lovers wrapped in white samite, so that she could not see their limbs or their faces. Then she said, 'Merlin, you have told me so much about these two that if I could be God for one hour, I would place their souls together in the joy that is everlasting. I delight so much in the remembrance of their deeds and their life that for love of them I shall stay here for the whole night.'

BELOW: *Merlin is tricked into entering the cave. From Malory's* Morte Darthur, *1529.*

'And I will stay with you,' said Merlin, 'to keep you company.'

Then the damsel ordered beds to be laid there and they both went to bed … and when Merlin lay down he fell deeply asleep, as if he had been enchanted and had already lost all sense and memory. The damsel knew this perfectly well, and she got up from her bed and came to where he slept, and she began to enchant him still more. And when she had so bewitched him that if one had struck him on the head he would still not have returned to himself, she opened the door of the chamber and called her servants … Then she had them take him by the head and the feet and throw him into the grave where the two lovers lay already. Afterwards they placed the stone on top, and then she began to cast spells to seal the stone on to the tomb, and by the strength of those charms no one would ever be able to remove it.

Then the damsel and her retinue left that place and closed the doors behind them. And no one ever knew what had become of Merlin until Bagdemagus accidentally found the tomb four years later. Meanwhile, the damsel felt very anxious about King Arthur, for she knew that Morgan his sister was plotting against him, and she wished to save his life.

SIR ACCOLON OF GAUL

ONE MONDAY MORNING, King Arthur went hunting in the forest of Camelot with his knights. They soon found a herd of deer and set their hounds on the strongest and swiftest hart ✦ King Arthur, his brother-in-law King Uriens of Gore and a knight called Sir Accolon of Gaul had better horses than the rest and quickly left behind all their companions. The hart was strong and nimble and they chased it more than ten miles without a rest.

✦ Hart: a male deer at least five years old; white harts are frequently hunted through the pages of medieval romance.

But then they had to stop, because their horses fell dead under them. When King Arthur got to his feet, he looked round and could see none of his men, except King Uriens and Sir Accolon, who were also on foot. 'My lords,' he said, 'what shall we do? … Tell me, do you see any of my men nearby?'

'None, Sire,' replied Sir Accolon.

They began to walk directly and, as night was falling, they came to a large river … and looking up the river, they saw a ship all hung with drapes of scarlet silk, right down to the water, so that the swiftly moving oars could not be seen. The ship glided towards them and stopped against a spit of sandy ground … The king called to his companions and said, 'Let us go in and see who is there.'

So they all entered the ship, and thought it the most beautifully adorned and refined ship they had ever seen. Then twelve lovely

CAMELOT

Ruins at Caerleon, one of the possible sites of Camelot.

CAMELOT WAS THE PLACE most often referred to in medieval Arthurian romance as Arthur's principal residence and court; other courts were held at Caerleon (his principal court according to Geoffrey of Monmouth) and Carlisle. The practical Malory stated flatly that Camelot is the city we now call Winchester, but this was probably because of the Round Table, which was hanging in the hall of Winchester Castle at the time he was writing. Other authors are much less forthcoming about Camelot's location, although they describe it in detail.

These descriptions are not much help in identifying a 'real' Camelot, though many people have tried. Cadbury Castle, an iron-age hill fort in Somerset, is a favourite candidate, since archaeological excavations carried out successively since 1966 show that the hilltop was refortified and occupied at approximately the right date — sometime after about AD 460 — and that the structures there were of a size and sophistication unequalled anywhere else in England and Wales. Another recent suggestion has been the old Roman city of Viroconium in Shropshire, which was also re-occupied in the fifth century.

If there was a 'real' Camelot, it would have been very different from the epitome of medieval gracious living exemplified in the romances. Apart from the fact that it lay in a wide plain beside a river and was surrounded by forest, the Camelot of the romances is a shadowy and mythical creation. This Camelot was all the more successful as the emotional and ideological heart of Logres for being an ideal city visible only in the imagination.

damsels came out of a chamber and knelt before King Arthur and welcomed him most courteously, inviting him and his companions, since it was now so late in the evening, to stay on board the ship. King Arthur agreed and the damsels brought many torches to light the chamber. Then he and his companions were given fresh robes to wear, richly woven, and water was brought for them to wash, and they were led to the most sumptuous feast that any of them could ever remember. They each ate their fill, and then, since they had ridden so hard all day, they became very sleepy, and the damsels led each of them away to a comfortable and richly decorated bedchamber, where they fell asleep at once and slept soundly all night.

But in the morning when they awoke, they were uncommonly disturbed to find that they were in quite different places, and had no idea how they got there. King Uriens found himself at Camelot in his own bed in the arms of his wife Morgan. Sir Accolon found himself in a meadow full of flowers, less than a foot away from the edge of a spring, from which a silver conduit fed water to a tall tower beside the meadow. When he awoke and found himself there, still clad in the same robe which the damsels had given him the evening before, he crossed himself and said, 'Holy Mary, what do I see here? Yesterday evening I lay down in the ship close to my lord, and now I find myself here at this fountain all clad in the robes I was given. O God! Where can my lord be, and King Uriens? ...'

Accolon felt as angry as he had ever been in his life. Then he saw a dwarf coming towards him, with black hair, a small nose and a huge mouth. And the dwarf greeted him saying, 'Greetings, my lord Accolon, from your lady Queen Morgan, who requests you to do battle for her tomorrow at the hour of tierce, ❦ with this sword.' And the dwarf put into his hands the sword Excalibur and its scabbard. Then many lords and ladies came out of the tower and joyfully welcomed Accolon, making him feel more at ease.

❦ Tierce: the third hour of the monastic daily round, about nine o'clock in the morning.

But King Arthur was not so fortunate, for when he awoke he found himself in a large, dark room with a number of other knights who moaned and lamented most miserably. When the king heard them wishing for death to take them, he asked the knight nearest to him where they all were, why they had been imprisoned, and why they could not get out. Then the knight told him that the lord of that castle, Sir Damas, needed to find a knight to fight on his behalf against his younger brother the good Sir Ontzlake. All the knights in the prison had been captured by force but had refused to fight for the lord; eighteen of them had already died of hunger, and the remainder were now so feeble that they could scarcely stand.

❦ *'God deliver you, in his mercy,' said Arthur.*

❦ Sir Thomas Malory, *Morte Darthur.*

Soon there came a damsel to King Arthur and asked him, 'What cheer?'

'I cannot say,' said he.

'Sir,' she said, 'if you will fight for my lord, you shall be delivered out of prison. Otherwise you shall not escape with your life.'

'Now,' said King Arthur, 'that is hard, yet I would rather fight with a knight than die in prison; if I may be delivered and all these prisoners, I will do battle.'

'Very well,' said the damsel.

Then she went and told Sir Damas and his knights what Arthur had said, and Sir Damas had Arthur brought before him. And when they looked at him, they thought he was a fine, strong, well-grown young man. So Sir Damas and Arthur came to an agreement that Arthur would fight for him against his brother and, if he won, he and the twenty imprisoned knights would be set free. Sir Damas swore an oath to do this, and Arthur swore to fight to the death. But Arthur did not reveal who he was. Then Sir Damas sent to his brother to say that he had found a knight to fight for him and that the battle should take place the next day.

ABOVE: *Medieval warfare from an early 16th-century woodcut.*

But Sir Ontzlake had been wounded in the thigh so that he could not fight. He was well acquainted with Morgan le Fay and he asked her what he should do. She told him that she would send him a good knight to fight on his behalf; and she sent him Sir Accolon, with King Arthur's sword Excalibur and its scabbard.

On the following day, King Arthur heard mass, armed himself and prepared for the battle.

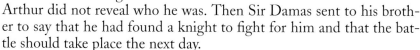 *And then came one of the damsels of Morgan and said to King Arthur: 'Sire, my lady your sister Queen Morgan salutes you and sends you this sword so that you can be certain to conquer in this battle.' When he looked at the sword, he believed that the shape of the scabbard and sword were just like Excalibur. But it was not Excalibur; it was another sword which counterfeited Excalibur so marvellously that on seeing them both together you would not be able to tell one from the other. Arthur thanked the damsel and also sent his thanks to his sister.*

Anon, Suite de Merlin.

Then King Arthur rode to the appointed place; and the two brothers swore openly to abide by the outcome of the battle, and each exhorted his knight to do his best. Twelve of the best knights of those parts were appointed to attend on the combatants; and when they were fully armed the battle commenced. They fought ferociously, but Arthur had the worst of it, because his sword did not bite like Accolon's, whereas Accolon gave Arthur terrible wounds with every stroke.

Arthur was so weary and exhausted from giving and receiving blows that he was forced to rest in order to get back his breath. He had been so busy that he had not yet noticed all the blood he had lost. When he was a

ABOVE: *King Arthur in battle.*

little rested, he chanced to look down at his feet and saw the grass all bloodied around him with the blood pouring from his wounds. And when he saw that he became afraid, for he perceived now that he had not his own sword, and that he had been betrayed and deceived.

Accolon, who felt much stronger than the king, urged him to defend himself and go to battle again. Then, with a tremendous effort, King Arthur gathered his strength and struck Accolon a powerful blow on the helm.

The king was very strong, and the helm was of good hard steel, but the sword was brittle and poor, so that it shattered at the blow just below the hilt, and the blade fell into the grass and the pommel remained in his hand. When the king saw this he was much dismayed, for he had lost his only means of defending himself, and … never before had he so feared to be shamed. But even so, he behaved as if nothing was the matter, and he did not care at all; and he covered himself as best he could with his shield and waited for the knight as if he could do him no harm. And when Accolon saw this he said to himself, 'Faith, this is either the most foolish or the most brave knight I have ever seen, for he is utterly at a disadvantage, and yet he is not in the least dismayed.' And he said to the king, to see if he could bring him down, 'Sir knight, … you cannot endure longer against me, for you have no weapon, and therefore I advise you in good faith because of the misfortune you have suffered to yield; for you are so good a knight that it would be a great shame to kill you.'

When the king heard this he felt very sad, but he replied: 'Sir knight, I should be much to blame and a great coward if I yielded to your request, for I am just as strong and agile as I was when I joined battle; therefore fear not, for I would rather die a hundred times, if I could, than to utter one cowardly word. I shall not yield to you while there is life in my body.'

'In that case,' said Accolon, 'you are come to your death.'

'Not yet,' said the king, 'nor shall I today come so close as you think.'

And Arthur smote Sir Accolon a great buffet with his shield, and he lost his balance and the sword fell out of his hand. Then Arthur sprang forward and picked up the sword and, as soon as his hand closed round the hilt, he knew it for his own sword Excalibur. 'You have been away from me too long!' he cried; and he snatched the scabbard where it hung at Accolon's side and flung it far away. And as soon as the scabbard came away from Accolon's body all his wounds began to pour blood.

'O knight,' said Arthur, 'this day you have done me great damage with this sword; and now you are come to your death … for much pain have you made me endure and much blood have I lost.' And at that Arthur rushed on him with all his might and pulled him to the earth and rushed off his helm, and gave him such a buffet on the head that the blood came out at his ears, his nose and his mouth.

Sir Thomas Malory, *Morte Darthur.*

And when he saw that he was in such great danger, he said: 'You can kill me, sir knight, if it please you, for I see that you have the upper hand. But I will never surrender; I would rather die.'

Anon, *Suite de Merlin.*

And then King Arthur thought that he recognized him as one of his court. And he said, 'Sir knight, I pray you to tell me who you are before I touch you again.'

And he replied at once, 'I am of the court of King Arthur and my name is Accolon.'

And the king was astonished, for he remembered that he had been enchanted with this man in the ship. Then he asked: 'I pray you tell me who gave you this sword.'

The other sighed deeply when he heard this question and said, ' … I shall conceal nothing from you, for I see that I am come to my death … Know then that Queen Morgan gave me the sword so that with it I should kill her brother King Arthur; for there is no one in the world whom she hates as mortally as she hates him.'

'And … did you promise to kill King Arthur?' asked the king.

'I did not,' replied Accolon, ' … I pray you tell me who you are.'. . .

'Know that I am that Arthur of whom you speak, who yesterday lay down with you in the ship where the damsels enchanted us.'

And when Accolon heard these words he cried aloud: 'O fair sweet lord, forgive me that I fought against you. I swear upon God and my own soul that if I had known it was you I would never have begun the combat.'

'Indeed, Accolon,' said the king, 'I forgive you, for I understand well by your words that you did not know me. And for that I should blame no one except my treacherous sister, who sought my death with all her power, when I have done nothing to deserve it. But if God allows me to come to Camelot healthy and whole, I shall take such a vengeance on her that after my death it will be spoken of throughout the realm of Logres.'

Then King Arthur called to the keepers of the field and told them who he was and what had happened, and when they knew he was the king everyone present fell on their knees and begged him to spare their lives. Arthur forgave them, and reconciled the two brothers with each other, inviting Sir Ontzlake to return with him to Camelot and join the Round Table. Meanwhile, he had himself and Accolon carried to a nearby nunnery for their wounds to be tended. There Accolon died of his wounds on the fourth day, for he had lost too much blood; but Arthur began to recover. After Accolon's death, Arthur instructed six knights to bear his body back to Camelot and present it to his sister Morgan with a message.

Meanwhile, on the day of the battle itself, Morgan was sure that Arthur would die.

Sir Thomas Malory, Morte Darthur.

She espied King Uriens as he lay in his bed sleeping. Then she called unto her a maiden of her counsel and said: 'Go fetch me my lord's sword, for I never saw better time to slay him than now.'

'O madam,' said the damsel, 'if you slay my lord you can never escape.'

'Do not concern yourself,' said Morgan le Fay, 'for now I see my time in which it is best to do it, and therefore hurry and fetch me the sword.'

Then the damsel departed and found Sir Ywain sleeping upon a bed in another chamber, so she went unto Sir Ywain and awaked him, and bade him, 'Arise, and wait on my lady your mother, for she will slay the king your father sleeping in his bed, for I go to fetch his sword.'

'Well,' said Sir Ywain, 'go on your way and let me deal.' Soon the damsel brought Morgan the sword with quaking hands, and she lightly took the sword, and pulled it out, and went boldly to the bedside, and awaited how and where she might slay him best. And as she lifted up the sword to smite, Sir Ywain leapt to his mother and caught her by the hand and said: 'Ah, fiend, what are you doing? If you were not my mother, I would smite off your head with this sword! Men say that Merlin was begotten by a devil, but I can say that an earthly devil bore me.'

'O fair son, Ywain, have mercy upon me, I was tempted by a devil, wherefore I cry you mercy; I will never more do so; and save my worship and discover me not.'

'On this covenant,' said Sir Ywain, 'I will forgive it you, so you will never again do such deeds.'

And she swore that she would not.

On the seventh day following the four knights carrying the body of Sir Accolon arrived at Camelot. Queen Morgan was sent for and when she appeared one of the four knights said:

Anon, Suite de Merlin.

'Madam, King Arthur your brother greets you in such a manner as you deserve, and sends you on this bier Sir Accolon, the knight whom you love with all your heart, and he lets you know that he has done to Accolon what Accolon was meant to do to him. And he would have you know that no treachery has ever been so well avenged as this will be; for no land will be far enough for you to flee to.'

When Morgan heard this she knew that they spoke the truth; but she hid this knowledge from them by replying: 'Truly, Sir, you are a foolish messenger to believe the things my brother ordered you to say. For he did this in jest, for amusement, to know how I would react.' And when they heard how boldly she acquitted herself, they did not think her at all guilty …

Then she asked leave of Queen Guinevere to travel into her own country, for she feared that if Arthur found her at court her death was certain. And the queen gave her leave to go. *So early in the morn, ere it was day, she took her horse and rode all that day and most part of the night, and in the morning at noon she came to the same abbey of nuns*

Sir Thomas Malory, Morte Darthur.

MORGAN LE FAY

MORGAN LE FAY makes her first appearance in the Arthurian legend in Geoffrey of Monmouth's *Life of Merlin*. In it the bard Taliesin recounts how he accompanied the dying Arthur by boat to the Isle of Avalon, where they were met by 'Morgen', leader of a sisterhood of nine sorceresses. Morgan tells Arthur that she can heal his wound, if he promises not to leave the island for a very long time. There is no suggestion that she is his sister, and no suggestion that she is anything other than benign in her magical powers. This Morgan derives from the Celtic triple goddess, Morrigan, Macha and Bodbh (pronounced Bowv). This deity already had a mixed character, compounding in her triple persona the archetypal female in relation to man: the mother who bears him, the bride who weds him, and the hag who lays him out for burial.

Chrétien de Troyes first associated her with Arthur's sister and, though he gave her a character as a skilled healer, did not say that she was wicked or hostile to her brother. It was in the prose romances of the Vulgate Cycle that her character began to deteriorate. The story of Morgan plotting her brother's death by stealing his sword and arranging for him to fight against her lover Accolon of Gaul appears in the Vulgate *Merlin*. In this account she is prevented from killing her own husband King Uriens only by the presence of mind of a damsel who fetches her son Ywain just in time to stop her.

Illustration by Aubrey Beardsley.

whereat lay King Arthur; and she, knowing he was there, asked where he was. And they answered how he had laid him in his bed to sleep, for he had had but little rest these three nights. 'Well,' said she, 'I charge you that none of you awake him till I do.' And then she alit off her horse, and thought for to steal away Excalibur his sword, and so she went straight unto his chamber, and no man durst disobey her commandment. There she found Arthur asleep in his bed, and Excalibur in his right hand, naked. When she saw that sword, she was passing heavy that she might not come by the sword without awakening him. Then she took the scabbard and went on her way.

When the king awoke and missed his scabbard he was wroth. 'Alas,' said Arthur, 'falsely you have watched me.'

'Sir,' said they all, 'we durst not disobey your sister's commandment.'

So anon the king and Sir Ontzlake were well armed and they rode after this lady, and ... within a while Arthur had a sight of Morgan le Fay, and then he chased as fast as he might.

When she espied him following her, she rode a greater pace through the forest till she came to a plain and, when she saw that she might not escape, she rode unto a lake thereby, and said, 'Whatever becomes of me, my brother shall not have this scabbard.' And then she threw the scabbard into the deepest of the water, so it sank, for it was heavy with gold and precious stones. Then she rode into a valley where many great stones were and, when she saw she must be overtaken, she shaped herself, horse and men, by enchantment into a great marble stone.

Soon came Sir Arthur and Sir Ontzlake, and the king could tell the forms of his sister and her men, and one knight from another. 'Ah,' said the king, 'here may you see the vengeance of God, and now I am sorry that this misadventure is befallen.' And he looked for the scabbard, but it could not be found, so he returned to the abbey whence he came. And when King Arthur was gone, she turned all into the likenesses as she and they were before, and said, 'Sirs, now we may go where we will.' ... And so she departed into the country of Gore, and there she was richly received, and made her castles and towns passing strong, for always she much feared King Arthur.

When the king had rested him well at the abbey, he rode unto Camelot, and found his queen and his barons right glad of his coming. And when they heard of his strange adventures, then all had marvel at the falsehood of Morgan le Fay; many knights wished her burned ... So on the morn there came a damsel from Morgan to the king, and she brought with her the richest mantle that ever was seen ... And the damsel said: 'Your sister sends you this mantle and desires that you should take this gift of her; and in what thing she has offended you, she will amend it at your own pleasure.' When the king beheld this mantle it pleased him much, but he said nothing.

With that came the damsel of the lake unto the king and said, 'Sir, I must speak with you in private.'

'Say on,' said the king, 'what you will.'

'Sir,' said the damsel, 'put not on you this mantle till you have seen more, and in no wise let it come on you nor on any knight of yours till you command the bringer thereof to put it on her.'

'Well,' said King Arthur, 'it shall be done as you counsel me.' And he said unto the damsel that came from his sister, 'Damsel, this mantle that you have brought me, I will see it upon you.'

'Sir,' she said, 'it will not beseem me to wear a king's garment.'

'By my head,' said Arthur, 'you shall wear it before it comes on my back, or on any man's that is here.' And so the king caused it to be put upon her, and forthwithal she fell down dead and burned to coals.

Then King Arthur was even more angry at his sister than he had been before, and he banished her from his court for ever; but always he loved and honoured her son Ywain and her husband Uriens.

LEFT: *Morgan Le Fay. Painting by the Victorian painter Anthony Frederick Augustus Sandys.*

SIR.LAVNCELOT.
AND.THE.WITCH.
HELLAWES.

PART II
THE KNIGHTS of THE ROUND TABLE

IN THIS PART OF THE STORY CYCLE we have a collection of the adventures of individual knights, those heroes of the Round Table who were the best, the bravest, the most chivalrous, and who made the Round Table famous by their deeds. It opens with the story of Sir Gawain and the Green Knight and it culminates in the greatest of quests, the Quest of the Holy Grail, in which all the Round Table knights swear to take part. Typically, the openings of these adventures are very similar; Arthur is holding court at one of his principal castles (usually Camelot, Caerleon or Carlisle) on one of the major feast days of the year (either Christmas, Easter, Whitsun or the Feast of St John). It is the custom for all the knights to assemble at the king's court on these feast days and Arthur also has a custom of not beginning his dinner until he has heard or seen a marvel. These elements are repeated time and again and are present in the earliest romances (though not in Geoffrey of Monmouth).

Similarly, convention often governs the scene of the adventures. Wandering knights are often wandering through the endless forest of medieval romance – sometimes named as 'Broceliande', but more often not localized. The courts, castles and towns they come to are isolated pockets of human habitation in the midst of the wild, unruly sea of an untamed, natural and, very often, supernatural world. At their overnight lodgings in castles, knights frequently relieve their hosts and hostesses from the cruel persecutions of neighbouring lords or giants, overcome opposition in order to abolish 'wicked customs', or dissolve long-standing enchantments. As long as the reader understands that the world of romance is not very closely related to the real world, these literary conventions, made powerful and resonant by repeated use over hundreds of years, can be enjoyed.

The sources of these stories include the Middle English *Sir Gawain and the Green Knight*, the romances of Chrétien de Troyes, Gottfried von Strassburg, Béroul, Thomas d'Angleterre and the anonymous authors of the great prose Vulgate Cycle.

❧ Sir Gawain and the Green Knight ❧

❧

One Christmas, the king held court at Camelot with jousting and tourneying, with carols and carnival, and fifteen days of feasting. On New Year's Day, the king and queen and all the knights and their ladies assembled in the great hall, to give one another new year gifts and make merry. Then everyone took their seats for dinner; Queen Guinevere sat at the king's dais, all hung with embroidered silks, between the king and his nephew Sir Gawain.

The first course was brought in, with a fanfare of trumpets, and all the knights and ladies were amply served. But it was the king's custom on feast days not to begin his meal until he had heard of some great feat of arms or a marvellous adventure. Scarcely had the noise of the trumpets ceased when there entered at the hall door an enormous knight, taller than any mortal man, massive and powerfully built, and yet handsome to look on. But the most remarkable thing about him, which caused all the knights to stare in amazement, was that he was bright green all over. Not only were his clothes green, but his horse was green, and the hair on his head, and his great beard that spread all over his chest, and even the skin of his face and hands, all were green! He wore no armour, but he held a holly bough in one hand, and in the other a massive battle-axe, its blade of green steel more than a yard wide. He rode his horse through the hall, staring about him, and then he called out: 'Where is the governor of this gang? I would be glad to see and speak with him.'

No one replied; throughout the hall was a deathly hush. At length, King Arthur greeted the green man courteously, welcoming him and bidding him join the feast.

'No, no,' replied the knight. 'I have not come to dine with you, but rather, because your knights are widely famed to be the bravest and the best, I have come to offer you some sport.'

King Arthur replied: 'If you seek single combat, Sir, we will not fail you.'

❧ *'Nay, I seek no combat, truly. There are none but beardless boys here on this bench; if I were clasped in my armour on my tall steed, no man here could match me, their force is too feeble. Therefore I crave a Christmas game in this court ... If anyone in this hall is hardy enough, so bold in blood, so rash in spirit, as to dare strike one blow for another fearlessly, I shall hand over to him this heavy axe to use as he thinks fit; and I shall abide the first blow, unarmed as I sit. If any man is so fierce as to try what I propose, let him leap lightly to me and lay hold of this weapon ... and I shall stand a*

ABOVE: *An early British woodcut of a feast.*

❧ The Gawain Poet, *Sir Gawain and the Green Knight.*

SIR GAWAIN : BRITISH HERO

SIR GAWAIN'S PERSONALITY changed during the 400 years of medieval Arthurian romance. In Geoffrey of Monmouth, Wace and Layamon, Gawain is already known as Arthur's nephew and is described as 'the bravest of all the knights'. He fights heroically in Arthur's war against the Romans, managing to engage Lucius the Roman general in single combat, and is killed during the first battle of Arthur's campaign against the usurping Mordred. These episodes stayed with Gawain until Malory. He is also said to have been brought up in Rome and to be very learned.

But after Geoffrey, Wace and Layamon, a curious thing began to happen. In French romances, Gawain began to appear as a foil to other, newer heroes – Lancelot, Ywain, Perceval. At first, in the romances of the great Chrétien de Troyes, Gawain was still a heroic figure noted for his courteous behaviour, but he appears more worldly and is often shown as a womanizer. It is clear, especially in the *Perceval*, that other heroes are being exalted at his expense. As time went by, his character deteriorated, sometimes into a joke, more often, as in the *Queste del Saint Graal* or the prose *Tristan*,

into a callous, brutal, selfish murderer, the epitome of all the worst aspects of knighthood. These qualities come through in Malory's mostly unattractive portrayal of Gawain.

While all this was happening in France, however, Gawain remained the pre-eminent Arthurian hero in Britain and the Low Countries, and in Germany was depicted much more favourably in romances based on French sources. In Holland, he was the hero of his own romance, *Walewein*, and in one German poem, *Diu Krone*, he became the Grail hero. In England, he was unquestionably the favourite Arthurian character – the majority of the surviving Arthurian romances in Middle English are about Gawain, whereas only one Scottish poem, *Lancelot of the Laik*, features the popular French hero in central position. Among the English romances is *Sir Gawain and the Green Knight*, a rich and delightful masterpiece which shows Gawain at his best – brave, generous, noble and too chivalrous to rebuff the lady's sexual advances discourteously. At the end of the poem, though Gawain turns out not to be absolutely perfect, the Green Knight admits that he is 'one of the most faultless fellows alive'.

ABOVE: *The Round Table fellowship at dinner. French Renaissance woodcut.*

stroke from him, unflinching on this floor, provided that you will adjudge me the right to deal him another in my turn;

> *And yet he'll have respite*
> *A twelvemonth and a day;*
> *Now haste and let us see*
> *If any man dare assay.'*

If he had stunned them at first, now they were even more silent. The man on his charger turned himself in the saddle, and his red eyes rolled ferociously around ... When no one would come to talk terms with him, he coughed loudly, drew himself up in a lordly manner, and spoke directly: 'What, is this Arthur's house?' said the man then, 'whose fame runs through so many realms? Where is now your pride and your conquests, your fierceness and your great boasts? Now the renown of the Round Table is overthrown by a single word of one man's speaking, for everyone cowers in fear without a blow being struck!'

With this he laughed so loud that the lord grieved, the blood flooding into his fair face for shame:

> *He grew as wrath as wind*
> *As did all who were there.*
> *The king, by nature bold,*
> *Then to the knight drew near.*

He said, 'By heaven, you're a fool to ask for this, and as you have sought folly, you deserve to find it. No man here fears your threats. Now give your axe to me, for God's sake, and I shall grant you the boon you have asked.' ... Proudly the other man dismounted. Now Arthur took the axe, gripped the handle, and sternly swung it, like one about to strike a blow. The strong man stood before him, towering tall, higher than any in the hall by a head and more. With a grim expression he stood there, stroking his beard, and quite unmoved he drew down his tunic, no more daunted or dismayed at Arthur's powerful swings than if a man at the bench had brought him a drink of wine. ❧

❧ i.e. the Green Knight is not lowering his head for the blow and, since he is far too tall for Arthur to reach his neck, leaves the king swinging the axe in the air and looking fairly foolish.

> *Gawain from his place made a bow;*
> *Everyone heard him say:*
> *'I beg you in plain words now*
> *To grant me this mêlée.'*

He rose from his seat beside the queen and said: 'If you will permit me, Sire, I would like to request that this foolish challenge be given to me; because if I am killed it will be the least loss.

The king invited Gawain to step down, handed him the axe, and gave him his blessing.

Then the Green Knight spoke: 'First, tell me your name.'

'I am called Gawain,' he said, 'and I am offering to give you this blow, whatever happens next, and will accept another blow from you a year from now.'

'Good,' said the Green Knight, 'I am pleased to find that you have repeated correctly the terms of our agreement. Now, take the weapon, and let us see what you can do with it.'

The green knight took his stand promptly; he bowed his head a little, and laid his lovely long locks over his crown, uncovering ... his naked neck. Gawain gripped his axe, and gathered it up on high and, setting his left foot forward, he brought it swiftly down on the bare neck, so that the man's own sharp blade cleaved his bones asunder, sank through the fair flesh, and sliced it in two ... The handsome head hit the ground, and many spurned it with their feet where it rolled about; blood spurted from the body, bright against the green. But for all that, the man neither faltered nor fell, but stoutly strode forward on his sturdy legs, and fiercely he reached out, seized his splendid head, and quickly lifted it up; and, turning afterwards to his horse, he swung himself up into the saddle, holding his head in his hand by the hair, as if nothing at all was the matter!

> *He turned his trunk about,*
> *That gruesome body that bled;*
> *Many felt dread and doubt,*
> *By the time his say was said.*

For now he held up his head in his hand .. and lifted up its eyelids, and stared with wide-open eyes, and spoke as you may now hear with its

SIR GAWAIN AND THE GREEN KNIGHT

THIS POEM SURVIVES in only a single manuscript, together with three other poems written by the same author. We do not know who he was, but we know he came from the North Midlands – probably Derbyshire or Staffordshire – and was writing in the last quarter of the fourteenth century. With the whole great treasury of medieval romance to draw on, he chose to write about the favourite British hero, Sir Gawain; but he turned his story into a sparkling comedy which can also be read as a sly critique of other romances.

For, in order to understand the point of what happens to Gawain, the reader must be familiar with his character as it appears in French, not English, romances. French authors developed Gawain's character into a notorious silver-tongued seducer, with whom no woman was safe. This stock situation is turned on its head in *Sir Gawain and the Green Knight* where, finding himself being blatantly seduced by the wife of his host – a situation the French Gawain would lose no time in taking advantage of – the hero's main concern is how to preserve his virtue and his perfect courtesy. The hostess, not surprisingly, is completely puzzled by this behaviour since she has heard of Gawain's reputation, and cannot believe it is really him.

OPPOSITE: *The Green Knight addressing the court after Sir Gawain has cut off his head. One of four illustrations in the only surviving manuscript of* Sir Gawain and the Green Knight.

Michaelmas: 29 September, The festival of St Michael. All Saint's Day: 1 November, when masses are sung for the souls of the dead.

BELOW: *Sir Gawain sets out on a quest, from a late 13th-century French manuscript.*

mouth: *'See to it, Gawain, that you are prepared to go as you promised, and search faithfully until you find me, as you have sworn in this hall in the hearing of these knights. Choose your way to the Green Chapel, I charge you, to receive a blow just like the one you have given - you have deserved to be promptly repaid on New Year's Morning. Many men know me - the Knight of the Green Chapel; therefore, if you seek to find me, you will not fail. So come, or you'll deserve to be called a coward.'*

With that, he turned his horse and clattered out of the hall. The axe was hung on the wall behind the dais, where everyone could see and wonder at it.

SEASON BY SEASON the next year followed after, the new green leaves with spring, the full fairness of rich, blooming summer, the hurrying of harvest time before winter darkness falls again. Before Sir Gawain knew it, Michaelmas was here. Yet he stayed on at court until All Saints' Day

In the morning, he armed himself richly in his magnificent armour, chased with gold, and mounted his horse Gringolet. His squire handed up his helm and his shield, which was red with a gold pentangle on it. This device symbolized Gawain's ideal of knightly perfection, and in particular the five knightly virtues: generosity, fellowship, purity, courtesy and compassion. Inside the shield was painted the image of the Blessed Virgin Mary, which he looked on to give him courage in battle.

So he set off on his quest, riding alone through the realm of Logres, all the way up through North Wales, then crossing into the wilderness of the Wirral. He asked everyone he met about the Green Knight and the Green Chapel, but no one had ever heard of them. Many times he found himself beset by strange enemies – dragons, wildmen, wolves, bulls and boars and great shaggy bears, and even giants. He fought them all and, with God's help, won through *War did not worry him so much but that winter was worse – when the cold clear water was shed from the clouds, and froze before it fell to earth. Almost slain by the sleet, he slept in his irons, more nights than enough among the naked rocks, where the icy streams ran clattering down from the clifftops, and hung high over his head in hard icicles. Thus in peril and pain and great hardship, the knight carried on across country till Christmas Eve, all alone. Almost at the end of*

ABOVE: *Gawain attacked by wild beasts on his perilous journey through the wilderness of Wirral.*

27 December, St John's Day, Holy Innocents.

his endurance, he prayed to Jesus Christ and his mother Mary that he might quickly find a civilized dwelling to stay in. And soon after, he caught sight in the distance of a magnificent moated castle on top of a rocky promontory. Gratefully he offered up his thanks and made for the castle as quickly as he could. The lord of the castle, a big powerful man with a red-brown beard and hair, frank of face and commanding in manner, greeted him most courteously and invited him to stay for the whole Christmas feast. The lord was truly delighted to have as his guest someone so famous for prowess and for perfect courtly behaviour. Everyone secretly looked forward to seeing a display of masterly good breeding – the art of polished conversation, faultless manners – and perhaps even some lovers' talk.

After the meal, the lady of the castle came to meet Sir Gawain; she was the fairest he had ever seen, lovelier even than Guinevere. She was accompanied by an older lady, as hideously old and withered as the first was young and fresh. Sir Gawain addressed both ladies courteously, then kissed the young hostess with the greatest politeness, requesting to be her servant always. The next day – Christmas day – was entirely given up to feasting and pleasure. Gawain was seated by the beautiful lady at each meal and found her delightful company. All next day, and the next, the pleasures and festivities continued. On the morning after St John's Day , most of the guests departed at dawn, but when Gawain took his leave, the lord detained him and pressed him to stay longer. Gawain explained that he was on a quest, and must appear at the Green Chapel on New Year's Day; and he asked whether the lord had ever heard of it. Laughing, the lord replied, 'You need not trouble any longer about the Green Chapel, for it lies only two miles from this castle; and now you have no reason to leave us!'

Sir Gawain was very glad to hear this and readily agreed to stay on at the castle until the day of his appointed meeting. Then the lord said, 'I know you are still tired from your journey, and you need more food and more sleep to be perfectly refreshed. So you should stay in bed at ease tomorrow, come down to eat whenever you like, and my wife will entertain you. I myself shall go hunting. Let us make a bargain to exchange whatever each of us has won during the day when we meet in the evening.' To this game Gawain agreed with glad goodwill.

❧

EARLY THE NEXT MORNING, the lord of the castle was up and busy with his huntsmen and groom, horses and hounds; and when he had heard mass and eaten, he hurried off for a day's hunting. Deer – hinds not stags – were his quarry.

Meanwhile Gawain dozed in his comfortable bed, enclosed snugly behind curtains. Hearing a noise, he peeped cautiously out and was astonished to see the lady of the castle stealthily approaching.

'Good morning, Sir Gawain,' cried the lady, drawing the curtains and sitting down on the bed. 'How careless you are to let someone steal in while you sleep. Now you're my prisoner.' And she pinned him down by placing her hands on the covers on each side of him.

'Fair lady,' replied Sir Gawain, smiling, 'it seems I can do nothing but yield and appeal for mercy. But if you would allow me to get up and dress, I should have greater pleasure in our conversation.'

'Oh, no,' she said, laughing gaily, 'I'm not going to let such an opportunity slip away – such a famous knight in my power and my husband out for the whole day. I intend to enjoy myself – I am all yours, to do with as you please; after all, I am absolutely obliged to be your servant, and I shall perform your will.'

'Truly,' said Sir Gawain, 'you are too kind, and shower me with honours I do not deserve. But allow me to be your knight, and I will devote myself to your pleasure.'

'I assure you that I value your excellence as highly as possible; I know many ladies who would give all they possess to have you in their power as I have you now. I thank God for His grace in giving me what so many desire.'

'My lady,' said Gawain, 'your noble generosity is entirely the result of your own virtue, and not my desert; for though people are kind enough to speak highly of me, I am by no means worthy of it.'

'I do not think so,' said the lady, 'for the beauty and courtesy and happy manners, which I see you possess, qualify you to be chosen above all other men.'

'Indeed, my lady,' said Gawain, 'you have already chosen a better man. But I am proud that you value me so highly, and shall be your knight from now on.'

So they talked all morning, and the lady behaved all the time as if she adored him; but Gawain was on guard against her, though with perfect courtesy. He could not respond very gaily because his mind was too much on his fate; and when the lady finally took her leave he readily agreed. She laughed and bade him good day, adding, 'but I find it hard to believe that you are really Gawain'.

'But why?' he asked anxiously, afraid lest he had given offence.

'Because,' she replied, 'a knight such as Gawain is reputed to be, such an embodiment of courtliness, could not have been so long in a lady's company without asking for a kiss.'

'I bow to your command,' said Gawain, 'as your knight should do.'

Gawain tries to wriggle out of the trap that his reputation as a ladies' man has put him in.

BELOW: *The death of a hind in the hunt. A 16th-century woodcut.*

59

Then she leaned down over him and took him in her arms, and kissed him. Afterwards she left him, and he hurriedly rose and dressed, and went to mass, before joining the ladies till evening.

The lord had killed a great number of superb deer, and butchered their bodies according to the due forms of venery ✦ . Then he blew his horn and returned to the castle, and met Gawain before the fire in the hall. He had his huntsmen bring in the venison, and showed Gawain his winnings according to the terms of their agreement.

'This is the finest kill I have seen in seven winter seasons,' said Gawain, 'and in exchange, I freely give you what I have won in the castle today.' And he stepped up to the lord, clasped his arms round his neck, and kissed him.

'That may well be the greater prize,' said the lord, 'especially if you tell me how you came by it.'

'Oh no,' said Gawain, 'that was not part of our agreement!' And they laughed and went to supper; and the lord proposed that they should renew their compact the following day, to which Gawain readily agreed.

Next morning the lord was up betimes, and out with twenty couple of hounds on the trail of a truly ferocious boar. Meanwhile, in the castle, the lady came once more to Gawain's bedchamber, intent on a hunt of her own. Once again, she teased Gawain all morning with talk of love, asking him to teach her the terms of amorous discourse. But Gawain turned everything into a jest, yet without giving offence and, at the end of the morning, despite all temptations, all she had given him were two kisses.

In the evening, the lord returned to the castle with his kill, a huge and bristling boar. Gawain expressed his amazement at its size and ferocity and, without further ado, bestowed on him the two kisses he had gained during the day.

'By Saint Giles ✦ ,' laughed the lord, 'you will soon be rich if you go on like this!'

Once more they went to supper, with mirth and minstrelsy, drinking and dancing, Christmas carols and every kind of merriment. All evening the lady flirted outrageously with Gawain, so that he was troubled at heart, but he was too well-bred to repel her and treated her with unfailing courtesy. Before they went to bed, the lord and Gawain renewed their agreement for the following day.

In the morning, the castellan and his men again set off for the chase, as the sun rose over the frost-rimed forest. This time they were hunting the wily red fox, which dodged and doubled back on its tracks, and led them all a merry dance. And the lady, also, arose early, and went to visit her knight, determined that this time he would not escape her. She dressed in a beautiful long gown which exposed her bright throat and breast, and wove glittering gems into her long hair. Gawain was dreaming of how destiny would deal him his doom at the

✦ Venery: the art of hunting.

✦ St Giles, patron saint of cripples and lepers, was a hermit who lived in a forest near Nimes. In medieval art he is most often depicted in a scene in which King Childeric, out hunting, accidentally shoots him in the leg.

OPPOSITE: *A boar hunt in progress. Note the hunters taking cover in bushes – boars could inflict terrible wounds. A 15th-century French illumination.*

Green Chapel next day. *But when that beauty arrived, he recovered his wits, dragged himself from his dream, and hastily greeted her. The lovely creature came towards him, sweetly laughing, and gracefully leaned over to kiss his face; he welcomed her courteously with good cheer. When he saw her so glorious, so gaily clad, her features so fair and her skin so flawless, an ardent joy welling up warmed his heart. With sweet smiles they fell into merry speech, so that bliss burst out between them, all joy and delight:*

> *They lanced with wordplay good,*
> *Each with sincere delight;*
> *Great peril between them stood,*
> *Did not Mary mind her knight.*

For that peerless princess pressed him so hard, urged him so close to the limit, that he found himself forced either to accept her love, or give offence by refusing her. He was concerned for his courtesy, lest he behave boorishly, but even more for his evil plight if he should commit sin and be a traitor to that noble lord who owned the castle. 'God forbid,' said the knight, 'that shall not happen!' So with laughing love-talk he gently parried all the declarations of affection that darted from her mouth.

Then the lady said, 'I think you are at fault, not to give your love to me; now I will go and mourn my life away for unrequited love.' Sighing she reached down and kissed him, then said, 'At least allow me to give you this belt.' And she unfastened a green silk girdle from her waist and offered it to him. But he would not take it—not, he said, until God allowed him to accomplish his quest. 'Are you refusing it because you think it isn't worth much?' said the lady. 'Then you are deceived; for this girdle has the special power that, while anyone is wearing it, he cannot be killed.'

Then the knight thought for a moment, and it occurred to him that it would be of great value in the perilous adventure to which he was assigned: it would be an excellent device if, when he arrived at the Green Chapel to receive his blow, he could manage to escape being killed ... He assented, and she gave it to him gladly, but besought him for her sake, never to tell anyone about it, and especially to promise faithfully to conceal the gift from her lord. The knight gave his word that no one should ever know anything about it, but they two ❧.

❧ At this point Gawain has made conflicting promises; he must break his word either to the lady or to the host.

> *He gave her many thanks*
> *With all his heart and might.*
> *Then for the third time she*
> *Had kissed that doughty knight.*

❧ Gawain makes a false confession, not mentioning the girdle.

The lady took her leave and left him. Gawain swiftly dressed, and carefully put away the love-lace where he could find it again later. Then he went to the chapel and confessed his sins to the priest ❧ and received absolution. Thereafter, he joined the others in the hall, and was merrier than he had ever been before, throwing himself into the gaiety of the season with such recklessness that everyone noticed it.

Meanwhile, the lord of the castle was having a difficult time catching the cunning fox; but at last, swerving aside from the castellan's sword, he fell into the path of the hounds and they tore him limb from limb. In the evening, the lord returned to the castle to find Gawain waiting for him by the fire. Gawain greeted him gaily, and said, 'Tonight I shall be the first to fulfil the terms of our agreement,' and at once he embraced the lord and gave him three hearty kisses.

ABOVE: The lord returns home to his castle after a day's hunting. An early 16th-century German woodcut.

'You have done well, by God,' said the lord. 'I'm afraid my winnings are inferior, for I've hunted all day long and got nothing to show for it but this fox-skin – a poor return for three such kisses.'

Then they fell to talking, and afterwards passed the merriest evening they had yet had, full of joking and jesting and happy laughter. At the end of it, Sir Gawain thanked his host for his splendid hospitality, and reminded him that the following morning he must set off to keep his appointment at the Green Chapel. The lord promised him a guide and everyone retired for the night.

IN THE MORNING, the weather was wild, for storms had blown up during the night and now a bitter wind drove the snow and sleet bitingly down to the iron-hard earth. Gawain was up before the sun, dressed and armed, not forgetting to wear the green girdle the lady had given him for protection. Then he mounted the noble Gringolet and followed the guide out of the castle gate. Through wooded hills and on to high moorland they journeyed – mist shrouded the mountain tops and the bitter cold chilled them to the bone. At last the man turned and said, 'You are not far from the Green Chapel now, Sir, and I dare take you no further. But let me advise you not to go on, for the Green Knight is a truly evil and terrifying creature, who loves to kill and shows no mercy. You will never escape him alive. Why not just go home by another road? I swear I will never reveal to another soul that you did not keep your appointment.'

'I am grateful for your good wishes', replied Gawain, 'but I am a knight and I must keep my word. I shall go to the chapel and speak with that man, and take whatever fate sends me.'

'Please yourself,' said the other. 'If you're so keen to be killed, I

ABOVE: *Lud's Kirk in North Staffordshire, one of the possible sites of the Green Chapel.*

won't stand in your way. Take that path down into the valley, and to the left across the clearing you'll see the Green Chapel. Farewell, in God's name! I wouldn't be in your shoes for all the gold on earth!' Then he spurred his horse and galloped away, leaving Gawain all alone.

Sir Gawain spurred his horse Gringolet and went on down the path, pushing his way through trees into a small valley, very wild and rugged. He looked around for anything that could be the Green Chapel, but could see nothing except, some way off beside a large stream, a sort of mound. He rode up to it, then dismounted and tied up his horse to a tree. *He went to the hillock, and walked around it, debating with himself what it might be. It had a hole in one end and one at each side, and was all overgrown with clumps of grass; inside it was hollow, nothing but an old cave, or a fissure in an old crag – he could not rightly tell which.* 'Lord,' said Gawain, 'can this be the Green Chapel? It looks hellish – ugly, desolate, overgrown. I feel strongly that the Devil himself has lured me to my death.' Fully armed, he climbed up to the roof of the mound and heard a loud noise. It sounded exactly like someone sharpening a scythe on a grindstone, but because of the steep rocks all around it echoed and grew in a sinister and frightening way. *'By God!'* said Gawain, *'I believe these doings are directed at me, to honour me as a knight with due ceremony:*

God sort all! Now I'm here,
It's useless to grieve and sigh.
No din shall make me fear,
Even if I have to die.'

Then the knight began to shout out boldly: 'Who is the master of this place and keeps his tryst with me? For the good knight Gawain has now arrived. If any man wants anything, let him step smartly forward, now or never, to further his business.'

'Wait,' said someone on the hillside above his head, 'and you shall swiftly have all that I once promised you.' Still he continued with his noisy grinding for a while, and turned aside to his whetting before he would come down. Then he made his way by the crag and emerged from a hole, whirling out of a nook with a fearsome weapon, a Danish axe ❧ *new-honed, with which to deal the blow. It had a massive blade, curving back*

❧ He had left the original axe at Camelot.

64

towards the shaft, sharpened on a whetstone, fully four feet long ... And the knight garbed in green was just as before, both face and legs, hair and beard, save that now he went on foot ...

'Gawain,' said the Green Knight, 'God keep you! Truly you are welcome, Sir, to my place, and you have timed your journey as a true man should, knowing the terms of the covenant made between us; twelve months ago today you took what befell you, and I at this New Year shall promptly repay it. We are absolutely alone in this valley; here are no knights to separate us, however fiercely we fight. Get that helmet off your head, and take your just deserts; offer me no more argument than I gave you before, when you whipped off my head at a single blow ✑ .

'No,' said Gawain, by 'God who gave me a soul, I shall not bear you the trace of a grudge, whatever grief befalls me. Confine yourself to just one stroke, and I will stand still and offer no resistance ... '

> He inclined his head and bowed,
> Exposing the bare, bright skin,
> And acted as if uncowed;
> For he would not give in.

Then the Green Knight quickly got ready, heaving up his grim weapon to strike Gawain. With all the strength of his body he raised it up high, and swung it as mightily as if he wished to annihilate him. Had it driven down as heavily as he intended, the blow would have finished the ever valiant knight. But Gawain glanced sideways at the axe as it came gliding down to butcher him, and his shoulders shrank a little from the sharp edge.

The other man checked the bright blade with a sudden jerk, and then reproved the prince with scornful words: 'You are not Gawain,' he said, 'who is considered so great, who never feared any host by hill or vale, if now you flinch in fear before you feel any hurt! I never heard of such cowardice on the part of that knight. I neither flinched nor fled, man, when you aimed at me, nor made any objection in King Arthur's hall. My head flew to my feet, and yet I never winced; but you, before any harm has happened to you, quail in your heart. Therefore I think I should be acknowledged the better man.'

> Said Gawain, 'I shrank but once;
> I will do so no more;
> But if my head falls on the stones,
> I cannot it restore.

'But come on, man ... deal me my fate, and do it out of hand, for I shall stand still for your stroke and start no more till your axe has hit me – I give you my word.'

'Have at you, then!' said the other, and heaved his axe aloft, staring as fiercely as if he were mad. He swung a powerful blow at him, but did not

✑ The Green Knight is trying to intimidate Gawain: everything he says is provocative and insulting – reminding him that their agreement is legally binding and that he has no friends nearby to save him, and finally warning him not to try to talk his way out of the situation. Gawain's reply, by contrast, is polite but full of sorrowful dignity.

touch him, withholding his hand suddenly before it could do any harm. Gawain waited for the blow soberly, and no part of him flinched, but stood still as a stone ... Then again the man clad in green spoke playfully: 'So, now that you have a whole heart, I must strike. Now be true to the high order that King Arthur bestowed on you, and save your neck from this blow, if you can manage it.'

Gawain was furious at this and angrily exclaimed, 'Ah, get on with your blow, you thrustful fellow, you threaten too long; I think your heart quails with fear at your own self!'

'Indeed,' said the other, 'you speak so fiercely that I will no longer delay or put off our business.'

> He took his stance to strike,
> And frowned with lips and brow;
> Small wonder he felt dislike,
> Who despaired of rescue now.

He lightly lifted his weapon and let it drop straight down, with the cutting edge towards the naked neck. But though he hammered savagely, he did Gawain no injury, except for snicking him slightly on one side, just cutting the skin. Through the fair fat to the flesh sank the sharp blade, so that the bright blood sprayed on the ground over Gawain's shoulders. And when the knight saw his own blood gleam on the snow, he sprang with his feet together in a leap of more than a spear's length, swiftly seized his helmet and clapped it on his head and, shrugging his shoulders so that his shield shot round to the front of him, swung out his bright sword – he had never felt so utterly happy since the day his mother bore him – and ferociously cried, 'Stop your assault, Sir, give me no more blows! I have taken one blow in this place without resisting, but if you try to give me any more I shall quickly requite you, and give you them back with interest – you can be sure of that!

> But one stroke here should fall;
> The covenant shaped it so,
> That was framed in King Arthur's hall;
> Therefore no more ado.'

The knight stood back from him and rested on his axe, setting the handle to the ground and leaning on the blade. He gazed at the knight who stood before him in the glade, seeing how the hero stood there boldly, quite undaunted, armed and ready; and it warmed his heart. Then he spoke up gladly in his great voice, and said to Gawain in ringing tones: 'Brave knight, be not so fierce in this field. No one here has ill-used or insulted you, nor acted in any other way than as the covenant at the king's court laid down ... If I had been clever, perhaps I could have hit you much harder, a blow that would really have harmed you. First I threatened you playfully *with the feint, and did not wound you, which was fair treatment by the terms of the agreement we made on the first night, when you, faithfully and honestly keeping troth with me, gave me all your winnings, as a good man should. The second feint I offered you for the next day, when you kissed my fair wife, and bestowed the kisses on me:*

> *The true man keeps his word;*
> *No danger need he fear.*
> *But you failed at the third,*
> *And therefore I tapped you here.*

'For that embroidered girdle you are wearing belongs to me; my own wife gave it to you, as well I know. And I know all about your kisses and all your conduct, and my wife's wooing of you; I myself devised it. I sent her to test you, and truly you seem to me the most faultless knight ever to walk the earth. As a pearl is of greater value than a pea, so is Gawain, in God's name, in comparison with other fair knights. But here you failed a little, and you lacked loyalty; but it was ... only for love of your life, and I blame you much less for that.'

The other strong man stood for a while in deep thought, so overpowered by mortification that he shuddered inwardly; all the blood of his breast burned in his face, so that he absolutely writhed with shame at the knight's words. His first words were: 'A curse on cowardice, and on covetousness! ❧ *For you cause the baseness and vice that destroy virtue.' Then he seized the belt and, loosening the knot, flung it angrily towards the other man: 'Look! There is my falsehood, evil luck to it! Now I am false and forsworn, I who have always detested treachery and dishonesty—may sorrow and care betide them both:*

> *Knight, I do here confess,*
> *I have done very ill.*
> *In future I will sin less;*
> *But now let me know your will.'*

The other man laughed and graciously said, 'I think the harm I suffered has been amply paid for. You have fully confessed and acknowledged your misdeed, and you have done your penance at the point of my blade, so I consider you cleansed of that offence .. And Sir, I make you a present of the gold-hemmed girdle; because it is as green as my gown. You can remember our contest when you make your way back among high-born princes and, for all chivalrous knights, this will be a perfect token of the adventure of the Green Chapel. Now come back to my house for the New Year and let us joyfully celebrate the remainder of the feast.'

❧ These sins of which Gawain accuses himself are quite serious, but not the most obviously appropriate. He means he has been a coward, because fear of death in the ordeal led him to accept and then to conceal the Lady's gift of the girdle; and by covetousness he means the act of holding on to the girdle which, by the terms of the exchange of winnings agreement, is the property of his host. 'Theft' would be another way of putting it, but it doesn't alliterate.

BELOW: *Sir Gawain prepares himself for the Green Knight's blow.*

ABOVE: *Sir Gawain presents himself to Arthur and Guinevere. Illustration from the manuscript of* Sir Gawain and the Green Knight.

Baldric: a belt or sash, hung from one shoulder across the body to rest on the opposite hip.

Then pressing him the lord
Said, 'With my wife, I know,
You will be in accord,
Although she has been your foe.'

'As for the girdle,' said Gawain, 'I will keep it, if only to remind me of my failure, so that when I am tempted to feel proud of my prowess, I shall never forget how easy it is to fall into sin. Before I depart, I pray you tell me your true name.'

'I am called Bertilak de Hautdesert,' replied the other. 'Everything I have done has been devised and achieved through the magical powers of Morgan le Fay, who dwells in my house; she is the very old lady whom you met. I entreat you to return and meet her; everyone in my house bears you nothing but good will.'

But Gawain would not go back; so they embraced one another, and Gawain set off for Arthur's court. When he arrived, everyone was overjoyed to see him safe and sound. He told them everything that had passed. The wound in his neck had healed, but he wore the green girdle across one shoulder like a sash; and he confessed with a blush of shame how he had failed in faith and the punishment he had received. 'This girdle,' said Gawain, 'is a token of the blame I bear, for cowardice and untruth. I shall wear it always as a reminder of my fault and my failure.

But the king comforted him with kind words, and all the other knights laughed at Gawain and agreed that for the sake of good fellowship they would all wear a bright green baldric over their breasts. This was done, and ever afterwards to wear such a badge was a sign of great honour.

THE FIRST TALE OF SIR LANCELOT

DOLOROUS GARD

IT BEFELL ON THE FEAST OF ST JOHN that the Lady of the Lake came to King Arthur's court at Camelot, leading a very fair youth all armed in white and riding a white horse. She asked King Arthur to knight the youth that Sunday, and said he would do him great honour in the years to come.

'Gladly, lady,' replied King Arthur, 'but what is his name?'

'That shall be revealed in good time,' said the Lady, 'but I shall not tell you now; for he does not know it himself.' She kissed the youth fondly and gave him a magical ring, explaining that it had the power to reveal enchantment; then she rode away. The king knighted the youth in his great church the following day, but when he was about to gird on the sword, the new-made knight found to his shame that he had forgotten to bring it with him. With great presence of mind, Queen Guinevere brought him a sword, thus preventing him from being shamed before the court.

'Thank you, my lady,' said the new-made knight. 'For this deed I shall ever be your own knight, now and always.' And he could not take his eyes from the queen, nor she from him.

Soon the new-made knight rode from the court to seek adventure and fame, and test his prowess. Before many days had passed, he met a maiden, weeping and lamenting. He asked her why she grieved, and she told him that her lover had just been killed attempting the adventure of Dolorous Gard, where there was an evil custom. Any knight trying to enter there would be challenged by a knight from the castle; but if the castle knight was defeated, another would come immediately in his place, and another, and another, until the challenger was exhausted and killed.

'Truly, lady,' said the new-made knight, 'that is an evil custom indeed. But show me the way to this castle, and I will try what I may do.'

Then the damsel brought him before a very large, fair castle, which

BELOW: *Sir Lancelot captures Dolorous Gard with the aid of a new shield sent to him by the Lady of the Lake. From a 15th-century manuscript of the French* Prose Lancelot.

had two gates in an inner and an outer wall. Before the first gate was an open space, much scored and marked with signs of battle. The new knight stood before the gate and demanded entry to the castle. All the townspeople, hearing this bold challenge, came out of their houses to watch; and many sighed to see so young and handsome a knight go to his death.

But soon they changed their ideas, for the new knight was strong and swift and he fought like a lion. The first knight to emerge from the castle he impaled through the body with his lance, leaving him dead on the ground. The second he unhorsed and broke his arm. The third knight was dispatched by a massive blow over the helm; the fourth was borne out of his saddle by the lance and, falling directly in front of the new knight, was trampled to death under his horse's hooves. At length ten of the knights of the castle had been killed or forced to surrender; and the first gate was opened.

The townsfolk hoped that here was the knight destined to undo the evil customs and enchantments of the castle, for no one had ever succeeded in passing the first gate before. But the young knight was beginning to feel weary, and his shield was so battered and pierced that it was almost useless. At the second gate waited another ten knights, intending to set on him all at once. Just then, the damsel who had brought him there offered him a new shield, white with a red diagonal across it. When he put his arm into the straps, the knight felt all his strength and more come flooding back; for this was an enchanted shield, which gave to its wearer the strength of three men and, although he did not know it, it had been sent to him by the Lady of the Lake.

BELOW: *Sir Lancelot rides forth to do battle, from a 15th-century Italian woodcut.*

❧ Anon, *Prose Lancelot.*

He looked up towards the second gate, and on the battlements he saw a huge copper statue of a knight. As he looked, it toppled and fell on to the knights below, crushing one of them to death. With a fierce cry, he flung himself upon the other nine, dispatching four of them so convincingly that the remainder surrendered the gate to him, and before evening he entered the castle as its conqueror. He was met by the townsfolk, who handed him the keys to the castle and led him to a sad little graveyard. Here he found the tombs of all the knights who had perished trying to enter the castle, including many from King Arthur's court, and their heads were impaled on spikes above each grave. The new knight wept at this terrible sight. ❧ *And in the middle of the cemetery was a massive metal slab, marvellously worked in gold and precious stones and enamel. On it were letters which read:*

THIS SLAB SHALL NEVER BE RAISED BY THE EFFORTS OF ANY MAN'S HAND BUT BY HIM WHO SHALL CONQUER THIS DOLOROUS CASTLE, AND THE NAME OF THAT MAN IS WRITTEN HERE BENEATH.

SIR LANCELOT

HOW. FOVR. QVEENS.
FOVND. LAVNCELOT.
SLEEPING.

Sɪʀ Lᴀɴᴄᴇʟᴏᴛ FIRST APPEARS in Chrétien de Troyes's poem *Le Chevalier de la Charrette*, composed in about 1170. He also features in the German poet Ulrich von Zatzikhoven's *Lanzelet* (*c.* 1194-1204), which is based on a separate Old French poem that did not mention Lancelot's love affair with Guinevere. Chrétien says that the story was given to him by Countess Marie of Champagne, his patroness, and we know that the story pre-existed, though not with Lancelot as the hero. Perhaps Countess Marie proposed that Chrétien combine the existing story of Guinevere's abduction with the theme of a lover's obedience to his lady. Some motifs of the latter appear in other romances – for example, the episode of the blood-stained sheets occurs in *Tristan* – but we cannot say which came first.

In Chrétien's poem, Lancelot behaves like a text-book lover; in true troubadour fashion he venerates Guinevere with a religious intensity which at times borders on blasphemy, and at times on farce. In Ulrich's poem Lancelot has three sweethearts and eventually marries the third, Yblis. In the *Prose Lancelot* the hero, untroubled by guilt, fulfils part of his heroic destiny by falling in love with Guinevere. The love affair is something he achieves, in much the same way as a religious quest, and the progress of the affair is described in loving detail.

The *Prose Lancelot* was incorporated into the Vulgate Cycle not long after it was written, and many further adventures were added in which Lancelot becomes aware that his love for the queen is sinful and will prevent him from achieving the Grail quest; a concept quite foreign to the intentions of the non-cyclic version, which wanted to show secular chivalry and courtly love as the finest and best of aristocratic culture.

ABOVE: *Sir Lancelot lifts the stone of his own predestined grave, and learns for the first time his name and parentage.*

Many people had attempted to raise this tomb, both by strength and by skill, in order to learn the name of the good knight. The lord of the castle had often gone to great pains to learn who the knight was, for he would have had him killed, if he could. They led the knight over to the tomb, still armed in his full armour, and they showed him the writing, which he knew well how to read, for he had spent a long time learning. When he had read it, he looked carefully all round the slab, and saw that even if it had been free-standing in the middle of a road, four of the strongest knights in the world would still have had enough to do to lift up the smaller of the two ends. Then he seized it around the larger end in his two hands, and he heaved it up so high that it was a good foot above his head. And then he saw letters which read:

HERE SHALL LIE LANCELOT DU LAKE, THE SON OF KING BAN OF BENWICK.

He replaced the slab again, knowing that it was his own name he had seen.

Then the people of the town raised a great outcry, for the wicked lord of the castle had seized a horse and escaped. Without the lord, they told Lancelot, the only way to bring the enchantments of the castle to an end would be for him to stay there for forty days and nights without setting foot outside or, alternatively, to fetch the keys to the enchantments. They urged him to do this, because the enchantments were so many and so troublesome that they could not sleep through a night or finish a meal without being tormented by them.

Lancelot chose to fetch the keys, and they led him to a small chapel from where he descended into a vault, utterly dark. As he passed along, he heard unearthly sounds, moaning and roaring, which made his flesh shudder and crawl; and the walls and floor shook so that he could scarcely keep on his feet. At the end of the vault was another doorway, guarded by two massive copper knights, with swords raised. Lancelot put up his shield and swiftly leapt between them; but he was not fast enough to escape their blows, and one of the swords fell heavily on his shoulder and wounded him. Nevertheless, he had got through, and found himself in another chamber, in which lay a vast well, six feet across; from it issued a vile stench of putrefaction. Behind the well stood a hideous guardian, whose head was as black as ink, with red eyes like burning coals, blue flames leaping from his mouth, and armed with a huge battle-axe. Lancelot threw himself upon the creature, knocking it off-balance, and seized it round the throat. So strong were his hands that he quickly squeezed the breath out of the creature and threw its body down the well. Then he saw a damsel of copper, with keys in her hand. Near her was a locked coffer, from which issued the loud moaning and roaring he had heard earlier. *He blessed himself, then went to unlock the chest. He saw that thirty copper pipes protruded from it, and out of each pipe came a truly terrifying voice, each one louder than the next. From these voices came all the enchantments and marvels of this place. He put the key into the chest; when he opened it, a great whirlwind flew out, and there was such a dreadful din that he thought all the devils of hell must be there. And he was right, for they were devils. Then he fell in a swoon. When he returned to himself, he looked round, and the well had vanished away as if it had never been; but he saw the ... copper damsel tumble down to the ground and the two knights who had guarded the door all broken in pieces.*

Then he returned to the cemetery and the people greeted him joyfully, for all the wicked enchantments of the castle were ended. And Sir Lancelot made that fair castle his own residence, and he changed its name to Joyous Gard.

SIR TURQUINE

SIR LANCELOT THEREAFTER did many great deeds and became known as the best and noblest knight of the Round Table. He saved his lord King Arthur in battle more than once, and he saved Sir Gawain, who had been captured by the wicked knight Sir Carados. And ever the love between Sir Lancelot and Queen Guinevere grew greater as the years passed.

One day, Lancelot rode out into the forest with his young cousin Sir Lionel. In the heat of the day, he grew sleepy and he lay down to rest beneath an apple tree ❧ . Sir Lionel kept watch while Lancelot slept, and before long he saw a huge, strong knight driving before him three other knights, all stripped and shamefully tied to their own saddle bows ❧ . He thought he would try to rescue them without waking Sir Lancelot, so he followed the strange knight and challenged him. But the strange knight was too strong for him, and soon he had joined the sad procession, slung over his own horse.

When Sir Lancelot awoke, there was no sign of his young cousin, but not far away he found trampled and blood-stained grass, and feared the worst. He followed the tracks until he caught sight of a forester on the path ahead of him. He asked him whether he had seen a knight pass that way, and described Sir Lionel's arms.

'Sir,' replied the forester, 'that knight was but lately taken by Sir Turquine, who hates all knights of the Round Table and, wherever he may, he captures them and imprisons them in a deep dungeon.'

'How may I find this knight?' asked Sir Lancelot.

'Sir, if you ride down to the river, you will find a ford, and growing beside it a fair tree, all hung with the shields of conquered knights. Hanging on the tree is a copper basin; strike it with the butt of your spear and you will soon hear tidings of him.'

Sir Lancelot thanked him and rode on to the river. There he found the ford and the tree; and hanging from the branches of the tree he found displayed many knights' shields, among them those of Sir Kay the seneschal, Sir Brandel, Sir Marhaus, Sir Galind, Sir Brian de Listenois, Sir Aliduke, his own brother Sir Ector de Maris and his cousin Sir Lionel. Furious at this insolent display, he struck the copper basin with the butt of his spear but nothing happened. He struck again, louder, and then he was aware of a huge, strong knight riding

---

❧ A very dangerous thing to do in romance, because it puts you in the power of the faeries. Here, however, the danger is to Lionel.

❧ Saddle-bow: the raised, reinforced rear of a knight's saddle, which helped him to keep his seat under the impact of striking a target with his lance.

towards him, leading another horse with a naked knight shamefully bound and thrown across its back. He recognized the bound knight as Sir Gaheris, one of Sir Gawain's brothers; he was bleeding from many wounds and in great pain.

☙ *'Now, fair knight,' said Sir Lancelot, 'put that wounded knight off the horse and let him rest awhile, and let us two prove our strengths; for I have been informed that you do and have done great despite and shame to knights of the Round Table, therefore defend yourself.'*

'If you are of the Round Table,' said Turquine, 'I defy you and all your fellowship.'

'That is overmuch said,' replied Sir Lancelot.

Then they put their spears in the rests and came together with their horses as fast as they might run, and either smote other in the midst of their shields, so that both their horses' backs broke under them. The knights were both stunned and, as soon as they might avoid their horses, they took their shields afore them, and drew out their swords, and came together eagerly, and either gave other many strong strokes ... And so within a while they had both got grimly wounds, and bled passing grievously. Thus they fared two hours and more ... then at the last they were both breathless, and stood leaning on their swords.

'Now, fellow,' said Sir Turquine, 'hold your hand a while, and tell me what I shall ask you.'

'Say on.'

Then Turquine said: 'You are the biggest man that I ever met with, and the best breathed ☙ , and like one knight that I hate above all other knights; so be it that you are not he I will lightly accord with you, and for your love I will deliver all the prisoners that I have, that is three score and four, if you will but tell me your name ...'

'It is well said,' said Sir Lancelot, 'but ... what knight is he that you so hate above all others?'

'Faithfully,' said Sir Turquine, 'his name is Sir Lancelot du Lake, for he slew my brother Sir Carados of the Dolorous Tower, who was one of the best knights alive; and therefore I make my vow, may I once meet with him, the one of us shall make an end of the other. And for Sir Lancelot's sake I have slain a hundred good knights, and as many have I maimed all utterly that they might never after help themselves, and many have died in prison, and yet I have three score and four; and all shall be delivered, if you will tell me your name, so long as you are not Sir Lancelot.'

'Sir knight, at your request,' said Sir Lancelot, 'I would have you know that I am Lancelot du Lake, King Ban's son of Benwick and knight of the Table Round. And now I defy you; so do your best.'

'Ah,' said Sir Turquine, 'Lancelot, you are unto me more welcome than ever was knight, for we shall never depart till one of us is dead.'

Then they hurled together like two wild bulls, thrashing and lashing with their shields and swords, that sometimes they both fell over their noses ... Then, at the last, Sir Turquine waxed faint, and gave somewhat aback,

☙ Sir Thomas Malory, *Morte Darthur.*

☙ Breathed: able to fight in full armour for a long time without getting out of breath.

75

Beaver: the lower face guard.

and bare his shield low for weariness. That espied Sir Lancelot, so he leapt upon him fiercely, got him by the beaver *of his helmet, and plucked him down on his knees, and then he pulled off his helm and smote his neck in sunder.*

Then Sir Lancelot untied Sir Gaheris and told him to release the prisoners from Sir Turquine's dungeon. *Gaheris went into the manor, and there he found a yeoman porter keeping many keys. Anon Sir Gaheris threw the porter unto the ground, and took the keys from him. Hastily he opened the prison door, and there he let out all the prisoners, and every man loosed the others of their bonds. And when they saw Sir Gaheris, they all thanked him, for they saw that he was wounded.*

'Not so,' said Sir Gaheris, 'it was Lancelot that slew Sir Turquine worshipfully with his own hands. I saw it with my own eyes.'

THE BEGETTING OF GALAHAD

RIDING OUT AFTER the following Whitsun Feast, Sir Lancelot chanced to cross the Bridge of Corbenic and found himself riding towards a fine, handsome castle. Gathered before it were all the townspeople, and as he approached they all called out to him, *'Welcome, Sir Lancelot du Lake, the flower of all knighthood, for you shall help us out of danger.'*

'What mean you,' said Sir Lancelot, 'that you cry so upon me?'

'Ah, fair knight,' said they all, 'here is within this tower a dolorous lady who has been there in pains many winters, for she is ever boiling in scalding water ... '

'Well,' said Sir Lancelot, 'then show me what I shall do.'

Then they brought Sir Lancelot into the tower; and when he came to the chamber where the lady was, the doors of iron unlocked and unbolted. And so Sir Lancelot went into the chamber that was as hot as any stew. And there Sir Lancelot took by the hand the fairest lady that ever he saw, and she was as naked as a needle; and by enchantment Queen Morgan le Fay and the Queen of Northgales had put her there in those pains, because she was called the fairest lady of that country, and never might she be delivered out of her great pains until the best knight of the world had taken her by the hand.

Then the people brought her clothes ... Presently this lady said unto Sir Lancelot, 'Sir, if it pleases you, will you go with me hereby into a chapel, that we may give thanks to God?' ...

So when they came there all the people gave thanks unto God and him, and said, 'Sir knight, since you have delivered this lady, you shall deliver us from a serpent that is here in a tomb.'

Then Sir Lancelot took his shield and said, 'Bring me thither and what I may do ... I will do.'

So when Sir Lancelot came thither he saw written upon the tomb letters of gold that said thus:

HERE SHALL COME A LEOPARD OF KING'S BLOOD, AND HE SHALL SLAY THIS SERPENT, AND THIS LEOPARD SHALL ENGENDER A LION IN THIS FOREIGN COUNTRY, THE WHICH LION SHALL PASS ALL OTHER KNIGHTS.

So then Sir Lancelot lifted up the tomb, and there came out a horrible and fiendly dragon, spitting fire out of his mouth. Then Sir Lancelot drew his sword and fought with the dragon long, and at last with great pain Sir Lancelot slew that dragon. Therewithal came King Pelles, the good and noble knight, and saluted Sir Lancelot and he him again.

'Now, fair knight,' said the king, 'what is your name? I require you of your knighthood to tell it me.'

'Sir,' said Sir Lancelot, 'wit you well my name is Sir Lancelot du Lake.'

'And my name is King Pelles, king of the foreign country and near cousin to Joseph of Arimathea.' And then they made much of each other, and so they went into the castle to take their repast. And so the king and Sir Lancelot led their life the greater part of that day together. And gladly would King Pelles have found the means that Sir Lancelot should have lain by his daughter, the fair Elaine, and for this intent: the king knew well that Sir Lancelot should beget a virgin youth upon his daughter which should be called Sir Galahad, the good knight, by whom all the foreign country should be brought out of danger; and by him the Holy Grail should be achieved.

Then came forth a lady named Dame Brisen, and she said unto the king, 'Sir, wit you well Sir Lancelot loves no lady in the world but Queen Guinevere. And therefore work by my counsel. I shall make him lie with your daughter, and he shall not know but that he lies by Queen Guinevere.'

'Ah, fair lady,' said the king, 'can you bring this about?'

'Sir,' said she, 'upon pain of my life, let me deal.'

For this Dame Brisen was one of the greatest enchanters that was that time in the world. And so at length by Dame Brisen's art she made one to come to Sir Lancelot that he knew well, and this man brought a ring from Queen Guinevere as if it had come from her, and such a one as she was accustomed to wear. And when Sir Lancelot saw that token, wit you well he was never so glad.

'Where is my lady?' said Sir Lancelot.

ABOVE: *Sir Lancelot slays the 'horrible and fiendly dragon'. The frontispiece to a 16th-century edition of Malory's* Morte Darthur.

'In the castle of Case,' said the messenger, 'but five miles hence.'

Then thought Sir Lancelot to be there the same night. And so this Dame Brisen, by the commandment of King Pelles, had Elaine sent to the castle with five and twenty knights. Then Sir Lancelot rode at night unto the castle, and there he was received worshipfully with such people, it seemed to him, as were about Queen Guinevere intimately. So when Sir Lancelot had alighted, he asked where the queen was. And Dame Brisen said she was in her bed. And then the people went away and Sir Lancelot was led into her chamber. And then Dame Brisen brought Sir Lancelot a cup of wine, and as soon as he had drunk that wine he was so enamoured and maddened that he might make no delay but went at once to bed. And so he thought that the maiden Elaine was Queen Guinevere; and wit you well that Sir Lancelot was glad, and so was that lady Elaine that she had got Sir Lancelot in her arms, for well she knew that the same night would be begotten upon her Sir Galahad, that should prove the best knight of the world.

And so they lay together until the middle of the morning; and all the windows and holes of that chamber were stopped, that no manner of daylight might be seen. And at length Sir Lancelot remembered him and arose

BELOW: *Elaine of Corbenic discovers Lancelot asleep under a tree in her garden. Drawing by Beardsley.*

78

and went to the window, and as soon as he had unshuttered the window the enchantment was past.

'Alas,' he said, 'that I have lived so long, for now am I shamed.'

And he took his sword in his hand and said, 'You traitoress! Who are you that I have lain by all this night? You shall die right here at my hands!'

Then this fair lady Elaine skipped out of bed all naked and kneeled down before Sir Lancelot and said, 'Fair courteous knight Sir Lancelot, you are come of kings' blood, and therefore I require you to have mercy upon me! And as you are renowned the most noble knight of the world, slay me not, for I have in my womb begotten of you what shall be the most noblest knight of the world.'

'Ah, false traitoress! Why have you betrayed me? Tell me at once,' said Sir Lancelot, 'who you are.'

'Sir,' said she, 'I am Elaine, the daughter of King Pelles.'

'Well,' said Sir Lancelot, 'I will forgive you.' And therewith he took her up in his arms and kissed her, for she was a fair lady and thereto lusty and young, and wise as any that was that time living. 'So God me help,' said Sir Lancelot, 'I cannot blame this on you; but she who made this enchantment upon me, if I may find her, that same Dame Brisen shall lose her head for her witchcrafts, for there was never knight deceived as I have been by her this night.'

And then she said, 'My lord, Sir Lancelot, I beseech you, see me as soon as you may, for I have obeyed me unto the prophecy that my father told me. And by his commandment to fulfil this prophecy I have given the greatest riches and the fairest flower that ever I had, and that is my maidenhood that I shall never have again. And therefore, gentle knight, you owe me your good will.'

And so Sir Lancelot arrayed him and armed him and took his leave mildly of that young lady Elaine. And he departed and rode to the castle of Corbenic where her father was. And as soon as her time came, she was delivered of a fair child and they christened him Galahad.

ABOVE: *Sir Lancelot runs amok. From Caxton's edition of Malory's* Morte Darthur, *published in 1529.*

But at the next feast of Camelot, Queen Guinevere discovered that Lancelot had fathered a child upon the lady Elaine; and she spoke harsh words to him, calling him false traitor knight and forbidding him ever to come into her presence again, that he swooned for sorrow; and when he awoke from his swoon, he ran mad and leapt from the window. He pulled off all his clothes and ran into the forest where, scratched with briars and soiled by mud, he lived as a wild man for almost two years.

ABOVE: *Lancelot and Elaine accompany the young Galahad to the monastery where he is to be educated. From an Italian manuscript, c. 1270.*

At length it chanced that in his wild wanderings he came once more to the castle of Corbenic, where the lady Elaine was still living with her father King Pelles and her little son Galahad. Sir Lancelot fell asleep in the garden of the castle beside a well. The lady Elaine, recognizing him, ran to tell her father, and the king had him carried into the room of the castle where dwelt the Holy Grail, and by virtue of that holy vessel, he was cured of his madness. And he dwelt there with the lady Elaine and his son Galahad a little while, and then he returned to the court and was reconciled with Queen Guinevere.

TRISTAN AND ISOLDE

RIVALIN, THE LORD OF LYONESSE, entrusted his lands to his loyal steward Rual li Foitenant, and crossed the sea to visit King Mark of Cornwall. While he was at Tintagel, he saw and fell in love with the beautiful Lady Blanchefleur, King Mark's sister. Blanchefleur was also smitten with love for Rivalin; she gave herself unto him and she conceived a child. A little later, Rivalin heard that his own lands had been invaded and he returned, taking Blanchefleur with him. He married her with due honour and then he went to battle. In the battle he was slain; and the tender lady's grief brought on her labour. She gave birth to a boy child; but she was too weak to survive the agony of birth. Rivalin and Blanchefleur were buried together. The baby, left in the care of loyal Rual, was christened Tristan, because of the sorrow attending his birth.

Tristan was blessed by God with great gifts; he was fair, strong and elegant of body, and clever at his books, speaking many languages with ease. He was very accomplished in courtly pursuits, from hunting and jousting to dancing and chess; but he excelled at playing the harp and singing.

One day he was buying goods on their ship from some merchants of Norway, who determined to steal him into slavery, for they could ask a high price for a youth so beautiful and so talented. They set sail, but no sooner had Tristan discovered what they had done than a fearful storm blew up, which drove the ship hard before it for a day and a night and cast it up on the coast of Cornwall. Tristan's looks, talent and courtly manners soon led him to the royal court at Tintagel; and King Mark was so impressed and delighted with the comely youth that he took him into his household, quite unaware that the boy was his closest kin.

Meanwhile, Rual left his home and set off on foot to search for the boy. For three long years he travelled through Europe, till at last he came to Cornwall, and heard that a youth answering Tristan's description was with King Mark at Tintagel. At once he journeyed to Tintagel and revealed to King Mark that the young man he had taken to his heart was his own sister's son. And Tristan was knighted, and set his heart on winning a knight's renown.

BELOW: *Tristan's mother Blanchefleur dies in childbirth, a woodcut from a 15th-century edition of Malory's* Morte Darthur.

LYONESSE

LYONESSE IS THE IMAGINARY COUNTRY of which Sir Tristan's father was king. In some versions of the story, the young hero must cross the sea to reach Cornwall, suggesting that his homeland is somewhere in France – for example Leonais in Brittany. Gottfried von Strassburg, however, calls this country Parmenie. An alternative identification is Lothian in Scotland, which was Loenois in Old French. Later romances clearly place Lyonesse as a stretch of land joining Cornwall to the Scilly Isles. This corresponds to a legendary country in Cornish folklore known as Lethowstow, which once linked the Scilly Isles to the mainland and filled up Mount's Bay, but which has now been sunk beneath the sea for generations.

There may be some factual basis for this legend. Part of Mount's Bay was once dry land, and archaeologists have discovered signs of human habitation dating from as late as 1,000 BC. Similarly, there are remains of stone walls and post sockets below water in the Scillies which suggest that some of them might once have been linked together. These remains are much later – early Christian – not so far removed from the time of Arthur. In addition, a tantalizing Latin reference records the Emperor Maximus banishing a heretic to 'the Isle of Scilly' in the fourth century – but this could be a scribal error.

When King Mark was only a child, Cornwall had been conquered by King Anguish of Ireland, and every five years since then Anguish's champion, his brother-in-law Morold, had been sent to collect a tribute from the Cornish: thirty young men of noble birth, to be given up to serfdom. Otherwise, someone must face Morold in single combat. But he was such a terrifying warrior that no one dared to fight him. The time of the tribute now approached, and Tristan challenged Morold to single combat, though he was still young and untried.

The duel was to take place on a small island off the coast. Each knight ferried himself over in a boat; Morold moored his boat on the island but, when Tristan arrived, he cast his adrift on the sea.

'Why did you do that?' asked Morold.

'Because only one of us will leave this island alive,' answered Tristan. Morold only laughed; to him Tristan seemed too young and inexperienced to fear as an opponent, and when they began fighting he soon wounded Tristan in the upper part of his thigh.

'That wound will be fatal,' said Morold. 'My sword blade is poisoned with a venom unknown to any doctor; only my sister Queen Isolde can save you now. If you surrender I will take you to her.'

'I shall not,' said Tristan. 'Even if I have to die in the end, the combat is not over yet!' And he ran to attack Morold once more, striking him a terrible blow to the head, so that his helmet split, and the sword lodged in his brain pan. Tristan wrenched out the sword and it broke, leaving a large splinter in the skull. This was Morold's death wound; he fell to the ground, and Tristan struck off his head.

Mourning, the Irishmen returned home with their dead lord; and Morold's sister, Queen Isolde, finding the splinter of steel lodged in his skull, removed it and kept it in a casket.

Meanwhile, Tristan's wounded thigh festered and putrified until no one could endure the stench of it. Tristan knew that only Queen Isolde could heal him; but he also knew that she would rather kill him than live herself. At last he took ship for Ireland, taking only his harp. When he came to Dublin, he dressed in filthy old rags and played so sweetly that he soon attracted a crowd. He told everyone that he was a musician named Tantris, and that he had been wounded by pirates. His fame quickly spread, and soon he was fetched to the palace on the orders of the queen. She was so impressed that she undertook to heal his wound, on condition that he would teach music to her young daughter, the Princess Isolde.

The princess was entrancingly beautiful, and quick to learn whatever Tristan taught her, so that the days flew past in mutual pleasure. When Tristan was fully cured he returned to Cornwall, to King Mark's great joy. He told of Dublin, and how the queen had cured him, but most of all he spoke about the radiant Princess Isolde.

BELOW: *Tristan, disguised as the minstrel Tantris, takes his leave of Queen Isolde and her daughter Princess Isolde.*

ABOVE: *Tristan plays the harp before the Princess Isolde. From a 14th-century manuscript of the French* Roman de Tristan.

⚜ Gottfried von Strassburg, *Tristan and Isolde.*

Now Tristan was so honoured that some of the barons began to be jealous of him. It was rumoured that Mark would make him his heir; so these evil councillors badgered Mark day and night to marry and beget sons of his own.

'Very well,' said King Mark at last, 'and whom do you advise me to marry?'

'Princess Isolde of Ireland,' said the barons, arguing that this would make peace for ever between the two kingdoms and that Tristan should be sent to ask for her hand. Secretly they hoped that the Irish would kill him in revenge for Morold's death.

'I forbid it!' said Mark. 'Tristan has almost died saving your sons from slavery!'

But Tristan volunteered to go; and Mark could not keep him against his will. He sailed with a hundred companions to Wexford, disguised as a merchant. While he was bargaining there, he heard that a fiendish dragon was infesting a valley near by, and that the king had offered his daughter as a prize to the man who could kill it. Early the next morning, Tristan armed and rode off to search for the beast. Soon he found it, and at the first charge he thrust his spear into its open mouth ⚜ *and down its throat, so that it stopped just short of the heart. He and his horse crashed into the creature so violently that the horse fell dead under him, and he only just escaped. The dragon attacked the horse, burning it and then devouring it, until the monster had eaten up the front half of its body as far as the saddle. But then the spear caused it such agony that it left the horse, and headed for a rocky place, with Tristan its adversary hard on its heels.* Tristan attacked it, but it spewed out burning hot flames and poisonous smoke, till he was almost overcome. He fought on until the wounded serpent sank to the ground, exhausted, and he thrust his sword into its heart. In its death throes the dragon let out a roar that shook the whole countryside.

When Tristan saw that it was dead, he forced its jaws open by main strength, and with his sword cut off as much of the tongue as he could, stuffed it inside his breastplate, and let the jaws snap together. Then he went into the wilderness, intending to rest in hiding during the day so as to recover his strength, and when night fell to return to his countrymen. But the heat he had endured, both from his own struggles and from the beast, had so exhausted him that he was almost dead of it. He noticed the gleam of a cold stream pouring into a large pool from a rock. He fell into it, in full armour, and sank to the bottom, leaving only his mouth above the water. He lay there for a day and a night! The foul tongue he carried with him took away his senses, for the fumes it gave off robbed him of his strength and vigour.

Meanwhile, the king's seneschal had long loved Princess Isolde and wanted to win her hand. He was near by when he heard the dragon's terrible death-cry. He reached the scene just as Tristan sank into the pool out of sight; seeing the half-eaten horse and the dead dragon, and no sign of a conquering knight, he thought he would claim the reward for killing the creature. After much struggling, he managed to hack off the dragon's head, and took it away with him back to court, as proof that he had done the deed.

The Princess Isolde was horrified, for she hated the seneschal. But the queen her mother comforted her: 'I am certain that the seneschal did not kill the dragon,' she said. 'He is far too cowardly. Let us go to the beast's lair and see if we

ABOVE: *Sir Tristan fights the dragon.*

can discover what really took place.' So they rode to the little valley where they found the headless body and the back half of Tristan's horse with its English-style saddle and trappings. Then the ladies knew that someone other than the seneschal had been there, and they searched until they saw the gleam of Tristan's helmet in the water. Carefully they dragged him out of the pool, laid him down and felt his feeble pulse.

'This man has been poisoned by the dragon's foul breath,' said the queen. 'We are only just in time to save him. Loosen his armour, give him air.' When they came to remove his breastplate, they found the dragon's tongue curled up behind it and rejoiced that the seneschal's claim was false. Tristan regained his colour and came to his senses, and they recognized him as their beloved minstrel Tantris. The queen was delighted, and swore to protect and help him in the future.

One day, as Tristan was taking a bath, Isolde had instructed a page to clean and repair all his armour and weapons, and she idly took up his sword to examine it. She noticed for the first time that a piece was broken from the blade and looked carefully at the shape. With trembling hands, she fetched the casket in which her mother had preserved the fragment of steel taken from her uncle Morold's head wound. To her horror, the splinter fitted perfectly. She was filled with anger and loathing at the way she and her mother had been deceived. *She grasped the sword and stood over Tristan as he was sitting in his bath:*

'So,' she said, 'Tristan, is it really you?'

'No, my lady, I am Tantris.'

'So you are, as I know perfectly well, both Tantris and Tristan; and the two are doomed: Tantris will have to make amends for what Tristan has done to me; you must pay for my uncle!'

'No, sweet maiden, no! For God's sake, what are you doing? Think of your good name and spare me; you are a woman, and a noblewoman. If people say of you that you have committed murder, then wonderful Isolde will for ever be dead to honour ...'

Just then the queen, her mother, entered at the door: 'Why,' said she, 'what is happening? Daughter, what do you intend doing with that? Is this proper behaviour for women?'

'Alas, my lady mother, remember what a terrible wrong has been done to both of us: this is the murderer Tristan, who slew your brother. Now we have a good opportunity to revenge ourselves on him and thrust this sword through his body – a better chance will never come our way!'

'Is this Tristan? How do you know?'

'I know, I am sure, this is Tristan. This sword is his; now look well on it, and on the splinter beside it ... Just now I inserted the fragment into the accursed space and – to my sorrow – I found that they were a perfect whole.'

'Isolde, what have you recalled to me? Oh, that my life was ever begun! If this is truly Tristan, how I have been deceived in him!'

Isolde once more ran at Tristan, and with that he once more cried out, 'Oh, fair Isolde, have mercy!'

In her heart, two contending feelings, two warring opposites, anger and womanhood, which match so ill with one another, were quarreling hard together. When Isolde's anger wanted to slay her enemy, then sweet womanliness would say softly, 'No, don't do it!' Thus her heart was in two minds: the same heart was both cruel and kind. The lovely maiden flung the sword away, and then snatched it up again. In her mind she did not know which of them to choose, evil or good. She wanted and did not want, she wished both to act and to refrain. This doubt bent her one way and

ABOVE: *Isolde nurses Tristan back to health after he has been poisoned by the dragon's tongue. Illustration by Beardsley.*

another, until at last sweet womanhood won the victory over anger, with the result that her deadly enemy lived, and her uncle was unavenged.

Then she flung the sword from her and, bursting into tears, she cried: 'Woe is me, that I should live to see this day!'

'My beloved daughter,' said the wise queen, 'I would rather endure one sorrow than two; my brother's death grieved me, but I would rather give up the feud than see you married to the seneschal, which we cannot prevent if we kill Tristan.'

'I promise you, my lady,' said Tristan, 'that if I have injured you in the past, I now wish nothing but your honour and advantage and, if you let me live, I will tell you how I plan to bring this affair to the happiest conclusion.'

Then Tristan informed the queen that his purpose was to win Isolde's hand for his uncle King Mark, thus ending all hostilities between Ireland and Cornwall. The queen was very pleased and undertook to gain the support of her husband.

The next day was the one appointed for judgement in the matter of the seneschal and the dragon. 'My lords,' said the seneschal before

GOTTFRIED VON STRASSBURG

ALMOST NOTHING IS KNOWN for certain about the life of Gottfried von Strassburg, one of the greatest poets in the German language. He came from, and possibly worked, in Strasbourg; later writers refer to him as 'meister', which implies that he had completed a course of studies at a university. But much more about Gottfried can be learned from his poem.

Tristan was written in about 1210. It is an astonishingly sophisticated piece of work. Gottfried had read more widely in the classics than most medieval poets – he often introduces classical myth and allusion, and can translate ornate Latin rhetorical devices into graceful German. It is often said that with this technical virtuosity and familiarity with classical poetry he anticipates the Renaissance.

Gottfried considered himself the equal if not the superior of an élite band of brilliant young German minnesinger and romance poets. In the earliest surviving passage of literary criticism in German, he praises the genius of Heinrich von Veldeke, Hartmann von Aue,

Bligger von Steinach, Reinmar von Hagenau and Walther von der Vogelweide. However, he reserves a passage of scathing criticism for a poet whom he does not name, but who is easily identified as his great contemporary Wolfram von Eschenbach, author of *Parzifal* and *Willehalm*. Gottfried accuses Wolfram, the 'friend of the hare', of 'skipping about' on the field of poetry, of making up spurious stories, and of being so obscure in his diction that he has to write notes to go with his poems.

Gottfried's attitude to religion itself often appears flippant, as for instance in his celebrated remark, when Isolde succeeds in tricking her way through a trial by ordeal, that 'Christ Almighty is like a sleeve blown in the wind.' But there is no doubting the sincerity of his belief that love makes life worth living. His Tristan is an accomplished courtier, a musician of genius, an expert huntsman, a poet and a diplomat; but, without love, it would profit him nothing, for 'he that never had sorrow from love never had joy from it either.'

the assembled court, 'I am here to claim what is mine by right, for the king promised that he who slew the dragon should win the hand of the Princess Isolde in marriage. I slew the dragon and here is its head to prove it.'

'Your majesty,' said Tristan, rising from his seat, 'examine the head and see if it contains a tongue.'

The dragon's jaws were opened and everyone could see that its tongue had been cut out. Tristan produced the tongue and explained what the cowardly seneschal had done. The seneschal was publicly shamed, and forced to withdraw in disgrace.

After that the agreement between King Anguish and Tristan about Isolde's marriage to King Mark was formalized, to the approval and delight of everyone. Tristan sought out as many as could be found of Cornish men who had been sent to Ireland as tribute and put them all in a ship. Then he made ready to return to his own ship, taking the Princess Isolde with him.

While Tristan and his companions were making ready, Isolde's mother, the wise queen, was preparing in a glass vessel a love potion so subtly devised and blended, and imbued with such power, that if a man and a woman drank it together, he must love her before all things, whether he wanted to or no, and she must love him alone. They would share one death and one life, one sorrow and one joy.

The wise lady took this drink and said quietly to Brangane: 'My dear niece ... you must go forth with my daughter. Take this flask with its potion, keep it close about you and guard it above all your possessions. Make sure that no one knows about it, and take especial care that nobody drinks any! When Isolde and Mark have been united in love, make it your special task to pour out this drink as wine for them and see that they drink it all. Do not allow anyone else to drink with them, and do not drink with them yourself. This potion is a love-charm.'

'Dearest lady,' answered Brangane, 'since you both wish it, I shall gladly accompany her and watch over her honour and all her concerns, as well as ever I can.'

So Tristan and Isolde and her ladies-in-waiting boarded their ships and set sail for Cornwall. Tristan visited Isolde in her cabin *and as he was sitting beside her and speaking about this and that, he ordered something to drink.*

BELOW: *King Anguish of Ireland hands over his daughter Isolde to Sir Tristan as affianced bride for his uncle King Mark of Cornwall. From the French prose* Roman de Tristan, *a late 15th-century manuscript.*

Now, apart from the princess, there was no one there except some very young ladies-in-waiting. 'Look,' said one of them, 'here is some wine in this little flask.' No, it did not contain wine, although it looked very similar. It was their eternal sorrow, their endless hearts' need, from which both were to die! But she was quite ignorant of all this; she passed the flask to Tristan and he passed it to Isolde. After a while, she reluctantly drank, then returned it to Tristan, and he drank it; and both of them believed it was wine. Just then in came Brangane and, recognizing the flask, she realized at once what had happened. She was so shocked and appalled that her strength ebbed from her and she turned as white as any corpse. With a heart that had died within her, she seized that sorrowful, accursed flask, carried it outside and flung it into the wild and raging sea!

ABOVE: *Tristan and Isolde drink the fatal love potion while crossing from Ireland to Cornwall.*

89

HOW SIR TRISTRAM
DRANK OF THE
LOVE DRINK

'Alas, alas!' cried Brangane, 'Oh, that I had never been born into the world! Unhappy creature, I have lost my honour and failed of my word! May God have pity everlasting that ever I came on this journey, and that death did not seize me when I was told to accompany Isolde on this fatal voyage! Alas, Tristan and Isolde, this drink will be the death of you both!'

Unaware of the poison they had innocently drunk, Tristan and Isolde began to feel the strong compulsion of love. They were forced to look at one another, to sigh, and to feel unbearable longing. Before the journey's end, they had confessed their feelings and acted on them too; and the tender passion possessed them utterly.

Only Brangane knew what had happened and, as she felt in part responsible, she helped the lovers as best she could. As the wedding day drew near, Isolde trembled to think of the wedding night because she was no longer a maiden. Brangane took her mistress's place in King Mark's bed and gave up her own maidenhead to hide Isolde's shame.

For many years, Tristan and Isolde managed to keep their love secret, with the help of the faithful Brangane. But this could not continue for ever; enemies of the pair began to spread rumours about them, even to the king. A spiteful and deceitful dwarf named Melot discovered that Tristan and Isolde used to meet sometimes by night in an orchard, so he and King Mark hid themselves in the branches of a huge, ancient apple tree overhanging a stream. Tristan and Isolde saw the reflections of the king and the dwarf in the water, and they cunningly pretended to have no love for one another at all, but to be discussing how they could counter the wicked scandal-mongers who were turning the king against them. Mark was reassured and regretted his suspicions; but before long Melot had persuaded him to try another trick. He advised the king to have Tristan and Brangane wait on himself and Isolde in their chamber, and to leave it himself to attend Matins ❧ . This the king did; and, as soon as he was gone, Melot sprinkled flour on the floor between Tristan's bed and Isolde's. Tristan saw this and knew that a trap was being laid, but his desire for Isolde was so great that he made a great leap between the two beds. Unfortunately, they had all been bled ❧ earlier that day so that with the exertion Tristan's vein opened and he bloodied all the sheets. Then he leapt back into his own bed and bloodied those sheets too. When King Mark returned, he saw the blood in his own bed and in Tristan's and, although Isolde claimed that she herself had bled on her own sheets, he was more and more certain that they were deceiving him. He decided that Isolde should publicly undergo a trial by ordeal.

King Arthur and a hundred of his noble knights travelled from Caerleon to be present at Isolde's trial. King Mark and his court were

❧ In the Middle Ages, this usually took place at midnight.

❧ They had had blood drawn from their veins by leeches, which was supposedly good for the health.

90

all there, including Isolde's three chief accusers, Denoalan, Ganelon and Godwin. Tristan had disguised himself, according to Isolde's instructions, as a leper, and he waited where she had told him, beside the marshy ground known as Malpas, which everyone had to cross.

When Queen Isolde arrived, she dismounted from her palfrey ✷ and sent it across the marsh ahead of her.

✷ *Then she went forward to the plank bridge [and spoke to the leper]: 'I want you to do something for me ... I do not want to dirty my clothes. You shall be my donkey and carry me gently across the planks.'*

'Nay, noble queen,' he said, 'don't ask me to do such a thing! I am a leper, a hunch-back, deformed.'

'Hurry up!' she said, 'Get into position. Do you think I will catch your disease? Have no fears, I shall not.'

'Ah, God!' he said to himself. 'What is she going to do? ... ' He was leaning on his crutch all this time.

'Good lord, leper, you are very fat! Turn your face that way and your back this way; I shall climb on like a squire.'

Then the leper smiled to himself, turned his back, and she mounted; everyone was looking at them, kings and counts. Holding himself up with his crutch, he lifted one foot and planted the other on the ground. Often he seemed about to topple over and put on an air of great suffering. The fair Isolde rode him, legs astride ... The squires ran [to meet the leper]. King Arthur went over, and the others in succession. The leper bent his face as he arrived from the other side and Isolde let herself slip to the ground.

Then the fire was built up, and the iron put in it to heat till it was white hot.

A silken cloth of dark grey, worked with animal figures in tiny stitches, was placed before the king's tent and spread out on the green grass. The cloth had been bought in Nicaea. Not one holy relic remained anywhere in Cornwall from a treasury or a phylactery, a chest or box or other kind of reliquary ... they had all been placed on the cloth and arranged in order.

The kings drew to one side. They wished to make a just decision. King Arthur, always lively in speech, spoke first: '... The noble and virtuous Isolde does not wish for any respite or period of grace. I want those who have come to hear her trial to know for certain that I shall have them hanged if, after this trial, they repeat their nonsensical accusations out of envy. They will have deserved their death. Now listen, king: whoever is at fault, let the queen come forward so that both great and small may see her and, placing her right hand over these holy relics, she shall swear to the Heavenly King that she has never loved your nephew in any way shamefully or wickedly ... '

'My lord Arthur, what can I do? ... If anyone, after the queen has cleared her name in this meadow, ever speaks dishonourably of the queen, he will pay for it ... '

Then the counsellors separated. Everyone sat down according to their rank, except the two kings; Isolde was between them holding their hands.

✷ Palfrey: a standard riding horse for ladies; not big enough to carry a knight in full armour.

✷ Béroul, *Tristan.*

Gawain stood near the relics, and the celebrated household of Arthur was seated round the cloth.

Arthur, who was nearest to Isolde, began to speak: 'Listen to me, fair Isolde, and hear of what you stand accused: [you must swear] that Tristan has never loved you improperly or shamefully, or any otherwise than he ought to love his uncle's wife.'

'My lords,' she answered, 'by God's mercy I see holy relics here. Listen now to what I swear, and may it reassure the king: so help me God and Saint Hilary, and by these relics, in this holy place, and by all those relics that are not here and all the relics there are in the world, I swear that no man ever came between my thighs except the leper who carried me on his back across the ford and my husband, King Mark ... ❧ If I have not said enough, my lord, I will improve the oath in whatever manner you tell me.'

'Lady,' said the king, 'this will be quite sufficient, as far as I can see. Now take the iron into your hand and, in what you have just sworn to us, may God help you in your need!'

'Amen,' said the fair Isolde. In the name of God she grasped the iron, bore it, and was not burned. Thus it was openly shown and understood by all the world that Christ the Almighty is like a sleeve blown in the wind. He falls and moulds himself into shape, in whatever position you place him, as closely and smoothly as by rights he should. He can be commanded by every heart, whether for the truth or for deceit.

❧ Gottfried von Strassburg, *Tristan and Isolde*.

After this Mark's suspicions were laid to rest, but he advised Tristan to visit other courts. This Tristan did. After a few months had passed, Mark recalled Tristan to Cornwall. When he and Isolde saw one another again, their eyes sparkled and their cheeks and lips returned to their former fresh colour, where before they had both been pale and drawn from melancholy, and they could not keep their eyes from each other. Mark could see that they were in love, and he publicly banished them from his court and lands.

Tristan took Isolde by the hand and, bringing nothing but his harp, his sword, his hunting horn and bow, and his favourite dog Hudain, they left the court. They lived simply in the forest; outdoors all day, and curled up by night in a cave. They were blissfully happy. One day, as King Mark was hunting in the forest, he found the two of them sleeping in a sunlit glade. As luck would have it, they lay apart, and with Tristan's naked sword between them. King Mark was deeply moved when he saw this, for he took it to mean that they lived chastely and had not dishonoured him. Seeing a ray of sunshine beaming down through the leaves into Isolde's face, he took one of his gloves and entwined its fingers in a branch so as to shade her. Then he took Tristan's sword, leaving his own in its place, and tiptoed away.

Mark informed his barons that he wished to recall Tristan and Isolde as he was convinced of their innocence. He received them with great honour. But, though Mark behaved affectionately towards Isolde, he had her watched, and the lovers were compelled to act with

discretion. This was such a contrast to the freedom of the forest that they both grew wretched; the more they were watched and kept apart, the stronger grew their desire for one another. At last they risked everything to meet by night. Alas! King Mark came unexpectedly and

ABOVE: *King Mark surprises the lovers in bed together. From the late 15th-century French* Roman de Tristan.

93

ABOVE: *A woodcut of the scene in which Mark surprises Tristan in bed with Isolde.*

found them together in one bed. He went off to fetch his retainers and barons, in order to denounce them and imprison them; but Tristan saw him leaving and knew that the only way to save their lives was for him to leave the country at once. The lovers made a tender farewell, with many tears, and exchanged rings. Then Tristan took a ship for France.

To keep his mind from his grief Tristan now began a time of knight-errantry, travelling the courts of Europe and taking on whatever challenge or cause offered. He visited King Arthur and became a knight of the Round Table; many tales are told of his deeds of chivalry.

At last he came to Brittany, to help its duke overcome enemies who were invading his lands. Tristan stayed on at the court because he had made friends with the duke's son, Caherdin. This young man had a sister named Isolde of the White Hands, who soon fell into a love-longing for Tristan; but Tristan never looked at her but as the sister of a friend. One day as Tristan sat alone, playing his harp and singing a sad song of his love for Isolde, Caherdin overheard him and, believing that he had at last solved the riddle of Tristan's sadness, persuaded his father to offer Tristan Isolde's hand in marriage. At first Tristan would have refused, but seeing that he could not do so without either giving offence or revealing the secret of his love for his uncle's wife, he agreed. Isolde was by no means unwilling, and the wedding was celebrated quickly. But when Tristan lay down beside his wife, he knew that he could never take another woman in his arms except Isolde of Ireland; so the marriage was not consummated that night, or any other night. Out of pride, Isolde of the White Hands never complained of Tristan's coldness, or confessed to anyone that she was still a virgin; but she grew bitter that her beauty was thus despised.

One day, as Isolde and Caherdin were out riding together, her horse took fright and ran with her through a large stream. As they passed, some of the spray flew up and splashed Isolde between her thighs. She laughed and said, 'This water has been bolder with my person than any man I have known.' But Caherdin was close behind and overheard her remark. Shocked, he pressed her for an explanation, and at last she admitted the true state of her marriage. Caherdin was angry that his sister had been slighted and hurt; and he at once returned to the castle and confronted Tristan.

Tristan was grieved by his friend's anger and told him about Isolde the Fair, and how his passion for her would not allow him to be unfaithful, even with his own wife. Caherdin wished to see this paragon of beauty, so the two men disguised themselves as pilgrims and travelled to Cornwall. Tristan contrived to send a message to Isolde, and they spent one night together in the forest, where they renewed the joys of their love. But Isolde was jealously watched and it was dangerous to remain; so the two friends returned to Brittany. Isolde of the White Hands, seeing her brother would still not take her part against Tristan, fed her resentment in silence.

It chanced that Tristan fought a battle against the wicked knight Estult l'Orgillus; he killed him, but not before the other's poisoned spear had pierced deep into his thigh. Tristan returned in agony, the poison spreading through his veins until his whole body was infected. The best doctors in Brittany were sent for, but none of them could help him. Tristan recalled how his earlier wound had been healed by Queen Isolde of Ireland, whose skills had been passed down to her daughter. So Tristan asked Caherdin to cross the sea to Cornwall once again, bearing his ring, and beg Isolde to come to him. He told Caherdin to raise a white sail on his ship if he returned with Isolde, and a black one if he was alone. Isolde of the White Hands overheard them talking together. Her heart swelled with anger and jealousy, but she kept it all within, pretending to know nothing and behaving with tender concern towards her husband.

Caherdin succeeded in gaining an audience with Queen Isolde. He gave her Tristan's message and the ring. She had no doubt in her mind about what to do. At once she prepared her remedies and made ready to leave with Caherdin. They took ship the same night and made for the rocky shore of Brittany. Just outside the bay they were becalmed and could make no headway.

❧ *Tristan was wretchedly unhappy; often he mourned, often he sighed, for Isolde whom he so yearned to see. Tears rained from his eyes, his body tossed about, and his longing almost killed him. While he was in this state of anguish and misery, his wife Isolde came before him. Intending great deceit, she said, 'My love, Caherdin is on his way. I have seen his ship on the sea, and I saw it sail with great difficulty; but none the less I could see it well enough to recognize it as his. Please God, may it bring news to give your heart new strength.'*

At this news, Tristan started up trembling, and said to Isolde, 'Fair love, do you know for certain that it is his ship? Then tell me, what kind of sail does it bear?'

Then Isolde said: 'Certainly I know. The sail is quite black; they have hoisted it high up, because they lack wind.'

At this, Tristan felt such agony that he never had and never would feel a greater pain. He turned his face to the wall, and said, 'God save Isolde and me! Since you did not wish to come to me, I shall die for love of you. I can cling on to life no longer; I am dying for you, Isolde, my fair love.' Then three times he said, 'Isolde, my love'; and at the fourth he rendered up his spirit.

❧ Thomas d'Angleterre, *Tristan.*

95

THE VERSIONS OF TRISTAN AND ISOLDE

THE TRISTAN LEGEND was one of the earliest and most popular of medieval romances. All surviving versions ultimately derive from one source, the 'Tristan archetype', a poem which has not survived, but the content of which can be reconstructed from its derivatives. It was composed in about AD 1150, before the works of Chrétien de Troyes or any other surviving Arthurian romance. The verse romances which survive today are all fragmentary, but between them they make up a complete story. I have taken the beginning and main part of the tale from Gottfried von Strassburg's masterpiece *Tristan und Isolde*, the scene of the tricked ordeal from Béroul's *Roman de Tristan* and the ending from Thomas d'Angleterre's *Tristan*.

Béroul's poem, and the *Tristan* of Eilhart von Oberg, are closest to the archetype. They depict the lovers as victims of an appalling tragedy, in that they are noble characters compelled through the accidental drinking of the love potion to behave in a very ignoble way.

Béroul employs irony to make this point, referring to the lovers as 'noble' and 'virtuous', whenever they are about to do something especially deceitful or self-indulgent.

Thomas d'Angleterre, who may have been attached to the court of Henry II in England, conceived a more courtly idea of the lovers. He explores romantic love as an overmastering passion which, no matter how destructive and anti-social, is yet in its way an ideal form of behaviour, which exalts the lovers and ennobles them through suffering. In his poem, the love potion is more symbolic than causal.

Gottfried was emphatic in preferring Thomas's version, but he goes far beyond it, and raises romantic love to cult status. He deliberately echoes the liturgy and employs the language that the mystic divine poets, led by St Bernard of Clairvaux, used to describe the intense personal devotion of a monk for Christ or Mary. He applies it, however, to an adulterous and treasonable love affair.

Then the knights and companions wept throughout the house. They cried aloud and made great dole. Knights and sergeants arose and bore his body from the bed. They laid him on a cloth of samite and covered him with a striped pall.

Then the wind rose on the sea and blew itself into the middle of the sail, bearing the ship to land. Isolde disembarked from the ship, and heard

ABOVE: *A composite illustration. Tristan drinks the love potion; Isolde, in a ship with black sails, arrives too late to save him. From the prose* Tristan, *c. 1470.*

97

the great lamenting in the streets and the bells of minsters and chapels. She asked the people for news, for whom the bells were tolling. An old man answered her: 'Fair lady, so God help me, we have here a greater grief than anyone has had before. Tristan the noble, Tristan the valiant, is dead; never has this region suffered such a catastrophe.'

As soon as Isolde heard this news, she could not speak a word, for grief. His death afflicted her so greatly that she passed uncovered through the streets, ahead of the others, to the palace. ... Isolde came to where Tristan's body lay. She turned to face the east and prayed for him pitifully: 'Tristan, my only love, now that I see you dead, I have no reason to live any longer. You are dead through love of me, and I am dying, my love, of sorrow, because I could not come in time to cure you of your wound. My love, my love, I shall never be consoled for your death ...'

She embraced him and, lying beside him on the bed, she kissed his lips and his face, clasping him tightly in her arms, body to body, mouth to mouth; she gave up her spirit at that moment, and died beside her beloved, for sorrow at his death.

Afterwards, so the stories tell, the bodies of the two lovers were brought back to Cornwall, where King Mark buried them beside each other at Tintagel. From their two bodies grew a vine and a rose, which entwined their branches around one another so closely that it was impossible for anyone to separate them.

THE SECOND TALE OF SIR LANCELOT

GUINEVERE ABDUCTED

ON ASCENSION DAY, King Arthur held court at Camelot  as was his custom, and after the feast the noble knights and ladies fell to pleasant conversation. Suddenly there came before them a stranger knight, fully armed for battle, who said: 'King Arthur, I have many knights and ladies from your lands imprisoned in my castle. Neither you nor any man here is rich or powerful enough to release them. But I offer you this one chance: if there is just one knight here whom you trust enough to let him accompany the queen after me into the forest, I swear that if he can defend the queen against me, then will I deliver up to him all the prisoners that I hold. So shall he and the queen and the prisoners return unhurt.' With that he turned and left the hall.

The court was in an uproar after hearing this insolent message. Then Sir Kay the seneschal came before the king, and announced that he would leave his service immediately. King Arthur was deeply distressed at this, for Kay was his foster-brother, who had been with him all his life. He tried to persuade Kay not to leave, but Kay was adamant. Then the king went to Queen Guinevere and asked her to persuade Kay to stay at the court. The queen went to him and earnestly begged him not to go, but he would not listen. At last the queen got down and prostrated herself full length on the ground at his feet, affirming that she would not rise until he gave his word not to leave. At that Kay promised her that he would remain, but only on condition that she and King Arthur would grant him one request. She undertook that they would do so and brought him before the king saying, 'I have had hard work to persuade Kay to stay with us; and I bring him to you with the assurance that you will grant whatever he is about to ask you.' With tears of joy in his eyes, the king promised at once to grant Kay's request.

'My thanks, Sire,' said Sir Kay. 'This is what you have agreed to grant me – that the queen shall be entrusted to my safe keeping, and that we go after the knight who awaits us in the forest.'

The king was trapped, for he could not break his word; but his grief and anger showed clearly in his face. He took the queen by the hand – she had turned white – and said, 'My lady, there is no help for it. You must go with Kay.'

⚫ This is the first mention made in Arthurian literature of Camelot, Arthur's principal castle. Chrétien does not give any description or clue about its location, except that it was 'in the region of Caerleon'. This was Arthur's principal castle in Geoffrey of Monmouth.

BELOW: *King Arthur holds court at Camelot according to his custom.*

99

ABOVE: *Sir Kay rashly leads Queen Guinevere into the forest after the stranger knight.*

'Trust me,' said Sir Kay confidently, 'I will bring her back quite safe and happy.' And he led her away to the courtyard where their horses were being made ready for them. The knights and ladies followed them outside, appalled. Not one of them had any faith in Sir Kay's ability to protect the queen, and they all began to lament as if she were already lying in her coffin, for they were certain that she would never come back alive.

Sir Gawain then said to his uncle the king: 'This is a very foolish thing you have allowed to happen. I think we must go after them.' The king agreed and a large party of knights armed themselves, called for their horses and prepared to search for Sir Kay and the queen.

Gawain set off, accompanied by two squires, each leading a fresh horse. As they neared the forest, they saw Kay's horse come running out, riderless, with broken reins, a shattered saddle-bow and stirrup leathers all stained with blood. Then they feared the worst. Gawain was some way ahead of the rest and shortly he saw coming towards him a knight, whose horse was panting hoarsely and lathered in sweat. Recognizing Gawain, the knight stopped and said, 'My lord Gawain, as you can see, my horse is at the end of his strength and I cannot ride him further. I pray you lend or give me one of your two spare horses; I promise to pay you back later.'

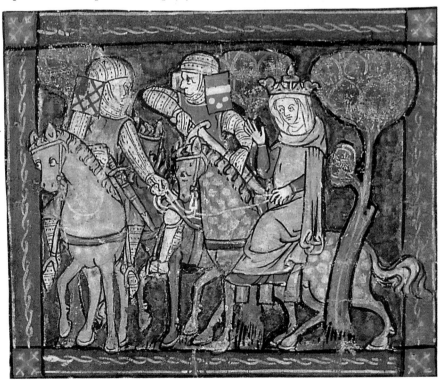

RIGHT: *The same scene, from an English manuscript of Chrétien's* Lancelot.

100

And Gawain replied, 'Certainly. Take whichever one you prefer.' The knight leapt on to the nearest horse and dashed off in frantic haste. The horse he had been riding fell dead from exhaustion, and Gawain followed him at a slower pace. He had not gone far when he saw the horse he had just given the knight dead on the ground. All round were signs of a tremendous fight. A little further on he saw the knight himself on foot, still fully armed, coming up to a cart.

In those days carts were used as pillories are now; and each large town, where now there are more than three thousand carts, in those days had only one. Like our pillories, the cart was for all criminals, for traitors and murderers, for those who had lost trials by combat, for those who had stolen someone else's goods by theft or seized them by force on the highway. The guilty person was taken and made to mount the cart and was dragged through the streets. He lost all his legal rights and was never afterwards heard at any court, nor invited or honoured there. Because carts were so feared in those days, there was a saying: 'Whenever you see a cart cross your path, make the sign of the cross and think on God, lest evil befalls you.'

The knight, on foot and without his lance, hurried after the cart and saw on the shafts a dwarf who held a long switch in his hand, like a driver. 'Dwarf,' he said, 'for God's sake tell me if you have seen my lady the queen pass this way?'

The base, low-born dwarf would not tell him anything, but said, 'If you want to climb into this cart I'm driving, you'll know tomorrow what has become of the queen.' He continued on his way, not waiting for the knight, who hesitated for only two steps before getting in ... Gawain quickly caught up, and was astonished to find the knight sitting in the cart.

He too asked the dwarf about the queen, but when the dwarf invited him to sit in the cart, he declined, saying that he would follow it instead. So they went along and at nightfall they came to a town, where all the people mocked the knight in the cart cruelly, asking the dwarf in what gruesome fashion he was to be executed. The dwarf said nothing, but took the knights to an inn and left them there. They were greeted by a beautiful damsel, who received Gawain courteously, although she was cold and scornful to the knight of the cart.

The following day, as they were standing by the window in their lodgings, they saw the queen pass by below them, led by a tall, strong knight and accompanied by a bier with a wounded knight lying in it. As fast as they could,

*Gawain's courtesy and generosity were proverbial. A knight's horse, like a top-of-the-range car today, would cost a year's income.

*Chrétien de Troyes, *Le Chevalier de la Charrette (Lancelot).*

BELOW: *Sir Lancelot riding in the cart, with Sir Gawain following on behind. From a French manuscript.*

⁌ Gorre, where Meleagant and Bagdemagus live, and where all the prisoners from Logres have been taken, probably derives from the Celtic Otherworld. One of its characteristics is that it is very difficult for mortals to enter and impossible for them to leave.

⁌ The frozen sea was supposed to be the end of the world in the extreme north.

⁌ The magic ring given to Lancelot by the Lady of the Lake, by means of which Lancelot can tell if any of the dangers he encounters are only magical illusions. Chrétien is delightfully ambivalent about this – perhaps the ring proves that the lions were an enchantment. Or perhaps Lancelot and his companions just imagined them in the first place.

they put on their armour, thanked the damsel, took their leave and followed in the same direction as the queen. At about midday, they came to a crossroads and met another fair damsel who told them that the queen had been abducted by Sir Meleagant, the son of King Bagdemagus of Gorre ⁌ . 'It is not easy to enter that land without the king's permission,' she said. 'There are only two ways – by the Underwater Bridge, which is as far under the water as it is above the river bed; or by the Sword Bridge, which is fashioned from the blade of a sword, and just as thin and sharp.' She then showed the knights which of the two roads led to which bridge, and they discussed with one another which direction to take. The knight of the cart gave Gawain free choice and he opted for the less dangerous, the Underwater Bridge. They took their leave of each other and each rode off along his chosen path.

It took the knight three days to reach the Sword Bridge, during which time he met with several adventures and, everywhere he went, was reminded of his shame and humiliation for riding in the cart. At last, with two companions, he reached the bridge in the late afternoon of the third day. *They dismounted and saw the treacherous water, black and boiling, rough and dense, as hideous and terrifying as if it were the Devil's own river, and so deep and dangerous that if anything fell in, it would be lost for ever as certainly as if it had fallen into the frozen sea ⁌ . The bridge across it was unlike any other ... it was a sword, sharp and bright, but the sword was strong and straight, and as long as two lances. On each bank was a large tree trunk, into which the sword was firmly thrust. No one need be afraid to fall because it might break or bend, for it was so wonderfully made that it could bear a heavy weight. What made the knight and his two companions most uncomfortable was that they thought there were two lions, or leopards perhaps, at the head of the bridge on the other side, tied up to a stone ...*

The knight prepared himself as best he could to cross the gap, and he did a very strange and surprising thing by removing the armour from his hands and feet – he would not be in one piece when he reached the other side! He was going to support himself on the sword, which was sharper than a scythe, on his bare hands and feet – for he left nothing on his feet, not even shoes and stockings. It did not concern him much if he hurt his hands and feet; better to maim himself than to fall from the bridge and bathe in the water from which no one ever emerged. It caused him terrible agony, but he crossed, in pain and distress, wounding himself in the knees, hands and feet. But Love, who guided and led him, also healed and relieved him, so that his very suffering was sweet. On hands, knees and feet he crept across to the other side. Then he remembered the two lions he thought he had seen before he crossed. He looked around; but there was not so much as a lizard there to do him harm. He raised his hand before his face, gazed at his ring ⁌ , and proved that, since neither the two lions nor any other living thing was there, he had been deceived by enchantments. He

CHRÉTIEN DE TROYES

CHRÉTIEN DE TROYES wrote the five earliest surviving Arthurian romances – *Erec et Enide, Cligès, Le Chevalier de la Charrette (Lancelot), Le Chevalier au Lion (Yvain)*, and *Le Conte du Graal (Perceval)*.

Geoffrey of Monmouth in his *History of the Kings of Britain* (c. 1136) concentrated on the political and military aspects of Arthur's reign. Chrétien's poems are more courtly, more personal, more imaginative; and in them all the themes central to the Arthurian legend are fully developed – the Quest for the Holy Grail, the supreme Arthurian hero Lancelot and his adulterous passion for Queen Guinevere, the everyday supernatural events, the courtly manners, the tournament. Chrétien addresses a sophisticated audience and his poems include a subtlety and irony all too often lost in later works.

What makes Chrétien's writing so special is that, behind all the plot-twists and supernatural paraphernalia, he is exploring serious themes in a way which combines lighthearted wit with acute psychological insight. The subject to which he returns again and again is the conflict between the demands of romantic love and a knight's concern for his worth. Chrétien tells us that his patroness, the great Countess Marie of Champagne, had dictated to him the subject matter of *Lancelot*. It may be that he did not agree with its theme of adulterous love, since he left it to be finished by someone else (Godefroi de Leigny). All his other poems explore an idealized state of married love, even *Cligès*, in which the heroine fakes her own death to escape from her husband and start a new life with her true love. None the less, many critics agree that *Lancelot* is Chrétien's finest achievement.

Chrétien dedicated his final and unfinished poem, *Perceval*, to Count Philip of Flanders, another great patron of the arts. Philip left France with the Third Crusade in September 1190 and died at Acre in 1191. This provides an end-date for Chrétien's literary activities; either because of Philip's death or his own, the poem was left unfinished, to be continued by other, lesser poets. It still became a central part of the Arthurian cycle.

ABOVE: *A composite illustration of Sir Lancelot crossing the sword bridge; he fights with the lions, then with Meleagant, watched by Guinevere and Bagdemagus.*

bandaged his bleeding wounds with his shirt and looked up to see a strongly fortified tower. Watching him from its windows were King Bagdemagus and his son Sir Meleagant.

The noble King Bagdemagus was impressed by the knight's courage and prowess in crossing the Sword Bridge and advised his son Meleagant to make peace with him and return Queen Guinevere at once; but Meleagant rudely refused. The king retorted that he would offer the knight his protection and furnish him with a horse and arms if he wished to do battle for the queen. Meleagant replied that he could do as he pleased. King Bagdemagus rode out of the castle to meet the knight, who was wiping the blood from his wounds.

'Welcome, sir knight,' said Bagdemagus. 'I am the king of this country, and I freely offer you my aid and counsel. I presume that you have come to find the queen.'

'Sir,' he replied, 'no other cause brings me here.'

'You are hurt, Sir,' said the king, 'come into the castle and have your wounds treated, and allow them time to heal before you do battle. Do not worry about the queen; I have her securely confined so that my son cannot come at her.'

'I thank you for your kindness,' answered the knight, 'but I am in no pain and I would rather do battle immediately, in the armour I am wearing, for I wish to waste no time.'

'You ought to wait at least two weeks, my friend; nor will I allow you to fight without full armour,' said the king.

COURTLY LOVE

COURTLY LOVE is a term coined by the French critic Gaston Paris in 1883 for the concept which the Provençal troubadours called *fin' amors*. Gaston Paris wrote a study of Chrétien de Troyes's *Le Chevalier de la Charrette*, considering how it had been influenced by the poetry of the troubadours, and comparing its treatment of romantic love with an extraordinary Latin treatise by one Andreas the Chaplain, called *Ars honeste amandi* ('The Art of True Loving'). Andreas claimed to have written it for Countess Marie of Champagne, whom he often quotes in the text, and whom he portrays as so fascinated by the intellectual problems posed by true love that she held courts of love and handed down judgements on various historical and literary lovers.

Most of Andreas's treatise could be reconstructed from Chrétien's poem, and the two may have known one another if they worked together at Marie's court. Andreas defines courtly love, giving thirty-one infallible rules, such as that the lover must turn pale and tremble in the presence of his beloved, be unable to eat or sleep, and be obedient to her every wish.

The Art of True Loving is written in three books. The first contains a collection of love debates. The second contains the general theory, the circumstances in which and the persons between whom true love can or cannot exist. For example, Andreas claims that love is impossible between a husband and wife, because love cannot exist without jealousy and one cannot be jealous of one's spouse. He cites many judgements on love made by Countess Marie or her mother Eleanor of Aquitaine, all tending to show that true love is so morally improving that it is the duty of lovers to engage in extra-marital affairs. The third book is a complete refutation of the first two.

For many years, this treatise was taken quite seriously as describing genuine practices and attitudes; people now tend to see it as ironic, parodying a bizarre literary convention. The problem is how to read the poems of the troubadours and romances like *Lancelot* and *Tristan* in the light of this doctrine of love. It is unlikely that many of the passions celebrated in the troubadours' poems were consummated in real life – one of the greatest acts of treason any man could commit was to sleep with his lord's wife.

Whether the poems reflect merely a literary convention of love-worship intended to flatter and honour noble ladies, or an account of illicit love affairs, the cult of love as dedicated service to a beloved lady was and continued to be a huge influence on the culture of Western Europe.

'Sir, I need no more armour,' said the knight, 'nor do I seek any delay; but to please you, I will wait until tomorrow.'

The king agreed to this and brought the knight into the castle, ordering his men to see to all his needs. Then he returned to his son and attempted to persuade him once more to give up the queen without a battle. But Sir Meleagant called his father a meddling old fool and refused to listen. With a heavy heart, the king sent his most learned doctor to tend the knight's wounds, and gave him a splendid horse and fine weapons.

By the next morning, a huge crowd had assembled from far and wide to watch the battle. Bagdemagus watched from the tower, seated beside Queen Guinevere. The two knights charged together with a great clash of steel; both their spears splintered against their breasts, and both were unhorsed. At once they leapt to their feet and flung themselves into battle like two wild boars. Savagely they hacked at each other till the blood ran down from rents in their armour. They were equally matched, but the wounded knight began to weaken after a while.

When she saw him falter beneath Sir Meleagant's blows, one of the queen's damsels thought that he would fight with renewed courage if he knew the queen was watching him. The damsel rushed to the window and cried out in a loud voice: 'Lancelot! See who is watching you!'

Lancelot looked up and saw the queen seated in the window, and at once he manoeuvred Meleagant round between him and the keep, so that he could fight and look at the queen at the same time. He felt ashamed of his former weakness and began to fight like a man possessed. Lancelot pursued Meleagant relentlessly all over the square, always keeping the queen in sight; Meleagant could not defend himself from the brutal blows, but staggered about like a blind man. King Bagdemagus saw that soon his son would be killed and he took pity on him, for he loved him despite his evil temper. He beseeched the queen, for the sake of the respect and kindness he had always shown her, to ask Lancelot to spare his life.

'I have no love for your son,' replied the queen, 'but I will do as you ask for your sake, and say that I wish Lancelot to refrain.' Lancelot and Meleagant both heard these words, and at once Lancelot, perfectly obedient to his lady's bidding, put up his sword and refused to touch Meleagant. Meleagant, furious because his father had intervened, struck Lancelot with all his strength.

'For shame!' cried King Bagdemagus and ordered his barons to restrain his son. Then he negotiated a truce – much against Meleagant's will – that bound the two knights to fight again in a year's time at the court of King Arthur; if Meleagant should beat Lancelot then, no one would prevent him from taking the queen back to Gorre. The queen and Lancelot agreed to the terms, and the two knights were disarmed. The king announced that, according to the truce, all his captives were now free to leave. Overjoyed, they pressed round Lancelot to thank him, but he could think of only one thing – he begged the king to bring him to Guinevere.

The king led him at once into the hall where the queen was waiting. When the queen saw the king holding Lancelot by the hand, she rose before the king and, seeming angry, she glanced down and said nothing.

'Madame, here is Lancelot,' said the king, 'who has come to see you. You must be very pleased and happy.'

'Me? Sir, he cannot please me; I have no desire to see him.'

'By my faith, Madame,' said the king, who was exceedingly noble and courteous, 'why have you taken this attitude? Indeed, you are too scornful of the man who has served you so well, who on this journey has often placed his life in mortal danger for your sake, and who has rescued you and defended you from my son, who would never willingly have given you up.'

'Truly, Sir, he has employed his time poorly; for my part, I shall never deny that I am ungrateful to him.'

Lancelot was utterly dumbfounded at these words, but he answered her most politely, as became a noble lover: 'Madame, truly this grieves me, nor do I dare to ask you the reason for it.'

Lancelot would have lamented bitterly, if the queen had listened to him; but in order to pain and embarrass him, she would not answer a single word. Instead, she went into another room ... His heart, which was its own lord and master, was able to follow after her, while his eyes, filled with tears, remained outside with his body.

The king said to him privily, 'Lancelot, I am astonished at this behaviour and wonder what it means that the queen cannot bear to see you, and refuses to speak to you ... Now tell me, if you know, for what reason, what misdeed, she treats you in this fashion.'

'Sir, I was quite unprepared for this manner of welcome ... it deeply grieves and troubles me.'

The king then took him to see Sir Kay, who was still suffering from his wounds, but he likewise had no idea why the queen had acted so coldly towards her rescuer. Lancelot decided to leave in search of Sir Gawain, and many of the captives whom he had freed accompanied him. But the queen stayed behind.

The people of that country were very dismayed to hear that all the foreign prisoners had been released and could come and go as they pleased. Thinking to please the king by recapturing his prisoners, they decided to ambush Sir Lancelot a day's journey from the castle. They took them all without difficulty for, never suspecting treachery, neither Lancelot nor his companions were armed. They tied Lancelot on to his horse and set off for the castle. Rumour, flying ahead, reached the king that his people had captured and slain Sir Lancelot. He swore that they would die for this deed. The rumour also reached the queen as she sat down to dine. She left the table, went to her room

ABOVE: *Queen Guinevere, falsely informed of Lancelot's death, gives way to her grief.*

OPPOSITE: *William Morris's painting of Guinevere is redolent of sexual guilt – from the tense, troubled expression of her face, and the clasping (or unclasping) of her girdle, to the rumpled bedclothes.*

and gave herself up to grief, reproaching herself with bitter tears for her cruelty. *'When he came to me smiling, expecting me to make great joy of him, and when I shunned him and refused to look at him, was not this a mortal blow? ... Oh, God! Can I ever make amends for this murder, this sin? No, truly; all the rivers and seas shall run dry first. Alas! How much it would have eased and comforted me, if just once, before he died, I had held him in my arms. How? Yes, naked, flesh on flesh, the better to take our pleasure ...'*

Thus the queen mourned for two days, neither eating nor drinking, so that everyone thought she must die. There are plenty of people who would rather carry bad news than good; to Lancelot came the news that his lady and his love was dead. So great was his despair on hearing this that he contrived to slip the rope that bound him round his neck and to fall from his horse, intending to be dragged to death on the road. But his companions saw him fall and they lifted him up, cut the noose and revived him. As he rode along, he reflected on the reason for the queen's hatred. *'God, what could my offence have been? I believe she found out that I had mounted the cart. I don't know what she could blame me for if not for this. This has done for me ... but if she loved me, she should not think ill of me for doing that, she should call me her true love, for it seemed an honour to me to do whatever Love commanded, even getting into the cart ... But my lady was not pleased by this service, as I discovered by her manner. And yet only for her sake her lover did this deed for which he has many times been shamed and reviled and blamed ...'* Thus he lamented, closely watched by his men. Then news reached him that the queen was not dead. His joy on learning this was a thousand times greater than his previous despair.

Meanwhile, as his party approached the castle, news that Lancelot was still alive was brought to the queen. At once her beauty returned to her; she longed eagerly to see and speak with Lancelot, and thought no more about quarrelling with him. The king led Lancelot to the queen. This time she showed him great attention and courtesy, sat him beside her and spoke to him at length in confidence.

When Lancelot saw that all was well, and that everything he said pleased the queen, he asked her privately, 'Madame, I greatly wonder why you behaved as you did the day before yesterday, when you would not speak one word to me; you almost gave me my death, and I lacked the courage to dare to ask you what I am now asking you. My lady, I am ready to make amends, when you have told me for what crime I have been distressed.'

108

GUINEVERE

EITHER GEOFFREY OF MONMOUTH or Caradoc of Llancarfan (author of a *Life of St Gildas* written in about AD 1130) was the first writer to mention Arthur's wife and to name her Guinevere (Guenhumara in Geoffrey, Guennuvar in Caradoc). Caradoc mentions that she was abducted by 'Melwas, King of the Summer Country' (Somerset) and that Arthur raised an army and besieged Melwas at Glastonbury to get her back. Another very early source, the archivolt over the north door of Modena cathedral, also probably represents an episode in which Guinevere is abducted and subsequently rescued by Arthur and his knights. Clearly this is a tradition strongly associated with Guinevere, and substantially the same story is the basis of one of the earliest Arthurian romances, Chrétien de Troyes's *Chevalier de la Charrette*. Here Chrétien intro-

duces for the first time what was to become a dominant theme in subsequent literature, Guinevere's adulterous passion for Lancelot.

Though interpretation of the story and of Guinevere's character varied widely throughout Arthurian literature, from the chronicle tradition which represents her as reluctantly forced to marry Mordred, to the Breton lai *Lanval* in which she appears as a promiscuous seducer, the central tradition of Arthurian romance preserved her character very much as it had been drawn by Chrétien. He established her as a rather tormented person, whose moods swung between passionate tenderness and appalling cruelty; yet at the same time she was as regal and noble as a great queen should be. This tradition culminated in Malory's sympathetic portrayal of a complex woman, who in the final analysis was true to her love, if not to her husband.

And the queen said to him: 'What? Did you not feel shame and fear of the cart? You showed great reluctance to mount it when you hesitated for two whole paces. It was for that, truly, that I did not wish to see or speak to you.'

'Another time, may God prevent me from such a misdeed!' cried Lancelot. '... For God's sake, tell me if you can ever forgive me!'

'My friend,' said the queen, 'you are completely forgiven; most gladly do I pardon you now.'

'Madame,' he said, 'I thank you, but I cannot tell you here everything that I would like to say; I would willingly speak with you at more leisure, if it were possible.'

The queen indicated a window with her glance rather than with her finger and said: 'Come through the garden and speak with me at that window tonight, when everyone inside is asleep. You will not be able to gain entry or stay here; I shall be inside and you outside ... We cannot join together, for beside me in my chamber lies Kay the seneschal, still languishing from the wounds that cover him. And the door is never open, but is kept shut and well guarded.'

Lancelot promised to be careful and joyfully they parted. He waited impatiently for nightfall, and then made his way quietly through the garden to the window, which was protected with thick iron bars. Though the lovers could speak to one another, their desire to be together was painfully great. Lancelot suggested that, if only she wished it, no bars could keep him out. 'Wait until I have returned to bed,' she replied, 'and be careful not to wake Sir Kay; but I certainly don't wish to keep you out.'

Inspired by her words, Lancelot seized the iron bars and wrenched them out of their sockets. In so doing he slashed his fingers to the bone on the sharp metal, but he did not notice either the pain or the blood. He climbed through the gap, passed by the sleeping Kay, and the queen reached out her arms and drew him into her bed. There they passed the night in sweet amorous delight and were filled with the wondrous joy which is the reward of true lovers. All too soon came the dawn and Lancelot sorrowfully took his leave. He climbed out of the window and carefully replaced the bars. But neither he nor the queen realized that the blood from his wounded hands had soiled all the sheets of her bed.

In the morning, while the queen was still sleeping peacefully, Meleagant came to pay her a visit. He saw her sheets all spotted with red blood, and he saw too that Sir Kay's wounds had bled afresh during the night, staining his sheets with gore. 'Aha!' said Sir Meleagant, 'so much for my father's precautions! It's plain to see that Sir Kay has had his pleasure with you this night.'

The queen was confounded, but she replied that the blood on her sheets was certainly nothing to do with Sir Kay, but must have come from a nosebleed. Meleagant fetched his father to witness the evidence, before she could have the bedlinen changed.

'Lady,' said the king, 'it will go ill with you, if what my son says is true.'

The queen denied emphatically that either she or Sir Kay would dream of such a crime against their lord. Meleagant asked to be allowed to prove the queen's guilt in battle against Kay; but Bagdemagus would not permit Kay to fight. Secretly, the queen sent to Lancelot, and at once he presented himself as her champion. He

ABOVE: *Sir Lancelot wrenches the iron bars from the window of Guinevere's bedchamber with his bare hands.*

and Meleagant made ready for battle at once. Holy relics were fetched and Meleagant swore an oath upon them that Kay had slept in the queen's bed that night and taken his pleasure with her. Lancelot then knelt and swore that this was a lie, and further swore that he would fight to the death.

Once again, Lancelot in his implacable fury had the better of his opponent, and King Bagdemagus, seeing his son on the point of death, once again requested Guinevere to intervene. Once again she did so; and Lancelot instantly ceased to strike, despite the oath he had sworn. The king had the combatants forcibly separated.

Lancelot took his leave of the king and queen and set off to search for Sir Gawain. On the way, a hideous dwarf met him and asked him to accompany him, with many assurances of good faith. Lancelot left his companions on the road; they waited for him to return, but in vain, and at last they concluded that he was the victim of a plot. They suspected foul play by the wicked Meleagant and set off to find Gawain with heavy hearts. They were just in time to pull Gawain from the water into which he had tumbled while trying to cross the Underwater Bridge. When he understood that Lancelot was missing, he was full of disquiet. They returned to the castle; Bagdemagus sent messengers to seek him throughout his domain, but they could find no trace. After a while, they received a letter from Lancelot, saying that he had arrived safe and well back at King Arthur's court, and hoped they would join him there. Gawain and Guinevere recognized Lancelot's signature and joyfully set off for Camelot. But when they arrived, Lancelot was not there and had not been seen for weeks; and they realized that the letter had been forged.

In fact, Lancelot had been imprisoned by Meleagant in a tower built on a lonely island, the doorway of which had been bricked up. There Lancelot stayed, shackled, miserable and ill-fed, for a year. The day came when he was to have fought Meleagant at Arthur's court. Meleagant appeared at the appointed time, maliciously asking where his opponent was and claiming that he had fled from fear. Sir Gawain immediately offered himself in Lancelot's place if he had still not appeared in a month's time and Meleagant agreed. Then he went home and boasted to his father of what had passed at Camelot. King Bagdemagus was not satisfied and answered that if Lancelot had not appeared for battle then he must have been forcibly detained.

THE TROUBADOURS

THE 'TROUBADOURS', or 'finders', were poets writing in the Provençal language in southern France from the late eleventh century on. They were usually younger sons of good birth and education, though one or two were from very lowly backgrounds (such as Perdigon, the son of a fisherman), and one or two were very noble (such as Duke William IX of Aquitaine). The new kind of poetry they invented presented the first medieval treatment of 'courtly love'. Their surviving poems tend to exalt the beauty and noble qualities of the beloved lady, and to lament and yet celebrate the agonies of the poet's unfulfilled passion.

By the mid-twelfth century, this love poetry had become a well-established genre represented by poets of genius and sophistication such as Arnaut Daniel, Marcabru, and Bernard de Ventadour. It had familiar conventions, complex verse-forms and highly stylized sentiments. Love, according to the troubadours, is an irresistible force which refines and improves the noble heart. To love is exquisite pain and yet gives great joy. The object of his love is usually a married noblewoman, beautiful, unattainable and an expert in the manners of courtly society. The poet approaches his lady as an inferior, a humble supplicant, who wishes to serve her in order to be rewarded by her love. The lady may be kind and generous or capricious and cruel, but she is always the dominant one in the relationship and the lover must obey her every whim. Some poets are clearly aiming for physical consummation of their passion; others seem to prefer to keep it imaginary and cerebral.

This 'cult of love', with its quasi-religious worship of high-born ladies, was soon imitated in northern France by *trouvères* and in Germany by *minnesinger*; it was highly influential to the developing new literature of romance.

One of the king's daughters, a wise, prudent and beautiful damsel, heard what they said. She was convinced that, noble and fearless as Lancelot was, he would never flee from her brother and must be incarcerated in some dungeon. She resolved to find him and stole away from the castle. She sought far and wide in the land for two weeks, until at last she noticed the new tower Meleagant had built. Coming closer, she noticed it had no door, but only one small opening in the side. She listened underneath and heard Lancelot lamenting bitterly inside. She called his name, whereupon he dragged his starved and enfeebled body over to the window.

'Lancelot,' said the damsel, 'you once did me a good turn and therefore I shall repay you now.' She hunted around for a tool and passed him a pickaxe through the narrow opening. Lancelot hacked a hole large enough to crawl through. Then she placed his gaunt frame on her mule and led him to a nearby castle which belonged to her, and tended him carefully until he had recovered his health and strength. Then she gave him a magnificent horse and told him to set off for Camelot to save the queen from her brother.

Sir Lancelot arrived just as Meleagant was about to enter the lists against Sir Gawain and swiftly took his place. He was enraged with the coward who had held him prisoner for more than a year, and before long his superior strength enabled him to slice through Meleagant's right arm. Meleagant rushed at him with all his remaining strength, but Lancelot smashed his helmet into his face, breaking three of his teeth and then, as he lay stunned, unlaced his helm and sliced off his head. You may be sure the queen did not appeal for clemency this time. Everyone was delighted that the wicked traitor was dead and they rejoiced to have Sir Lancelot and the queen returned to them.

The Quest of The Holy Grail

ONE PENTECOST ✴ the knights were assembled at the Round Table after mass when a page came in and told the king of a great wonder he had seen: 'for, Sire, below your castle, there is a great stone floating in the water'.

The king and the knights at once came down to the river, and there they found a great slab of red marble, and held fast in it a sword, with its pommel inlaid with letters of gold, which read:

NO MAN SHALL TAKE ME HENCE BUT HE BY WHOSE SIDE I OUGHT TO HANG, AND HE SHALL BE THE BEST KNIGHT IN THE WORLD.

Sir Lancelot refused to attempt to draw it out, saying he was not worthy. Sir Perceval and Sir Gawain tried to draw the sword, at King Arthur's request, but neither could stir it, and no other knight was bold enough to try. Then the knights returned to their places, but no sooner was dinner served than all the doors and windows in the palace suddenly closed by themselves, yet the hall was not darkened. And there appeared in the middle of the knights an aged man clad in a white robe, leading by the hand a young knight in red armour who bore neither shield nor sword.

'Peace on all here,' said the holy man. 'King Arthur, I bring you this knight, who is nobly descended from Joseph of Arimathea, and who will achieve the greatest deeds yet seen in this land.'

'You are most truly welcome,' said King Arthur. And the holy man led the knight to the Siege Perilous. The letters of gold on the chair now read:

THIS IS THE SIEGE OF GALAHAD THE HIGH PRINCE.

'Here is your seat, sir knight,' said the holy man, and took his leave.

The knights realized that Sir Galahad was the son of Sir Lancelot, whom he had begotten upon the daughter of King Pelles. Then King Arthur said: 'Sir knight, it must be that God has sent you here today in order to achieve an adventure that none of my knights has been able to accomplish.' And he told him of the sword in the stone, and they went together to the water's edge.

'Small wonder,' said Sir Galahad, 'that none of your knights could draw this sword, for it belongs to me.' And with that he pulled it lightly and easily out of the stone and sheathed it in his scabbard. Then King Arthur's heart was filled with pride, and yet sorrow, for he felt that although this was the finest hour of the Round Table

✴ Pentecost commemorates the descent of the Holy Spirit upon the Apostles. Certain details from the biblical account are echoed in these scenes.

qil la uoulisent lesier en mille meni
ere. car il ma nul3 qi ne fust pauure.
et ce seroit trop grant desloiautez qi
de ce les uouldroit requere. par foi fet
li rois qe soi bien qe uos dites uoir.
Ores la granz amorz qe ge auoie auoc
et as autres les me roueues dire. Et
ne fust inchuenable chose ne se auz
qe le uouslisse bien. Car trop me grua
li de partimenz de uos donz. et des autres
opagnions

Ant ont parle entraux. qe li torz fu
leuz a esclaus alisolanz. or ia auqs
abatue la rosee. et li paluz comenca aen
plir des barons del roiaumes. Et la rine
qi si fu leuee. et uint la ou li rois estoit
et dit sur cil. chrs. nos atandoit leanz
por aler on messe. Atanc se leua li rois.
si esuesez iaus porce qe cil qe leue
ront ne sachient le duel qil or mene
Et mesire. Gau comande. qe len li aport
ses armes. et ausi fist lancelot. Et qnt
il sunt arme. de leur armes senz des esu
et senz des haumes. se uient el palez.
atrourent lor opagnos qil estoient a

apareillie por aler a le glesse

Vant il furent uenu au mostier. et
il ozent oi le sinse tot. isi arme ai
il estoient. et il furent retorne el palez
si salerent aseou liuns de les autre. cil
qi compignos estoiet de la queste. Si
re fet li rois. Batemagus au roi artu.
puis qe cist afaires est enpris si fiere
mat. qil ne puet mes estre leisiez. ielo
croie qe li saint fussant aporte si uen
ront le seuremant ausi com cil font qi
enqste doiuent entrer. Ge le uoil bien
puis qil uos plest fet li rois. puis qil
ne puet estre. autremat.

Ors furet as clere de leenz les sa
int aporter. sor coi enfesoit le seue
mant de la cort. et qant il furent apor
te deuat le matre dou. si apella li rois
mon seigneur. Gau. et li dit uos esme
ustes pmieremat ceste queste. Venez
auant et si ferez le seiremat qe cil
douoient fere. qi en ceste queste uot

Fellowship, yet they would never again be all together; and he called for all the knights to joust together in the meadow before Camelot. The tournament lasted all day, and Galahad showed himself to be indeed worthy to wear the sword of the best knight, for despite his youth he was very strong, and fast, and fierce, and no knight could keep his seat against him, except Lancelot and Perceval.

In the evening, all the knights returned to the castle to rest and wash, and hear mass, and then they came to the hall to dine. ❧ *The knights seated themselves in their places, as they had done that morning ... There was silence in the hall, when there sounded a roll of thunder so violent and deafening that it seemed to everyone that the castle would collapse. Suddenly a ray of sunlight shone through the hall with a clear radiance, seven times brighter than before. Everyone there seemed as if lit from within by the grace of the Holy Spirit; they looked at one another, filled with wonder. But they all remained silent, for they had been struck speechless, no matter who they were. A long while they remained thus, deprived of speech and gazing at one another like dumb beasts. Then the Holy Grail appeared, covered in white samite. No one could see who carried it. It entered through the great door, and immediately the hall was filled with fragrance, as if all the spices of the earth had been scattered here. The Holy Grail passed*

OPPOSITE: *The Knights of the Round Table all swear an oath to seek the Holy Grail. From a 14th-century French manuscript of* La Queste del Saint Graal.

❧ Anon, *La Queste del Saint Graal.*

BELOW: *The knights about to depart on the Quest for the Holy Grail. Tapestry designed by Burne-Jones and woven by William Morris & Co.*

through the hall, around each table, and where it passed, whatever each knight desired to eat appeared in his place. Then, when everyone had been served, the Holy Grail disappeared, no one could tell how or where. Presently, they recovered the power of speech, and most of them praised the Lord and thanked Him for the honour He had done them in filling them with the grace of the holy vessel.

When they had eaten and begun to speak of the wondrous thing that had befallen, Sir Gawain rose from his place and said: 'My lord king, indeed we have been honoured, to be served and graced by the Grail itself. But yet we were so blinded by our sins that we could not see it plainly, but only veiled and hidden. I now make this vow: to leave in the morning in quest of the Holy Grail, and pursue it as long as I may until I have looked openly upon this mystery, if I am worthy to do so; if not, I will return.'

Then all the other knights swore the like oath. *The king then fell into a reverie of a nature that made tears well up in his eyes, so that everyone could see his sorrow. Then he spoke in a loud voice for all to hear: 'Gawain, Gawain, you have filled my heart with anguish ... no king in Christendom ever had, nor ever will have again, so many valiant knights, or men of such great nobility and worth at his table as I have this day. Never again shall I see them reunited around this table as they have been today. And this grieves me more than anything.'*

As the news spread through the court, there was great weeping and lamenting by all the ladies whose lords and loved ones were preparing to set off on the quest, from which many would never return. In the morning the knights heard mass, then they armed, and each one embraced the king their lord and each other; and each knight departed his own way to follow the most high and holy quest.

BELOW: *A knight and his squire ride out on the quest. From an early 16th-century English woodcut.*

Sir Galahad rode through the forest until he came to an abbey, where he achieved his shield, which was white with a red cross marked upon it. He wandered on for many days without meeting any adventures and at length came to a great strongly fortified castle above the River Severn. He asked an old man what place it was and the man replied that it was the Castle of Maidens.

'And Sir,' added the old man, 'I advise you to turn back, for any knight who comes near cannot escape being brought down and butchered.'

'Thank you for your warning,' said Sir Galahad, 'nevertheless I will go on.'

Then he rode to the great gate, and shouted up to the porter to ask the custom of the castle. The porter gave a laugh. Soon the portcullis was heaved up and out rode seven huge, powerful knights, all brothers, fully armed and ready for battle. 'What, will you all have ado with me at once?' asked Sir Galahad.

'That we will,' answered the eldest and they spurred on their chargers. Sir Galahad set his spear in rest and, with the first onset, he unhorsed the leader and almost broke his neck; then the other six set on him all at once and killed his horse under him, and he had great work to defend himself. Yet he was so strong, and above all so fearless, and he attacked the knights so ferociously, that they turned and fled from him.

Then an old man clad in white came out and handed Sir Galahad the keys of the castle and he rode within. And there was a great crowd of maidens, who greeted him with joy as their deliverer. Then Sir Galahad asked what had been the origin of the evil custom of the castle, and the old man said: 'Seven years ago, good sir, came these seven brethren knights that you have here defeated to stay with the lord of this castle, Duke Lianor. And they fell to quarelling, because they

THE GENESIS OF THE GRAIL LEGEND

THE GRAIL STORY was probably based on a Celtic tale about a hero visiting the palace of a maimed king and restoring him to health by asking a significant question, but the exact form of this story can only be conjectured.

In the early thirteenth century, a Burgundian poet called Robert de Boron composed a sequence of poems explaining the entire history of the Holy Grail, how it was brought to Britain and the involvement of Arthur's court in the quest for it.

Robert writes that the Grail is the cup of the Last Supper, used by Joseph of Arimathea to catch Christ's blood from the cross. Joseph is imprisoned by the Jews for burying Christ's body, but the Grail feeds him miraculously. Many years later, the Emperor Vespasian journeys to Jerusalem, discovers Joseph still bricked up in his prison and frees him. Joseph then takes the Grail and, with his sister Enygeus and her husband Bron or Hebron (Bran?), sets up a small Christian community somewhere outside Judaea. Owing to the sin of lechery practised by some, their crops fail. Joseph is instructed to build a round table, a replica of the table at the Last Supper, and the Grail is placed on it, beside a fish caught by Bron (subsequently

known as the Rich Fisher). Only the pure members of the community can bear to sit at the table, where they are fed with the fish through the power of the Grail and filled with bliss.

Bron and Enygeus have twelve sons, of whom one, Alain, wants to remain celibate. Realizing that this means he will become the father of the Grail knight, Joseph trains him in the secrets of the Grail; afterwards he takes it to the far West (the west of Britain is implied, but Robert does not name Glastonbury).

Several subsequent authors elaborated Robert's version of the Grail story, but when the Vulgate Cycle was written, the author of *La Queste del Saint Graal* made profound alterations. He wanted to show the inadequacies of secular chivalry, and he wanted a Grail hero who was perfect, not the flawed character of Perceval. So he invented a new hero, Galahad, and followed the efforts of many knights in the Grail quest, showing what happened to those who failed as much as to those who succeeded. Of all the Knights of the Round Table only Perceval, Bors and Galahad achieve the Grail, but even their success is relative—only the pure Galahad reaches the peak of beatific ecstasy.

RIGHT: *The young Sir Galahad. Painting by G F Watts.*

would have taken his daughter by force; and they killed the good duke and his son and then defiled the daughter after. They seized the castle, with all its lands, and by force made all the duke's knights submit to their lordship or die. And the daughter of the duke, mortally wounded by her ravishment, then said to them that, as they had won the castle through a maid, so they should lose it to a maid, and the day would come when one knight would defeat all of them with his own hands. And then she died; but her younger sister is here yet. Since that day, no maid has passed by this castle but they would seize and imprison her, and that is how they have long held all these maidens in great cruelty and discomfort. And no knight passed the castle, but they would all seven set on him at once and hack him down.

Then Sir Galahad invested the duke's younger daughter that very day with the castle and all its lands and he made all the knights belonging to it swear fealty to her. And the maidens were released and went back to their homes.

ABOVE: *The old man hands over to Sir Galahad the keys to the Castle of Maidens.*

SIR LANCELOT

SIR LANCELOT RODE many days in the forest, meeting no one. At last, at a dark and lonely crossroads, he found an old stone cross carved with strange letters and, near to it, an ancient chapel, abandoned and half ruined. Lancelot tried to enter the chapel, but the way was blocked by an iron grille; inside he could see an altar richly draped with cloths of silk, upon which stood a tall silver candelabrum carrying six fair white candles. He felt a great desire to enter, but he could not pass the grille; so he unsaddled and tethered his horse to the cross, took off his helm and sword, and lay down to sleep on his shield. But it was a hard, cold bed, and he slept poorly.

Then it seemed to him, while he lay between sleeping and waking, that ✦ *he saw come by him two palfreys all fair and white, the which bore a litter, therein lying a sick knight. And when he was nigh the cross he abode there still ... and he heard him say, 'Oh, sweet Lord, when*

✦ Sir Thomas Malory, *Morte Darthur.*

121

WHAT WAS THE HOLY GRAIL?

WE NOW THINK OF THE HOLY GRAIL as the cup which Christ used at the Last Supper, but originally it was not imagined as a cup at all. Of the romance writers whose works have survived, Chrétien de Troyes is the first to mention the Grail and he introduces it most unpretentiously as 'un graal', a serving dish carried by a maiden in procession with other mysterious objects. The Old French word *graal* originally derived from the Latin word *gradale*, meaning 'gradually' or 'in stages', and was used to refer to a large, deep dish filled with sweetmeats which was carried round to the diners at the beginning of each new course at a banquet. It occurs in Old French writings from the early eleventh century. Chrétien clearly meant a large dish, for he mentions that the Grail contained not a pike or a lamphrey or a salmon—all large fish which would need to be served from a good-sized dish —but a mass wafer, with which the Fisher King's bedridden father has been miraculously sustained for fifteen years.

In addition, Welsh legend spoke of one of the treasures of Bran (son of the Celtic sea-god Llyr) as a platter (Welsh *dyscyl*) from which one received whatever food one desired. Another treasure was a drinking horn (Welsh *corn*), which magically provided whatever food or drink was required. The god Bran in later folklore became a king who sometimes fished from boats – very like the Fisher King in Chrétien's poem. *Graal* is the old French equivalent of the Welsh *dyscyl*. Although Chrétien describes the Grail once as 'holy' (*sainte*), there is nothing obviously sacred in his description.

In *Parzifal*, Wolfram von Eschenbach describes the Grail as a stone object, a *lapsit exillis* – a pseudo-Latin term which probably derived from *lapsit ex caelis* ('it fell from heaven'), since Wolfram reports that angels left it on earth before returning to the stars. Later it was entrusted to the family of the Grail King. The king himself could marry and have children, but the order of knights who guard the Grail are vowed to celibacy, and Wolfram calls them Templars. His Grail also miraculously produces food and drink, and prevents anyone who remains in its presence from dying. Inscriptions appear on the stone from time to time, naming children who are to be brought up at the Grail Castle. All this has given rise to some extraordinary theories, from the Grail as a meteorite, to the Grail being the tablet of stone bearing the ten commandments which in the Old Testament had been kept in the Ark of the Covenant.

shall this sorrow leave me? And when shall the holy vessel come by me, wherethrough I shall be blessed? For I have endured thus long, for little trespass.'

With that Sir Lancelot saw the candlestick with the six tapers come before the cross although he saw nobody that brought it. Also there came a table of silver and the holy vessel of the Sangrail ... ✤ *and therewith the sick knight sat him up, held up both his hands, and said, 'Fair sweet Lord, which is here within this holy vessel, take heed unto me that I may be whole of this malady.' And therewith on his hands and knees he went so nigh that he touched the holy vessel and kissed it, and anon he was whole; and then he said, 'Lord God, I thank Thee, for I am healed of this sickness.'*

✤ Sangrail: from *Saint Graal* ('Holy Grail').

When the holy vessel had been there a great while it went into the chapel with the chandelier and the light, so that Lancelot knew not where it had gone; for he was overtaken with sin, so that he had no power to rise in the presence of the holy vessel ... Then the sick knight dressed him up and kissed the cross; and his squire brought him his arms and asked his lord how he did.

'Truly,' he said, 'I thank God right well, through the holy vessel am I healed. But I have marvel of this sleeping knight that had no power to awake when this holy vessel was brought hither.'

'I dare say,' said the squire, 'that he dwells in some deadly sin which he has never confessed.'

'By my faith,' said the knight, 'whatever he is, he is unhappy, for as I judge he is of the Fellowship of the Round Table, which is entered into the quest of the Sangrail.'

'Sir,' said the squire, 'I have brought you all your arms save your helm and your sword, and therefore by my advice you may now take this knight's helm and his sword.' And so he did. And when he was fully armed, he took Sir Lancelot's horse, for he was better than his, and they departed. Then anon Sir Lancelot awoke and sat up, and he thought about what he had seen and whether it was a dream or not. ✤ *Then he heard a voice say to him: 'Lancelot, harder than stone, more bitter than wood, more naked and barren than the fig tree, how do you dare be present in the place where the Holy Grail abides? Leave this place at once, for the stink of your sins pollutes it.'*

These words afflicted him so grievously that he did not know what to do. He rushed away, blinded by tears, sighing and groaning and cursing the day that he was born, because he knew that he was dishonoured for ever, since the secret mysteries of the Holy Grail remained hidden from him.

ABOVE: *Sir Lancelot, still in a state of mortal sin, lays down to sleep near the half-ruined chapel. Woodcut from Malory's* Morte Darthur.

✤ Anon, *La Queste del Saint Graal.*

ABOVE: *The sick knight is carried to the chapel in a bier.*

However, he would never be able to forget the words he had heard as long as he lived, and he would never be at peace until he knew why he had been described thus. Reaching the cross, he found neither his helm nor his sword nor his horse, and he realized at once that it had been no dream. Then he gave way to his grief and burst into lamentations: 'Oh, God, here have my sins and my evil life been fully revealed! Above all my weakness has destroyed me, I now see ... but my blindness should not come as any surprise to me; ever since I was first knighted, not a moment has passed when I have not been swathed in the shadows of mortal sin, because more than any other man I have given myself up to lust and to the world's depravity.'

🙖 Sir Thomas Malory, *Morte Darthur.*

🙖 Thus he sorrowed till it was day when heard the fowls sing; then somewhat was he comforted. But when Sir Lancelot missed his horse and his harness, then he knew well that God was displeased with him.

124

Then he wandered into the forest until he came to a hermitage where he begged the hermit to hear his confession. He told the hermit of his failing at the chapel and the lifelong sin which was responsible; and the hermit gave him wise counsel how to amend his life. Lancelot wept in true and humble repentance and the hermit absolved him and gave him a penance, which was that he should ever wear a hair shirt next to his skin. And Lancelot remained there in prayer and penitence with the hermit.

SIR PERCEVAL

AFTER SEVERAL DAYS without meeting any adventure, it chanced that Sir Perceval saw on the road ahead of him twenty men at arms, who asked him whence he came. When he replied that he was of the court of King Arthur, they all cried out, 'Slay him!' and rushed to attack him. Perceval set his spear in rest and slew the first one as he came on, but then seven set on him at once and his horse was killed under him, and he fell to the ground. They were on him before he could get to his feet, and it was all he could do to defend himself with

---

A CISTERCIAN ROMANCE?

THE VERSION OF THE GRAIL QUEST in the Vulgate Cycle, *La Queste del Saint Graal*, is so infused by mystical symbolism that some scholars have suggested that it must have been written by a Cistercian monk. Its insistence on the supremacy of spiritual over secular chivalry is foreshadowed in the Vulgate *Lancelot*, where Lancelot comes to realize that his adultery with Queen Guinevere is a mortal sin which will prevent him from achieving the pinnacle of knightly excellence.

The author of the *Queste*, if not a monk himself, certainly knew a great deal about the Cistercian order and was familiar with the writings of the great St Bernard of Clairvaux, the most influential theologian of his day. The repentance and rehabilitation of Sir Lancelot, in particular, reflect the stages of contrition described by St Bernard in his treatise *The Steps of Humility* and a determination to start a new life of austerity and mortification. Lancelot and Bors both spend a long time with hermits repenting of their sins. Lancelot undertakes the rest of the quest in a hair shirt, while Bors keeps to a diet of bread and water.

The most 'Cistercian' element of the romance is the mystical visions granted to the successful questers, which derive from St Bernard's writings on divine grace and the mystical union of the soul with God. The Grail is a symbol of divine grace, which is freely dispensed by God to all men. But only the truly pure in heart can attain the ultimate gift of grace, a rapturous union with the heart of divine mystery, like that achieved by Sir Galahad just before his death.

his shield from their savage blows. He would soon have been hacked to death, if it had not been for Sir Galahad, who chanced to pass by and immediately joined battle to save him, though he could not see who Perceval was. Such was Galahad's prowess that with every stroke he cut down or wounded a man, until the rest fled into the forest. Then, seeing that the knight he had saved had no more need of him, Sir Galahad rode off into the forest.

Sir Perceval was very distressed, for he wanted desperately to follow Sir Galahad, but he had no horse. He ran as fast as he could on foot and before long he met a yeoman on a cob, leading a fine black charger. 'Friend, will you lend me that horse?' asked Perceval. But the man said that he dared not, for fear his master would kill him. Perceval would not take it by force, so he walked on, feeling very sad. Before long, a knight galloped past him on the black horse, and after him came the yeoman on the cob, crying out that he had taken the horse from him by force, and that his lord would slay him as soon as he found out.

'What can I do about it?' said Sir Perceval. 'If I had a horse, I could soon bring him back, but you see I am on foot.'

'Take my cob,' said the yeoman, 'and I will follow you on foot.'

So Sir Perceval mounted the sturdy cob and rode after the knight on the black horse. And before long he saw him, and called to him to turn and fight. They set their spears in rest and charged together; but the strange knight struck Perceval's cob through the chest with his spear so that it fell dead at once; and then rode off into the forest. Enraged, Perceval shouted after him, 'Coward, turn and fight!' However, the knight took no notice and was soon lost to sight. For pure anger, Sir Perceval tore off his helmet and sword and flung them away. He sat down under a tree, hid his face in his hands, and burst into tears. He stayed there until it was night. When he awoke at dawn, he found himself in a wilderness surrounded by water.

Two days and two nights he passed there, without food or water, unable to leave and impatient for deliverance. On the third day, he observed a ship, draped from stem to stern with rich cloths of black silk, coming swiftly towards the land. Seated at the entrance to the ship was a damsel of extraordinary beauty, splendidly dressed, who addressed him: 'Perceval, what are you doing in this wilderness where you will very likely die of hunger if you are not rescued?'

'How do you know my name?' asked Perceval in surprise.

'I know you well,' replied the damsel, 'for I have watched you for a long time, growing into a good knight. Now tell me,' she asked him, 'whether you have eaten meat today?'

'Not for these three days, damsel,' he replied.

'It is a great pity,' she said, 'that such a young and promising knight should starve to death and be eaten by wild beasts; I would like to help you, if I may.'

PERCEVAL

THE ORIGINAL HERO of the Grail quest, Sir Perceval, first appeared in Chrétien de Troyes's unfinished masterpiece *Le Conte du Graal (Perceval)*. Chrétien's Perceval is brought up in ignorance of everything to do with knighthood by his mother, who has lost her husband and two eldest sons through violence and wishes to preserve Perceval from their fate. One day, the youth sees five knights riding through the forest and, dazzled by their shining armour, takes them for angels. They explain that they are knights and Perceval determines to be knighted at once. He sets off for Arthur's court, leaving his mother to die of grief.

Perceval is fearless and enthusiastic; he quickly learns how to handle horse, weapons and armour. But because he is untaught he is slow to pick up the ethical and cultural aspects of a knight's education. Disparate pieces of advice given him by his mother and by Gornemanz, a good knight who teaches him how to ride and fight, take on disproportionate importance and he commits increasingly serious blunders. These culminate in his disastrous visit to the Grail Castle. He is welcomed by the maimed Fisher King and witnesses the Grail procession – the bleeding lance, the candelabra, the Grail and the silver platter – but, because Gornemanz had advised him not to be too talkative, he refrains from asking the crucial questions which would have healed the maimed king.

Perceval continues his wanderings and completes his knightly education. He falls in love with the beautiful Blancheflor, he befriends Sir Gawain and the romance then pursues their separate adventures by turn. He learns from a hermit that his failure at the castle stemmed from his sin in leaving his mother to die, and that he must atone for this before he can return. Chrétien's romance breaks off in mid-sentence, but was continued by at least four other writers.

Chrétien's poem was certainly the principal source for Wolfram von Eschenbach's great masterpiece *Parzifal*. Wolfram wrote his poem between about 1198 and 1210. He claimed that Chrétien had not done justice to the story, and that he had an alternative source, a Provençal poet named Kyot who had translated an Arabic version into French. This is unlikely to be true although *Parzifal* contains much that was not in Chrétien's poem. Wolfram brilliantly interweaves his complex storylines and never loses his grasp of their thematic significance. Gawain is the pre-eminent secular knight, best of Arthur's court and family. Parzifal is the pre-eminent knight of a more spiritual chivalry, based on the Grail court and the family of the Grail King. He is related to Arthur through his father and to the Grail King through his mother, so he has leanings towards both ideals, but ultimately learns that the service of the Grail is a higher calling.

'I would like to know,' said Perceval, 'who you are, that offer me such great kindness.'

'I am,' said she, 'a gentlewoman that am disinherited, who was once the richest woman in the world.'

'Damsel,' said Sir Perceval, 'who has disinherited you? For I have great pity of you.'

'Sir,' said she, 'I dwelt with the greatest man of the world, and he made me so fair and clear that there was none like me; and of that great beauty I had a little pride, more than I ought to have had. I said a word that pleased

him not; and then he would not suffer me any longer to be in his company, and so drove me from my heritage and disinherited me. He had never pity of me, nor of none of my council, nor of my court. And since, sir knight, it has befallen me so, through me and mine I have deprived him of many of his men and made them to become my men.'

They had been speaking together so long that midday passed and it was almost the hour of none. The sun blazed down and it was so hot that the damsel said, 'Perceval, in that ship there is a most beautiful silken pavilion. If you wish, I shall have it set up here to protect you from the heat of the sun.'

Perceval agreed at once, and she went on board the ship and ordered two servants to erect the pavilion on the beach. When they had finished their task as well as they could, she said to Perceval, 'Come now and rest here, sit in the shade till nightfall, for it seems to me that you are over warm.'

Perceval entered the pavilion and fell asleep at once, although not before the damsel had removed his helm, his hauberk and his sword. Thus stripped, she allowed him to sleep. After he had slept deeply and long, he awoke and asked to eat. The damsel commanded her servants to set the table and Perceval watched them heap upon it an extraordinary quantity of dishes. He and the damsel ate together; when he requested drink, they brought him wine, the best and strongest he had ever drunk ... The wine was so potent that Perceval became overheated with it; he looked at the damsel and she seemed to him to be the most beautiful damsel he had ever seen. Her exquisite gown, her charming speech, pleased and aroused him so much that he was inflamed beyond measure. He spoke to her of this and that, and finally begged for her love, assuring her that she had his.

At first she refused him as long as she could, for she intended to bring his desire to its height, and the young man never ceased pleading with her. At length, when she could see that he was burning with desire, she said to him, 'Perceval, understand that I absolutely refuse to do as you wish, unless you swear to be mine from this moment, to aid me against all my enemies, and to do nothing but at my command.' Eagerly he promised his obedience

'Do you swear to me on your honour as a knight?'

'Yes,' he replied.

'So be it,' she said, 'I agree to do whatever you wish. From the very first you should know that I have desired you even more than you have me, and that you are one of the knights I have coveted most in all the world.'

Anon, *La Queste del Saint Graal.*

None: three o'clock in the afternoon.

OPPOSITE: *Sir Perceval sees the Holy Grail for the first time and neglects to ask the crucial question. This painting by Ferdinand Piloty illustrates a scene from Wolfram von Eschenbach's* Parzival.

BELOW: *Sir Perceval is tempted by the beautiful damsel who feeds him a sumptuous feast prior to seducing him. From an Italian manuscript of the Grail Quest, c. 1400.*

Then she ordered her servants to prepare in the middle of the pavilion the most beautiful and sumptuous bed possible. That done, they undressed the young damsel and put her to bed, and Perceval lay down beside her. Then, just as he would have drawn the covers over them both, he chanced to catch sight of his sword, lying on the ground where the servants had left it. He stretched out his hand to lay it against the bed, and just then his eye fell on the vermilion cross engraved on the pommel. In an instant, he came to his senses and made the sign of the cross on his forehead. Immediately the pavilion collapsed around him, while black clouds of smoke blinded the young man, and all around him was such a disgusting stench that he believed he must truly be in Hell. 'Jesus Christ, my sweet Lord and Saviour, let me not perish thus, but succour me by Your grace, or I am lost!'

He opened his eyes, but he could see no trace of the pavilion where he had been lying that very same minute. Then he looked towards the sea, and he saw the ship as he had seen it earlier, and in it the damsel, who called out to him: 'Perceval, you have betrayed me!'

✤ *And so she went with the wind roaring and yelling, and it seemed all the water burnt after her.*

Then Sir Perceval made great sorrow and drew his sword unto him, saying, 'Since my flesh will be my master I shall punish it.' Therewith he rove himself through the thigh so that the blood spurted about him, and cried, 'O good Lord, take this in recompense for that I have done against You, my Lord.' Then he clothed him and armed him, and called himself a wretch, saying, 'How nearly I was lost, and nearly lost what I should never have gotten again, that was my virginity, for that may never be recovered once lost.' And he stopped his bleeding wound with a piece of his shirt.

✤ Sir Thomas Malory,
Morte Darthur.

Looking out to sea again, Perceval saw another ship approaching, this time bedecked with white silk. When it drew to the shore, he saw within a man clad like a priest. Perceval greeted the man in God's name and asked him what brought him to such a desolate spot.

'I have come here,' answered the man, 'to visit you and help you with wise counsel. How have you fared here, where God placed you in order to test your true knightly virtue?'

Perceval hung his head in shame and confessed how the damsel had nearly lured him into mortal sin. Then the venerable man explained to Perceval that the damsel had been none other than the Fiend himself, and that when she spoke of being disinherited by the greatest lord in the world, the Fiend meant God, who had flung him out of heaven for his foul sin of pride, and against whom he had been waging war ever since, ceaselessly striving to corrupt God's good vassals and knights and turn them against Him.

Then Perceval understood that everything the damsel had said to him had a double meaning, and he shuddered to think how close he had come to losing his immortal soul. He thanked God for His grace that had saved him; and when he looked round, he found that the venerable man had vanished away. But he heard a voice, which said to him: 'Perceval, you have triumphed over sin. Enter this ship and go wherever it brings you and fear not, for God will guide you.'

Then Perceval was filled with joy, and gave thanks once more to the good Lord; and he entered the ship, and wind filled its sails and it bore him swiftly away from the island.

Sir Bors

WHILE ALL THIS WAS HAPPENING, Sir Bors was also staying with a wise hermit, who heard his confession, absolved his sins and advised him to eat and drink nothing but bread and water until he should sit at table in Castle Corbenic and be served by the Grail itself. Wondering at the hermit's words, Sir Bors promised to do these things. As he was riding through the forest, he came upon a terrible scene. *At the meeting of two roads he encountered two knights who were leading his brother Lionel, naked but for his breeches, mounted on a big, strong hackney , his hands bound across his chest. The two knights each carried a branch loaded with sharp thorns, with which they were beating him so violently that the blood poured down from more than a hundred wounds in his back, and he was spattered with his own blood, both before and behind. But he, like one that was great of heart, said not a word, but endured their cruel blows as if he felt no pain. But, as he made ready to ride to his brother's rescue, Bors looked to his other side, and saw an armed knight abducting by force a beautiful damsel and making for the densest part of the forest so as to hide her from those who were coming to rescue her.*

And she, afraid of what would happen, cried out with all her strength, 'Holy Mary, succour your maid!' Then, perceiving Bors riding alone, she turned towards him and cried out as loudly as she might: 'Oh! Knight, by the faith you bear Him whom you serve as liegeman, I beseech you to come to my aid and suffer me not to be dishonoured by this knight!'

When Bors heard the damsel exhort him in the name of his liege Lord, he was so distressed that he knew not what to do: for if he left his brother in the hands of his captors, he thought there would be no chance of ever seeing him alive and unhurt again; and if he did not rescue the young damsel, she would be violated and dishonoured, and he would be to blame for refusing to help her. He raised up his eyes to Heaven and said, weeping, 'Sweet Lord Jesus Christ, whose liegeman I am, protect my brother so that these knights do not slay him, and I for mercy and for love of You shall save this maiden from the dishonour and rape that knight would subject her to.'

At once Bors galloped away in pursuit of the ravisher, spurring his horse so hard that blood flowed down the beast's flanks. As he came up he shouted out, 'Sir knight, let that maiden be, or you are but a dead man!'

Anon, *La Queste del Saint Graal.*

Hackney: a middle-sized riding horse, as opposed to a knight's war-horse, a charger or a small pack-pony.

131

il me semble qe al chr̄ la uoele despū
celez. et ēsi seroit ele maubaillie. et afolee.
Ors sadrece cele part ou li chr̄. en por
te la pucele et broiche le cheual des
esperons si duremāt. qil li fet le sanc
saillir de mādeus le coste; et qīt la pro
che se li crie. Sire chr̄. leissie; cele damo
isele ou nos estes mors. Et qīt al ot
ceste parole si met ius la damoisele. et
et il estoit armes de totes armes fors de
gleue. Il enbrace lescu et tret le spee et
la drece uers Boort. Et Boort le fiert si
duremāt. qe par mi le huiltre et par mi
le scu li met le gleue atot le fer et li
passe parmi le spaule. Mes il ne la pas
naure si fort qe il ne puisse bien guzir
legierement.
l enpuint bien come cil qi estoit
de mult gr̄t force se lalut del cheual
aterre. et au rettere qil fet de son gleue
se pasme cil de la gr̄t engoisse qe il sant
Et Boort uient ala damoisele se li dit.
damoisele il me semble qe nos estes de
liure de cest chr̄ qe uos plet qe ge face
plus.
Ir fet ele puis qe nos maue; garantie
de pore lenneu. et destre honie. ge uos
pri qe nos mene; me la ou cist chr̄ me
prist. Et il dit qe si fera il mult uolenti
ers Boorz prant le cheual. au chr̄ naure
se monte la pucele. et lesse le chr̄ gisant
aterre. Si en mene la pucele tote la uoie
qe ele li deuise. Et qīt il est auqes es
longie se li dit.

ge ne se onques par quel mēuere dela
uble lauoient si eschiuse. ace qe il me
prist bien main chies mon pere. celeemāt
et p̄ men portoit en cele forest plus espes
se por moi despuceller. et sil laust fere il
fust mors de pechiee et honi; del cors et
gen fusse ce sachiez desonoree a tos ior
mes.
Il demantiers qil parloient īsi. si uoiet
desai dis. chr̄. tos armes. qi queroient
la damoisele par mi la forest. Et qīt la
uoient. se le font si gr̄t ioie qe ce est
merueille aregarder. Et ele leur prie qil
facent feste acel chr̄. et le retiegnēt por
aler auec aus. car ele fust honie se deus
et il ne fust qil li dona la uolente de moi
aidier.
l le prenent au frain et li dient. Sire
nos en uandrez auec nos. car il le
uient īsi afere. Et nos nos en proions
qe nos uignez. car tant nos auez fait.
qe apenez le uos porriens guerredoner
Beaus seignour fet il ge ni iroie en
nulle meniere. qe tant ai afere aillors. qe
ne puis oreres demorer. Si uos pri por
deu qil ne nos pri por deu qil ne uos en
poist. car bien sachiez qe mult uoletiers
ialase. Mes li besoing test si gr̄t en droit
demoi et la perte si doleruse se ge reme
noie qe nus deus ne la me porroit resto
rer. Adonc leur conte. coment il lessa son
frere en peril de mort por secorr la damo
isele et deliuer del chr̄.

At these words the knight set the maiden down on the ground. He was well armed, but he had no lance; however he strapped on his shield, drew his sword and charged at Bors. But Bors struck him so hard with his lance that he pierced through shield and hauberk deep into his body. Then the knight fainted in his agony. Bors approached the maiden and said, 'Damsel, it seems that you are delivered from this knight. Now what more shall I do for you?'

The damsel asked Bors to return her to her home, and he gladly agreed to do so. The damsel's father was overjoyed to see her safe and sound, and begged Bors to stop with them; but Sir Bors, thinking of his brother, refused and rode hastily on his way. ✹ *Then Sir Bors rode after Sir Lionel, his brother, by the trace of their horses, and thus he rode seeking a great while.*

Then he overtook a man clothed in religious clothing, and he rode on a strong black horse, blacker than a berry, and he said, 'Sir knight, what seek you?'

'Sir,' said Bors, 'I seek my brother whom I saw a while ago beaten by two knights.'

'Ah, Bors, discomfort you not, nor fall into despair, for I shall tell tidings such as they be, for truly he is dead.'

Then he showed him a new slain body lying in a bush, and it seemed to him that it was indeed the body of Lionel. Then he made such sorrow that he fell to the earth in a swoon, and lay a great while there. And when he came to himself he said, 'Fair brother, since the company of you and me is departed, shall I never have joy in my heart, and now He whom I have taken as my Master, may He be my help.' And when he had said thus he took the body lightly in his arms and put it upon the arson [back part] of his saddle. And then he said to the man, 'Can you tell me the way to a chapel where I may bury this body?'

'Come on,' said he, 'here is one fast by,' and so long they rode until they saw a fair tower, and before it there seemed an old, feeble chapel. Then they both alit, and put the body into a tomb of marble.

Bors looked all around him, but he could not see any holy water, nor a cross, nor the least symbol of the presence of Jesus Christ.

'Leave the body here,' said the man, 'and tonight we will lodge in this tower, and tomorrow I shall conduct a service for your brother.'

Then the two of them went into the tower, where Bors was handsomely received, and given costly robes lined with ermine and all manner of comforts. Many ladies and damsels exerted themselves to cheer his spirits, and they had succeeded somewhat when a dazzlingly beautiful lady entered the hall, clad in a magnificent gown. Then said a knight to Bors, 'Sir, this is the lady we serve, who has loved you from afar for a long time and has waited for you to come, for she wants you and no other to be her lover.'

ABOVE: *The damsel, rescued from ravishment by Sir Bors, is reunited with her father.*

✹ Sir Thomas Malory, *Morte Darthur.*

OPPOSITE: *Sir Bors is forced to make the agonizing choice between rescuing his brother Lionel, or saving a damsel whom he sees being dragged away into the forest.*

How a devil in Woman's likeness would have tempted Sir Bors

ABOVE: *Ladies and damsels threaten to fling themselves from the top of the tower if Sir Bors refuses to grant the lady of the castle his love. Illustration by Beardsley.*

Bors was dumbfounded, but the lady came and sat beside him and they conversed pleasantly for a long time. At length she openly besought his love. Bors pitied the lady, but was determined not to break his vow of chastity; not knowing how to answer her, he remained silent.

'Will you not grant my request, just for one night?' asked the lady.

'Madam,' he replied, 'I would not do such a thing for any lady or damsel in the world; and I wonder that you can ask it of me, when my brother is lying dead outside in your chapel.'

'But you must grant me your love,' cried the lady, 'for if you do not, I shall die of grief!' And she wept and implored him to take pity on her. Then, seeing that he was unmoved, she ordered her men to hold him still, and said, 'I am going to kill myself; and the shame of my death shall be on your head.' And, taking twelve of her maidens with her, she climbed up on to the battlements of the tower.

One of the maidens cried out: 'Sweet sir knight, have pity! For we must all throw ourselves from the tower with my lady unless you grant her desire! How can you let us all perish for such a small thing?'

But Bors replied that, though he pitied them from his heart, he could not consent to mortal sin, even to save their lives. At this, all the damsels, and the lady, flung themselves from the top of the tower. Bors crossed himself; and at once there was a dreadful roaring and shrieking and the damsels and lady as they fell became fiends that flew off through the air.

Then Sir Bors looked around him and could see neither the tower nor any of the people; all that remained was the little tumbledown chapel and his own arms. He knelt to pray, thanking God for preserving him from the Fiend's temptations. Then he looked for his brother's body in the marble tomb; but it too had vanished, and he felt encouraged by this to hope that it had only been part of the illusion, and that his brother still lived. He rode on his way and came to an abbey. There the holy and learned abbot explained to him the meaning of all the things that had taken place that day.

In the morning, Bors mounted his horse and rode on. He had not gone far before he came to a little hermitage on the edge of the forest.

He turned towards it, and there he found his brother Lionel sitting on the steps of the chapel, unarmed ... It would be impossible to tell of the joy Bors felt when he saw his brother. He jumped down from his horse and cried out, 'Dear brother, when did you come here?'

Lionel knew Bors at these words, but he made no move towards him, and said; 'Bors, Bors, it was no thanks to you that I was not killed the other day by the two knights who were leading me off and beating me! You rushed off to help the maiden whom the knight was abducting, leaving me in mortal danger. Never has a brother committed such a foul betrayal; and for this crime I promise you that you shall die. Keep yourself from me from now on, for you can be sure that I shall seek your life wherever I can, as soon as I am armed.'

Deeply distressed by his brother's anger, Bors knelt down in front of him, his hands joined to implore him for mercy, and besought him in God's name to forgive him. But Lionel refused absolutely and swore to kill him if with God's help he could overcome him. Then, refusing to listen any further, he strode into the hermitage where he had left his arms and rapidly put them on. Fully armed, he mounted his horse and cried to Bors: 'Defend yourself from me! For, with God's help, if I can best you, I shall treat you as one should treat a felon or traitor. Never was a more cruel and false-hearted knight begotten by such a noble man as was King Bors of Ganis, our father! Get on your horse. If you do not, I shall kill you where you stand ... '

Bors did not know what to do ... Common sense told him he must mount his horse, yet he wished to try once more to win his brother's pardon. So he knelt down in front of Lionel's horse and, weeping piteously, said: 'Have mercy, dear brother, in the name of God! Forgive me my offence, and do not slay me; remember the great love which ought to be between us.'

But Lionel cared nothing for Bors's pleas, for the Fiend had excited in him a furious desire to kill his brother ... When he saw that Bors would not rise to fight him, but persisted in kneeling, he spurred his horse to the gallop and the chest of the horse struck Bors with such violence that he was dashed

Anon, La Queste del Saint Graal.

135

ABOVE: *Sir Lionel and Sir Calogrenant do battle. Woodcut from the 1529 edition of Malory's* Morte Darthur.

to the ground, cruelly injuring himself in the fall. Lionel rode right over him, breaking his bones under the horse's hooves. His pain was so extreme that Bors fainted, convinced that he would die unshriven.

Lionel, seeing him unable to rise, dismounted, intent on beheading him. He seized his brother by the helm and unlaced it in order to cut off his head. Just then, by God's will, along came Calogrenant, a knight of King Arthur's court and a companion of the Round Table. He paused, horrified, as he perceived Lionel on the point of slaughtering his brother ... He leapt from his horse, seized Lionel by the shoulders and dragged him back with all his strength, crying out: 'What does this mean, Lionel? Are you out of your mind, wanting to kill your brother, who is one of the noblest knights known? By God, no knight worthy of the name could permit such a thing!'

'What?' replied Lionel, 'are you minded to help him? If you persist I shall leave him and turn to you!'

Calogrenant was speechless with astonishment and stared at Lionel. Then he said, 'What, Lionel? Do you truly wish to kill him?'

'Certainly,' replied Lionel, 'and I shall do it, in spite of you or anyone else. He has done me such an injury that he deserves to die.'

He rushed upon Bors again and sought to strike him on the head, but Calogrenant put himself between them, declaring that if Lionel dared to offer his brother violence again, he must first do battle with him.

At this Lionel picked up his shield and attacked Calogrenant with all his strength; and Calogrenant defended himself ably. The battle raged for a long time. Bors at last awoke from his swoon. He was distressed to see the battle, but he was in such pain that he could scarcely move. After a while, he saw that Lionel was winning; Calogrenant was seriously wounded and had lost a great deal of blood. Calogrenant then saw that Bors was watching, and called out to him, 'Bors! Help me, for I am in peril of death, wherein I put myself to help you!' At this, Bors struggled to his feet and put on his helm, but he moved slowly, for he was nearly fainting. Meanwhile, Lionel had struck off Calogrenant's helmet and, realizing that he could no longer escape death, Calogrenant said, 'Sweet Lord Jesus Christ, forgive my sins and have mercy upon my soul, and let the pains I am enduring now count as my penance.' As he spoke, Lionel struck him to the ground and his body stiffened in the throes of death.

Without pausing, Lionel then rushed at his brother and struck him a staggering blow. Bors begged him for love of God to cease fighting; but Lionel would not listen. *Then Bors drew his sword, weeping, and said, 'Sweet Lord Jesus Christ, may it not be accounted sin if I defend my life against my brother!'*

With these words he raised his sword but, just as he was about to strike, he heard a voice which said, 'Flee, Bors, and strike him not, for you will slay him.' And immediately a flash of fire, like a thunderbolt, fell from the heavens between them, from which leapt such a fierce and searing flame that their two shields were burnt, and they were so terrified that they fell to the ground and lay there senseless for a long time. Presently they recovered their wits and looked long at one another, then at the ground between them all scorched red by the fire ... Then Bors heard a voice which said to him: 'Bors, arise and depart. Leave your brother and head for the sea without stopping along the way, for Perceval awaits you there.'

Then Bors found that his injuries were healed, and he mounted his horse at once and made for the sea. There on the beach he saw a marvellous ship all hung with white samite, and he dismounted and went on board, and at once the ship moved swiftly away from the shore. Inside the ship, Bors found Sir Perceval of Wales. They made great joy of one another, speaking of all the adventures that had befallen them.

ABOVE: *Sir Lionel, having decapitated the hermit who tried to plead for Sir Bors's life, now kills Sir Calogrenant. From an early 14th-century French manuscript of* La Queste del Saint Graal.

SIR GALAHAD JOINS THE OTHER KNIGHTS

MEANWHILE, Sir Galahad stopped for the night in a small hermitage in the forest. During the night there came a maiden, who asked for him, saying, 'If you come with me now, sir knight, I will show you the noblest adventure that any knight has ever seen.'

Sir Galahad armed and mounted, and followed the maiden; she led him down to the sea, where a beautiful ship all hung with white samite awaited them on the shore. On board the ship were Sir Perceval and Sir Bors who greeted Sir Galahad joyfully. Sir Galahad and the maiden entered the ship, and at once its sails filled with wind and it sped off across the sea.

In the ship they found all manner of marvels, which the maiden explained to them; and she told them that she was none other than the sister of Sir Perceval, daughter to King Pellinore, and a holy nun. With these high and noble histories the time passed, till at last the ship came to land. *They rode forth until midday and found themselves close to a fine, well-fortified castle ... They were a short distance from the*

ABOVE: *The three Grail knights – Sir Bors, Sir Perceval and Sir Galahad – meet together in the magical ship.*

principal gate when they were overtaken by a knight, who said: 'Sirs, is this damsel who rides with you a maid?'

'Assuredly, she is,' replied Sir Bors.

With that, the knight seized the maiden's horse by the bridle, and said, 'By the Holy Cross, you shall not escape me without yielding to the custom of this castle.' ... Meanwhile ten more knights, fully armed, came out of the castle, accompanied by a damsel, who carried a silver basin in her hands ...

'What is that custom?' asked Sir Galahad.

'Sir,' replied the knight, 'every young maiden who passes here must fill this basin with blood from her right arm. None who passes can escape complying.'

'A curse upon the wicked knight who established such a cruel custom!' cried Galahad. 'I promise you that, with God's will, while I have strength and she trusts in me, you shall not touch this damsel, and she shall not yield to your demands.'

'By my faith,' said the knight, 'then you will all die; for you could not endure against us even if you were the best knights in the world.'

Then they all fought together; but the three good knights overcame their ten opponents easily. Then sixty more knights came out of the castle, and they too fought the three companions. Mainly by the strength and skill of Sir Galahad, supported at each side by Bors and Perceval, those sixty knights also were all unhorsed and wounded or slain.

Then said the old knight who had spoken to them earlier: 'Come and lodge with us this night, good sirs, and we will return to this matter tomorrow. But I am sure that if you knew the reason for our request you would consent to the maiden giving her blood.'

Then they agreed a truce and the knights and the damsel rode into the castle, where they were courteously welcomed. Later, when they had eaten, they asked the old knight to explain the cruel custom. 'Gladly,' he replied. 'Two years ago, the lady of this castle, our beloved mistress, was taken ill with leprosy, and no treatment could help her. At last, a wise man told us that she could be healed only if she bathed in the blood of a clean maiden, pure in thought and deed and a king's daughter. Since then no maid has passed our gate without giving her blood, either willingly or not; but our lady is not yet cured.'

Then the damsel called the three companions to her, and said, 'Sirs, you see well that this lady is sick and that her health or harm depends on my decision. Therefore advise me what I must do.'

'Before God,' said Galahad, 'if you agree to this, you will surely die, for you are young and frail.'

'Truly,' said she, 'if I die in healing her, I and my kindred will have great honour and worship ... Tomorrow there will be no more battle, but I promise that I shall yield to the custom, like the other maidens.' Then the people of the castle thanked her sincerely, and there was great rejoicing.

In the morning, after they had all heard mass, Perceval's sister went to the castle and asked to see the sick lady whom she must cure with her blood. The lady's assistants ... went to fetch their mistress from her bedchamber. When the three companions saw her they were appalled, for her face was so corrupted and disfigured by the leprosy, such a mass of sores, that they wondered how she could endure to live through such suffering. They stood at her approach and asked her to sit with them; at once she asked the damsel to fulfil her promise. Bidding them bring the basin, Perceval's sister stretched forth her arm and allowed them to open the vein with a knife as sharp as a razor. Then, as the blood came gushing forth, she crossed herself and commended herself to God, saying, 'Madam, to heal you I am dying. In God's name, pray for my soul, for my end is come.' So saying, she fainted, for she had lost so much blood that the basin was full. The companions rushed to support her and tried to staunch the flow of blood.

She lay senseless a great while, and then, recovering her speech, she said to Perceval: 'Fair brother Sir Perceval, I die for the healing of this lady, but I pray you do not bury me in this country. As soon as I am dead, place me in a barge at the first port you find and let me float where destiny leads me.'

Perceval, weeping, promised to carry out her wishes.

Then the damsel received the last sacrament and departed her life. And the sick lady was anointed with her blood and healed of her leprosy that same day. Then Sir Perceval laid her in a barge, all hung with black silk; and the wind arose and drove the barge from the land, and they watched it until it was out of sight. The companions said prayers for her soul, and then with many tears they departed and went their separate ways.

THE QUEST ACHIEVED

MEANWHILE, SIR GALAHAD RODE through the realm of Logres releasing it from the many enchantments that had bound it for hundreds of years. He met again with Sir Perceval and Sir Bors, and together they journeyed to the castle of Corbenic, where they were joyfully welcomed by those who had long awaited them.

That same night they witnessed holy marvels in the hall of the castle. First came in the silver table bearing the Grail. Then a voice spoke, saying: 'All those not worthy to eat at the table of Our Lord Jesus Christ, arise, for now shall only true knights be fed.' Then all the people left, save for King Pelles and his son Eliazar, his niece and the three knights. Suddenly they became aware of the presence of the holy bishop Josephus, who had been consecrated bishop by Our Lord himself in the spiritual palace at Sarras more than three hundred years before. Then the chamber door opened and they saw a procession of

BELOW: *Sir Perceval's sister in the ship.*

angels. Two carried great candles, a third bore a cloth and the fourth carried a spear, down which ran great drops of blood that he caught in a bowl. These things they set down upon the table. After a while, the holy bishop took from the vessel a host made to look like bread. As he lifted it up in consecration, there descended from above the figure of a child, whose face glowed like flame. The child smote himself into the bread, so they all saw it take on human form; then the bishop returned it to the Holy Grail. Then Josephus said: 'Servants of the Lord Jesus Christ, who have endured so many sufferings in order to glimpse the mysteries of the Grail, take your place at this table where you shall be served by your Saviour's own hand with the most glorious and sublime food that any knight ever tasted.'

With that he vanished; and the knights approached the table and sat in prayer. *Then looked they and saw a man come out of the holy vessel, that had all the signs of the passion of Jesus Christ, bleeding all openly, who said: 'My knights, and my servants, and my true children,*

Sir Thomas Malory, *Morte Darthur.*

140

which are come out of mortal life into spiritual life, I will now no longer hide me from you, but you shall see a part of my secrets and my hidden things: now hold and receive the high meat that you have so much desired.'

Then took He Himself the holy vessel and came to Galahad; and he kneeled down, and there he received his Saviour, and after him so received all his fellows, and they thought it so sweet that it was marvellous to tell. Then gave He them His blessing, and vanished.

Then Sir Galahad went to the Holy Lance and dipped his fingers into the blood; with it he anointed the wounds on the legs and body of King Pelles, the maimed king. And the king was healed in that instant and leapt from his bed, crying, 'Thanks be to the Lord God, for I have so long waited for Your coming in pain and torment, and now my suffering is over, and I am healed through your hand.'

Then Galahad and Perceval and Bors took ship, with the Holy Grail upon its silver table, and sailed across the sea to the holy city of Sarras. But when they brought forth the Holy Grail into the city, the

ABOVE: *The Achievement of the Grail Quest. Sir Bors, Sir Perceval and Sir Galahad are depicted in this tapestry designed by Burne-Jones.*

ABOVE: *The achievement of the Quest. Only two of the three successful Grail knights are present in this illustration by Beardsley.*

people reported them to the king, who was a pagan and a tyrant, and he cast them all into a deep and noisome dungeon for a year. But the Holy Grail comforted them there and fed them daily with spiritual nourishment. After a year, the king fell sick and on his deathbed he sent for the three companions, and begged their forgiveness; and they forgave him as good Christian knights. After his death, the people chose Galahad to be their king. He had the Holy Grail encased in a shrine of gold and silver and precious gems, and every day he and Perceval and Bors would come before it to pray and hear mass.

Now at the year's end, and on the same day that Galahad had borne the crown of gold, he arose up early with his fellows, and came to the palace, and they saw before them the holy vessel, and a man kneeling in the likeness of a bishop, that had about him a great fellowship of angels as it had been Jesus Christ himself; and then he arose and began a mass of Our Lady. And when he came to the sacrament of the mass, he called Sir Galahad and said to him, 'Come forth the servant of Jesus Christ, and you shall see what you have much desired to see.'

Then Galahad began to tremble right hard when the mortal flesh began to behold the spiritual things. Then he held up his hands towards Heaven and said, 'Lord, I thank You, for now I see what has been my desire for many a day. Now, blessed Lord, would I not longer live, if it might please You, Lord.'

And therewith the good man took Our Lord's body between his hands and offered it to Galahad and he received it right gladly and meekly ...

And therewith he kneeled down before the table and made his prayers, and then suddenly his soul departed to Jesus Christ, and a great multitude of angels bore his soul up to heaven, that his two fellows might well behold it. Also the two fellows saw come from heaven a hand, but they saw not the body; and it came right to the vessel, and it took it and the spear, and so bore it up to Heaven. Since was there never man so hardy as to say that he had seen the Sangrail.

Then Sir Perceval and Sir Bors, sorrowing deeply, had Sir Galahad's body buried in rich state in the spiritual palace; and after that, Sir Perceval took himself to the religious life and lived as a

hermit in prayer and contemplation outside the city. And Sir Bors departed from the holy city of Sarras and took ship for Logres. And he rode until he came to Camelot where King Arthur's court was. The king and knights made great joy at his return; for he had been away for many years, and many knights had perished in the quest. Then King Arthur had all the adventures of the Holy Grail recorded in a great book, just as I have rehearsed them here.

ABOVE: *Sir Galahad is crowned king in the Holy City of Sarras.*

PART III
THE FALL of KING ARTHUR

THE ACHIEVEMENT OF THE Holy Grail forms the pinnacle of the quests of the Knights of the Round Table. The Knights return to Camelot and the focus settles on King Arthur whose own tragedies, betrayals and ultimate death form the moving and dramatic finale to the chronicles. The supreme story-teller of this final tragedy is undoubtedly Sir Thomas Malory, whose account of the bitter enmity between life-long friends, the unbearable loss of death and final part-ing, can move the reader as no other part of the *Morte Darthur* can. This retelling is based mainly on Malory, supplemented where Malory is very brief or obscure by passages from his source, the Old French *Mort Artu*, the final section of the great Vulgate Cycle, and from another translation of that, the Middle English stanzaic poem *Morte Arthur*, which Malory knew and used in his work.

⅄ Lancelot had amended his life to a state of 'perfection' by repenting of his sinful liaison with the queen and receiving absolution on condition that he did not sin any more.

⅄ As usual when Malory writes 'as the French book says', the French book actually says no such thing. *La Queste del Saint Graal* is generally much more severe on Lancelot than Malory.

BELOW: *'Sir Lancelot began to resort unto Queen Guinevere again, and forgot the promise and perfection that he made in the quest.'*

⅄*AFTER THE QUEST of the Holy Grail was fulfilled and all the knights that were left alive were come again to the Round Table, there was great joy in the court; and in especial King Arthur and Queen Guinevere made a great joy of the remnant that were come home, and passing glad they were of Sir Lancelot and Sir Bors, for they had been long away in the Quest of the Holy Grail. Then Sir Lancelot began to resort unto Queen Guinevere again, and forgot the promise and the perfection ⅄ that he made in the quest. For, as the French book says ⅄, had not Sir Lancelot been in his private thoughts so set inwardly to the queen as he was in outward seeming to God, there had no knight passed him in the Quest of the Holy Grail. But ever his thoughts were privily on the queen, and so they loved together more hotly than before and had such private courses together that many in the court spoke of it, and in especial Sir Agravain, Sir Gawain's brother, for he was ever open-mouthed.*

At the feast of Our Lady's Assumption, King Arthur announced a great tournament to be held at Camelot, where he and the King of Scots would joust against all comers.

When King Arthur made ready to depart, however, the queen would not go with him, for she said she was sick and could not ride. Many thought that she wanted to stay behind to be with Sir Lancelot. And the king was wroth at this; but he left her in London, and went with his fellowship towards Camelot. On the way, he lodged for the night in the castle of Astolat. And when he was gone, the queen called Sir Lancelot to her and said: 'Sir Lancelot, you should not stay behind my lord the king, for our enemies will say that you do so to have your pleasure with me.'

'Madam,' said Sir Lancelot, 'it is but lately you are grown so wise; but I will be ruled by your counsel and tomorrow I will go to Camelot.'

And in the morning early he heard mass, took his leave of the queen and departed. When he came to the town of Astolat in the evening, he arrived at the hall of an old baron named Sir Bernard of Astolat and, as he entered there to seek his lodging, it happened that King Arthur espied him from the castle. And the king smiled to himself and went into his lodging.

The old baron welcomed Sir Lancelot in the most courteous manner; but he knew him not. *'Fair sir,'* said Sir Lancelot to his host, *'I pray you to lend me a shield that is not openly known, for mine is well known.'*

'Sir,' said his host, *'you shall have your desire, for meseems you are one of the likeliest knights of the world, and therefore I*

shall show you friendship. Sir, wit you well I have two sons that were but late made knights, and the eldest is called Sir Tirre, and he was hurt the same day that he was made knight, so that he may not ride, and his shield you shall have . . . My youngest son is called Sir Lavaine and, if it please you, he shall ride with you unto that joust. Much my heart gives unto you that you are a noble knight, therefore I pray you, tell me your name.'

'As for that,' said Sir Lancelot, 'you must hold me excused at this time, and if God give me grace to speed well at the joust I shall come again and tell you. But I pray you, in any wise let me have your son Sir Lavaine with me, and that I may have his brother's shield.'

'All this shall be done,' said Sir Bernard.

This old baron had a daughter that was called the Fair Maiden of Astolat. And ever she beheld Sir Lancelot wonderfully and her name was Elaine. So thus as she came to and fro she was so hot in her love that she besought Sir Lancelot to wear upon him at the joust some token of hers.

'Fair damsel,' said Sir Lancelot, 'if I grant you that, you may say that I do more for your love than ever I did for lady or damsel.' Then he remembered him that he would go to the jousts disguised. And because he had never before that time borne any manner of token from any damsel, then he bethought him that he would bear one of her, that none of his blood thereby might know him, and then he said, 'Fair maiden, I will grant you to wear a token of yours upon my helmet, and therefore show me what it is.'

'Sir,' she said, 'it is a red sleeve of mine, richly embroidered with great pearls,' and so she brought it him.

Sir Lancelot received it and said, 'Never did I do so much for any damsel.' And then Sir Lancelot gave his shield into the fair maiden's keeping and prayed her to keep that until he came again; and that night he had merry rest and great cheer, for ever the damsel Elaine was about Sir Lancelot all the while she might be suffered.

In the morning, Sir Lancelot and Sir Lavaine made them ready for the jousts; each of them carried a white shield, and Sir Lancelot carried with him the red sleeve. They set off for Camelot, and found it packed full of kings, dukes, earls, barons and many noble knights.

Then the jousts began. King Arthur watched from a scaffold to judge who did the best and Sir Gawain with him. The King of Scots and the King of Ireland fought on King Arthur's party; and against them fought the King of Northgales ❧, the King with the Hundred Knights, the King of Northumberland and Galahaut the Haut Prince. Sir Lancelot and Sir Lavaine withdrew themselves to a little wood, where they might watch the fray. Sir Lancelot fastened the red sleeve to his helm. Then both the parties came together with a great clash of swords and lances, and mighty blows were struck; but King Arthur's party was ever the stronger and at last the party of the King of Northgales began to give ground.

Then Sir Lavaine said to Sir Lancelot, 'Sir, which side shall we fight on?'

❧ Northgales: North Wales.

147

'Let us join the weaker,' replied Sir Lancelot, 'because it will do us no honour to join the stronger side.'

The two rode out into the thickest of the fighting, and Sir Lancelot smote down five knights of the Round Table with one spear, and Sir Lavaine smote down two. Then Sir Lancelot's spear broke, and he laid about him with his sword and unhorsed several more knights, until the knights of King Arthur's party were forced to draw back.

'What knight is that,' said Sir Gawain, 'that does such marvellous deeds of arms?'

'I know who he is,' said King Arthur, 'but I shall not name him now.'

'Sir,' said Sir Gawain, 'I would say it was Sir Lancelot by his riding and by his great blows, but that he bears a red sleeve on his helm; for I never knew Sir Lancelot to wear a token from any lady or damsel.'

And King Arthur smiled and said nothing.

Then Sir Bors, Sir Ector and Sir Lionel called to them all the other knights of Sir Lancelot's blood, and they all joined the fray mightily, for they were indignant at being put to shame (as they thought) by an unknown knight. They hurled together with Sir Lancelot's party and they smote down many knights of Northgales and Northumberland. On seeing this, Sir Lancelot seized a great spear *and there encountered with him all at once Sir Bors, Sir Ector and Sir Lionel, and all three smote him at once with their spears. And with the force of themselves they smote Sir Lancelot's horse to the earth; and by misfortune Sir Bors smote Sir Lancelot through the shield into the side, and the spear broke, and the head was left still in his side. When Sir Lavaine saw his master lie on the ground, he ran to the King of Scots and smote him to the earth; and by great force he took his horse and brought him to Sir Lancelot, and in spite of all of them he made him to mount upon that horse. And then Sir Lancelot got a spear in his hand, and there he smote Sir Bors, horse and man, to the earth. In the same wise he served Sir Ector and Sir Lionel.*

Then he drew his sword and laid about him with the last of his strength; and altogether he smote down thirty knights that day, most of them knights of the Round Table. And Sir Lavaine smote down ten knights.

Then the king blew the horn for the end of that day's jousting and the heralds awarded the prize to the knight with the white shield that wore the red sleeve. But Sir Lancelot groaned piteously and rode away at a gallop with Sir Lavaine until he came to a wood. *And when he saw that he was near a mile away from the field, so that he was sure he might not be seen, he said with a high voice, 'O gentle knight, Sir Lavaine, help me that this truncheon were out of my side, for its sticks so sore that it almost slays me.'*

'O mine own lord,' said Sir Lavaine, 'I would gladly do what might please you, but I dread me sore if I pull out the truncheon that you will be in peril of death.'

'I charge you,' said Sir Lancelot, 'as you love me, draw it out.' Therewith he descended from his horse, and right so did Sir Lavaine, and forthwith Sir Lavaine drew the truncheon out of his side, and he gave a great shriek and a grisly groan, and the blood burst out almost a pint at once, so that he sank down and swooned, pale and deathly.

At last Sir Lancelot revived a little and begged Sir Lavaine to bring him to a hermitage he knew of near by, where the hermit, who had been a knight in his younger days, was a skilled surgeon and healer. Sir Lavaine put him on his horse and together they rode to the hermitage, and the hermit received them both kindly, gently undressed Sir Lancelot and laid him in the bed.

ABOVE: *Jousts performed before King Arthur and his court. Miniature from a fragmentary copy of the* Romance of Guiron le Courtois.

Meanwhile, at Camelot, King Arthur asked for the knight with the white shield that wore the red sleeve: 'Bring him here so that he may be honoured and receive his prize.'

Then came the King with the Hundred Knights and told King Arthur how the knight with the white shield had been almost mad with the pain of his wound and had ridden off, he knew not where.

'Alas,' said the king, 'I would rather lose all my lands than hear that that knight is dead.'

'By my head,' said Sir Gawain, 'he is one of the noblest knights that ever I saw handle a spear and sword; and if he can be found, I shall find him, for he cannot have gone far from here.'

Straight away Sir Gawain took a squire and rode all about Camelot for six or seven miles; but no trace of the knight with the white shield could he find. Two days later, King Arthur and his fellowship returned to London, by way of Astolat; and Sir Gawain stayed in the hall of Sir Bernard of Astolat, the old baron. And when they knew who he was, the baron and his daughter came to keep him company, and asked him who had won the prize at the tournament.

'There were two knights,' said Sir Gawain, 'bearing white shields, but one of them carried a red sleeve on his helm, and he was one of the best knights I have ever seen.

'I thank God,' said the fair Elaine, 'that he did so well, for I truly love that knight.'

THE TOURNAMENT

TOURNAMENTS EVOLVED PARTLY as an opportunity for combat training. Knights could practise the handling of their horses and weapons, the tactics of defence and attack, and of co-ordinating their actions with a team of companions. They would also have the opportunity to display their skills before ladies, and before potential employers, and they could, if they were successful, make a great deal of money from forfeited horses and armour and the ransoms of those they captured.

The first recorded tournament took place in 1066 in France. Early tournaments were fairly unregulated free-for-alls; two or more teams of knights would fight one another all day long over a large range of ground, with the object of defeating and capturing as many members of the opposing teams as possible. Weapons and armour in the early days were the same for tournaments as for wars; only the acknowledged intention of fighting for sport distinguished early tournaments from real battles. They were extremely violent, and mêlées often resulted in death and injury. Yet they became more and more popular with knights, some of whom would bankrupt themselves, or risk excommunication or imprisonment to go on taking part.

The joust, an encounter between two individual knights, became popular in Germany towards the middle of the twelfth century and spread to France and England, where it was incorporated into the tournament before or after the mêlée or team fighting took place. During this period rules intended to make tournaments safer were introduced. These included such safeguards as the use of blunted weapons and the erection of barriers to separate the galloping horses of jousting knights; but casualty rates remained high.

Tournaments were banned by the Church for much of this period, but this ban was widely flouted, and eventually it was revoked. Individual rulers also imposed bans from time to time; King Henry II of England forbade tournaments during his reign and his son Henry the Young King, with his tutor William Marshal – both tournament addicts – had to go to France to indulge their passion. Later, King Edward I, a keen tourneyer himself in his youth, had to forbid his knights to hold tournaments during his campaigns against the Scots and Welsh, because knights kept sneaking away from camp to attend them.

Eventually tournaments became highly regulated. The area in which the fighting took place – the lists – was fenced in; attacks were not permitted on, or by, knights who had surrendered, and heralds played important roles identifying and judging the competitors. By the close of the Middle Ages, tournaments were more associated with grand state occasions than with a robust sport that provided useful military training.

'Do you know his name?' asked Sir Gawain.

'No, I do not,' she replied, 'but I have his shield, for when he came here he borrowed my brother's shield and left his own in my chamber. If you wish I will take you to see it.'

'Not so,' said Sir Bernard to his daughter, 'have it sent for.' ✾ When the shield was brought, Sir Gawain recognized it at once as Lancelot's.

'Damsel,' said Sir Gawain, 'if the knight who owns this shield is your love, then you are loved by the noblest knight in the world; and never before did he ever wear any lady's favour at any tournament. This shield belongs to Sir Lancelot du Lake. I hope and pray that you two may have joy of one another; but that is in God's hands, for I fear you may never see him again in this world.'

'Alas,' said she, 'what do you mean? Is he slain?'

'No,' said Sir Gawain, 'but he was grievously wounded.'

'Father,' said Elaine, 'give me leave to ride and seek Sir Lancelot, for I cannot rest until I have found him.'

'Very well,' said Sir Bernard, 'see what you can do, for I am sorry indeed to hear that that noble knight is hurt.'

So the maid rode off in search of Sir Lancelot; and the next day Sir Gawain joined King Arthur and told him that he had discovered the identity of the knight with the red sleeve.

'I knew it was Sir Lancelot, because I saw him at Astolat,' said King Arthur, 'but I saw that he wished to keep it secret.'

'He may have another secret,' said Sir Gawain, 'and I will tell you what it is, but it must be only between the two of us.' Sir Gawain drew King Arthur with him into a little garden and told him how the Fair Maid of Astolat had said that Lancelot was her love, and that it was her sleeve he had worn in the tournament. 'And even if she is not very highly born,' added Gawain, 'it would not surprise me to hear that Lancelot loves her, because she is one of the most beautiful women I have ever seen.'

Queen Guinevere was standing at an open window above the little garden and she overheard everything. Now she leaned forward and asked, 'Who is this beautiful creature you are talking about?'

'Madam,' replied Gawain, 'she is the daughter of Sir Bernard of Astolat.'

At this the queen abruptly went into her chamber and lay down upon her bed. She wept and wailed with woe, for she believed that Gawain spoke the truth, that Sir Lancelot had fallen in love with the Fair Maid of Astolat. And when she had wept, she swelled with anger; and she sent at once for Sir Lancelot's cousin, Sir Bors. When he came, she said: '*Ah, Sir Bors, have you heard how falsely Sir Lancelot has betrayed me? . . . He is a false traitor knight.*'

'*Madam,*' said Sir Bors, '*I pray you say not so, for wit you*

✾ Malory is alluding to Gawain's reputation as a womanizer here. Sir Bernard very wisely will not trust him alone with his daughter in her bedchamber. At this point in *Mort Artu*, Gawain is actually trying to seduce her.

BELOW: *Sir Lavaine tends the badly wounded Lancelot.*

well I may not hear such language of him.'

'Why, Sir Bors,' said she, 'should I not call him traitor when he wore the red sleeve upon his head at Camelot, at the great joust?'

'Madam,' said Sir Bors, 'I sorely regret that sleeve-bearing, but I dare say he did it for no evil intent, but for this cause he wore the red sleeve, that none of his blood should know him.'

'You will hear no more about it from me,' said she, ◆ *'but this much I will tell you—I will never forgive Lancelot.'*

◆Anon, *Mort Artu.*

'Indeed, Madam,' said Bors, 'that grieves me; and since you have taken such a great hatred towards my lord, our men have no good reason for remaining here. And therefore, Madam, I take my leave of you and I commend you to God; for we shall leave in the morning. And when we are on our way, we shall search for my lord until we can find him, if it please God. Know therefore, Madam,' he went on, 'that we would not have stayed in this country as long as we have, had it not been for the love of our lord, and nor would he have stayed so long after the Quest of the Holy Grail, except for you; and know for sure that he has loved you more faithfully than any knight ever loved a lady or a damsel.'

When the queen heard these words, she was more distressed than ever she had been before, and could not prevent tears from coming into her eyes. When she could speak, she said that the hour should be accursed that ever such tidings came to her; 'for,' she said, 'I am in a sorry plight because of it'.

Then Sir Bors left the queen and told his kinsmen what had passed between them; and they all left the court to search for Sir Lancelot. Meanwhile the fair Elaine was also seeking Sir Lancelot, and her brother Sir Lavaine brought her to him.

◆Sir Thomas Malory, *Morte Darthur.*

◆*And when she saw him lie so sick and pale in his bed she might not speak, but suddenly she fell to the earth in a swoon, and there she lay a great while. When she awoke, she shrieked and said, 'My Lord, Sir Lancelot, why are you in this plight?'*

Then she swooned again . . . and when she came to herself Sir Lancelot kissed her and said, 'Fair maiden, why fare you thus? You put me to pain, wherefore make no more such cheer, for if you are come to comfort me you are right welcome; and of this little hurt that I have I shall be right hastily whole by the grace of God.' . . .

So this maiden Elaine never went from Sir Lancelot, but watched him day and night, and did such attendance on him, that the French book saith there was never woman did more kindlier for man than she. And at last, after much care, Sir Lancelot was recovered enough to be able to ride without his wound bursting open and he decided to return to court. First he and Sir Lavaine and the fair Elaine returned to Astolat. When she knew that he was about to leave, Elaine came to him and said: *'My lord, Sir Lancelot, now I see you will depart; now fair and courteous knight, have mercy upon me, and suffer me not to die for your love.'*

'What would you that I did?' said Sir Lancelot.

'I would have you to my husband,' said Elaine.

LANCELOT AND GUINEVERE

WE HAVE ALREADY COME ACROSS LANCELOT in *Le Chevalier de la Charrette* of Chrétien de Troyes, written about 1175-80. In this poem he is utterly besotted with Queen Guinevere. Although this passion is, in its way, exemplary and admirable, it is also clearly intended to seem rather comical; for example, when Lancelot falls into a trance on catching sight of a couple of Guinevere's hairs caught in a comb, or considers throwing himself out of an upstairs window because the queen is no longer in view from it – luckily, the sensible Gawain is on hand to restrain him.

Chrétien's brilliant verse contains all the major features of later versions – Lancelot's complete devotion to the queen, which she tests to the utmost, her fiery temper and desire to punish him for the slightest shortcoming, and Lancelot's rescue of her from a shameful death after she has been accused of adultery. From this moment on, Lancelot became the supreme champion of Arthur's court, at least in French romance.

Chrétien, too, created the archetypal version of the queen; her passionate love for Lancelot, tempered by her great pride, are as much part of her as his devotion to her is part of him. Chrétien described with acute psychological insight a sequence of the queen being furious with Lancelot for hesitating to debase himself in order to save her, then bitterly repenting her coldness and cruelty when she thought he was dead, and a tender and passionate reconciliation.

In *La Mort le Roi Artu* Guinevere becomes more jealous and demanding, given to fits of jealousy and spite, while Lancelot responds with an unvarying gentlemanly devotion which makes him appear quite saintly. Malory's version of the lovers is more human. His Lancelot appears disenchanted with Guinevere's jealous tantrums, but remains loyal to her in almost the same way as he is loyal to Arthur. His Guinevere is as tormented by love as Lancelot, unable to stop herself betraying her lord by more and more flagrant indiscretion.

'Fair damsel, I thank you,' said Sir Lancelot, 'but truly, I never cast me to be wedded man.'

'Then, fair knight,' said she, 'will you be my paramour?'

'Jesu defend me,' said Sir Lancelot, 'for then I rewarded your father and your brother full evil for their great goodness.'

'Alas,' said she, 'then I must die for your love.'

'You shall not so,' said Sir Lancelot, 'for wit you well, fair maiden, I might have been married if I had wanted, but I never applied me to be married yet; but because, fair damsel, you love me as you say you do, I will for your good will show you some goodness, and that is this, that when you bestow your heart upon some good knight that will wed you, I shall give you together a thousand pounds yearly to you and to your heirs. Thus much will I give you, fair madam, for your kindness, and always, while I live, to be your knight.'

'Of all this,' said the maiden, 'I want nothing, for unless you wed me, or else be my paramour at least, wit you well, Sir Lancelot, my good days are done.'

'Of these two things,' said Sir Lancelot, 'you must pardon me.'

Then she shrieked shrilly and fell down into a swoon . . . Then came Sir Bernard to Sir Lancelot and said to him, 'I cannot see but that my daughter Elaine will die for your sake.'

'I can do nothing about it,' said Sir Lancelot, 'for that I sore regret, for I ask you to judge that my offer is fair. And I am sorry,' said he, 'that she loves me as she does; I was never the causer of it, for your son can tell you that I never offered her bounty or fair behests. As for me, I dare do all that a knight should do that she is a clean maiden for me, in deed and in will. And I am right heavy of her distress, for she is a full fair maiden, good, gentle, and well taught.'

'Father,' said Sir Lavaine, 'I dare make good she is a clean maiden as for my lord Sir Lancelot; but she does as I do, for since I first saw my lord Sir Lancelot, I could never depart from him.'

Then Sir Lancelot and Sir Lavaine took their leave of Sir Bernard and rode until they came to London to the court; and great was the rejoicing at the court when they saw Sir Lancelot whole and well. But Queen Guinevere swept out of the hall to her room as soon as Sir Lancelot entered, and sent word that she was ill and could not speak to anyone. But later on she sent for Sir Lancelot and said: 'Sir Lancelot, I see that your love for me begins to dwindle and fade, for you have no pleasure in my company, but are always out of the court and keeping company with other ladies and damsels.'

'Madam,' said Sir Lancelot, 'you must hold me excused for three reasons. First, I was but lately in the Quest of the Holy Grail, when it was told to me that I would have seen as great mysteries as my son Sir Galahad and Sir Bors, had it not been for our sinful love. Second, you must know that many knights are talking about us, such as Sir Agravain and Sir Mordred, and lying in wait for us, and I dread to see

you dishonoured; and third, if we are too open we shall bring great shame and slander on ourselves and on this noble court.'

At this the queen burst out weeping and sobbing. When she could speak, she accused Lancelot of being unfaithful, saying: '*Now I understand your falsehood, and therefore I shall never love you more. And never be so foolhardy as to come in my sight; I forbid you my fellowship, and upon pain of your head you shall see me no more.*'

Sir Lancelot left at once in great sorrow. He called for Sir Bors, Sir Ector and Sir Lionel, his kinsmen, and told them how the queen had forbidden him the court. But Sir Bors advised him privately not to leave the country: 'Remember who you are, my lord, and remember

ABOVE: *Queen Guinevere and The Maid of Astolat. Cartoon for a stained glass window by William Morris.*

ABOVE: *Sir Lavaine brings his sister Elaine to the bedside of the wounded Lancelot.*

✠ Sir Gawain had killed Sir Lamorak in revenge for the death of his father, King Lot, who had been killed by Sir Lamorak's father, King Pellinore.

also that women often do things in haste which they regret afterwards. This is not the first time that the queen has quarrelled with you, and she has always relented in time. By my advice you should ride to the hermitage of Sir Brastias near Windsor, and wait there till I send you better news.'

Sir Lancelot agreed to do this, and left the court full of sorrow, and no one knew where he had gone except Sir Bors. And after his departure the queen was bitterly sorry for her hasty words, but she was too proud to show her grief and pretended to everyone that she was happy as ever. To show that she had as much joy in other knights as in Sir Lancelot, she made a dinner for twenty-four knights of the Round Table in London, including Sir Gawain and his brothers.

Sir Gawain was very fond of fruit, and especially apples and pears, so the queen ordered plenty of fresh, ripe apples for him. Sir Pinel le Savage hated Sir Gawain because he had killed Sir Lamorak de Gales ✠, and he poisoned some of the apples so as to kill Sir Gawain. By misfortune the queen offered the fruit to Sir Patrise, a cousin of Sir Mador de la Porte, and he took a poisoned apple; when he had eaten it, he swelled up until he burst and fell down dead. All the knights leapt to their feet in anger; for they had all seen Queen Guinevere hand the apple to Sir Patrise and there was no escaping her guilt.

Then they all came before King Arthur, and Sir Mador de la Porte openly accused the queen of murder. 'Fair lords,' said King Arthur, 'I cannot take the queen's part, because I must be the judge, but surely some good knight will be her champion and fight on her behalf in a trial by combat.'

'My gracious lord,' said Sir Mador, 'you must hold us excused, but none of us knights that were at the dinner will take the queen's part.' And all the knights agreed with Sir Mador that the queen was guilty.

'Alas,' said the queen, 'I report me unto Almighty God, that I had no evil intent when I made the dinner, but only good.'

Sir Mador insisted that he would have justice and King Arthur had to name a day fifteen days hence when trial by combat would determine the queen's guilt or innocence. And if no one would come forward to fight for her, there was no help for it but she must be burned at the stake. King Arthur spoke in private with the queen and asked her how this had befallen. The queen answered: 'Before God, on my very soul, I know not.'

'Where is Sir Lancelot?' said the king. 'What ails you, that you cannot keep Sir Lancelot on your side? But I advise you to go to Sir Bors and require him to do battle for you for Sir Lancelot's sake.'

The queen was very loth to ask this favour of Sir Bors, after the harsh words that had passed between them, but there was no help for it. She sent for him to her chamber and begged him to help her.

'Madam,' said Sir Bors, 'if I take your part then suspicion will fall upon me. And now you should be sorry that you drove Sir Lancelot away, for he would not have failed you in right or in wrong.'

'Alas, fair knight,' said the queen, 'whatever I have done amiss, I will amend it as you advise me.' At that she kneeled down and begged Sir Bors to have mercy on her.

Just then came King Arthur and found the queen on her knees, and Sir Bors bade her rise and said, 'Madam, you do me great dishonour.'

'Ah, gentle knight,' said the king, 'help my queen, for I am certain that she is falsely defamed. Therefore promise me to do battle for her, I require you for the love of Sir Lancelot.'

'Sire,' said Sir Bors, 'if I do battle for the queen I shall anger many of my fellow-knights. But, for Sir Lancelot's sake, I will undertake to be the queen's champion, unless a better knight than I comes to do battle for her.'

Then the king and the queen thanked him heartily. And Sir Bors secretly departed from the court and rode to the hermitage and told Sir Lancelot what had befallen.

'Ah, Jesu,' said Sir Lancelot, 'this has fallen out just as I would wish. I pray you, make ready to do battle on the appointed day, but tarry till you see me come.'

'It shall be as you say,' replied Sir Bors, and he departed and returned to the court.

Meanwhile the Fair Maid of Astolat took to her bed and neither slept, nor ate, nor drank, and when she had endured thus for ten days everyone could see that she was dying. A priest was sent for to hear her confession, and he absolved her of her sins and gave her the Holy Sacrament. But ever would she complain of Sir Lancelot. *Then her ghostly father bid her leave such thoughts.*

Then she said, 'Why should I leave such thoughts? Am I not an earthly woman? And all the while the breath is in my body I may complain me, for my belief is I do none offence, though I love an earthly man; and I take God to my record, I loved never any but Sir Lancelot du Lake, nor ever shall, and a clean maiden I am for him and for all other.

BELOW: *Queen Guinevere accidentally offers a poisoned apple intended for Sir Gawain to Sir Patrise of Ireland.*

157

And since it is the will of God that I shall die for the love of so noble a knight, I beseech the Higher Father of Heaven to have mercy upon my soul . . . for sweet Lord Jesu, I take thee to record, on thee I was never an offender against thy laws; but that I loved this noble knight, Sir Lancelot, out of measure, and of myself, good Lord, I might not withstand the fervent love wherefore I have my death.'

Then the fair maiden asked her father that she might dictate a letter, and that, when she was dead, the letter should be put in her hand, and she should be laid in a barge on the River Thames, and steered down the river to Westminster, to the court. And all this was done as she had requested. So the barge came to Westminster, and it happened that King Arthur and Sir Gawain saw it hove to at the bank and wondered what it meant. They entered the barge and found a bed adorned with rich brocades, and lying on the bed the dead body of a beautiful girl. ❧ *They regarded her for a long time and, when Sir Gawain had looked well at her, he recognized her as the beautiful damsel . . . who had said that she would never love anyone but Lancelot. He said to the king: 'Sire, I know who this damsel was . . . Do you remember the beautiful damsel of whom I told you before, with whom Lancelot was in love?'*

'Yes,' said the king, 'I remember well . . .'

'Sire,' said Sir Gawain, 'this is the damsel we were talking about.'

'Indeed,' said the king, 'that saddens me, and I would dearly like to know the reason for her death, because I believe she died from grief.'

The queen came on board to join them and ❧ *espied a letter in her right hand, and told the king. And the king said, 'Now I am sure this letter will tell us who she was, and why she is come hither.' . . . Then the king broke the seal of the letter and caused a clerk to read it, and this was the intent of the letter:*

> *Most noble knight, Sir Lancelot, now has death made us two at debate for your love. I was your lover, that men called the Fair Maid of Astolat; therefore unto all ladies I make my moan, yet pray for my soul and bury me at least, and offer my mass-penny; this is my last request. A clean maiden I died, as I take God to witness. Pray for my soul, Sir Lancelot, as thou art peerless.*

This was all the substance of the letter. And when it was read, the king, the queen and all the knights wept for pity. And Sir Gawain said to the queen: ❧ *'Madam, oh madam, now I know well that I slandered Sir Lancelot when I told you he loved the Maid of Astolat and that he was staying with her; for certainly if he had loved her with such a great passion as I implied, she would not be dead now, but Sir Lancelot would have done all that she required him to.'*

'Sir,' said she, 'many good men are the subjects of gossip. It is a shame, for they lose thereby much more than is generally believed.'

Then the king decided to have the beautiful damsel buried with

❧ Anon, *Mort Artu.*

❧ Sir Thomas Malory, *Morte Darthur.*

❧ Anon, *Mort Artu.*

158

TENNYSON

TENNYSON made an enormous contribution to the Victorian fascination with medieval culture in his Arthurian poems with their focus on King Arthur and the Round Table Fellowship. He wrote the first of these, *Morte d'Arthur*, in 1834 when he was only twenty-five years old. He began with the end of the story, for this poem deals with the king's final hours. When he wrote the *Idylls of the King*, much later, he incorporated this earlier poem with scarcely any changes.

The passion for a new, contemporary version of medieval chivalry, which was to culminate in the Eglinton Tournament of 1838, had already been roused by the tremendously influential book *The Broad Stone of Honour* by Kenelm Digby, and was being fed by the popular novels of Walter Scott. This passion was so widespread that it influenced all major artistic and cultural endeavours in Victorian Britain, and in many other countries too. Tennyson became Poet Laureate in 1850 and, shortly after, began work on his own version of the Arthurian legend, *Idylls of the King*.

He published four idylls together in 1859: *Enid, Vivien, Guinevere* and *Elaine*. Tennyson wanted to explore the question of private morality influencing public well-being. To do this he concentrated on the way in which King Arthur's world was destroyed from within by its own corruption and vice. Enid, the patient and loving wife of the jealous Geraint, represents all that women should be; Vivien, the evil and scheming seductress of Merlin, all that they

should not be. Guinevere, a more human creation, very much based on Malory's portrayal, is by turns noble and good, yet selfish and demanding. For Malory, there was no conflict in being noble and at the same time sinful. Tennyson's position was much more moral and judgemental – the worm in the bud, which eventually destroys the whole edifice of Arthurian chivalry and everyone in it, is Guinevere's adulterous love for Lancelot. Tennyson invented a final interview between Arthur and Guinevere just before the final battle, in which Arthur makes clear just how Guinevere's selfish sensuality is responsible for corrupting a generation of knights whom he had hoped to lead to the realization of their highest ideals.

Four more tales followed in 1869 and Tennyson continued to add to them until the complete edition appeared in 1886. He based his vision of Arthur and Camelot largely on Malory, whose *Morte Darthur* he had read from boyhood and loved. Tennyson brings to the legend the agonized moral consciousness of the nineteenth century, when it appeared to many people that the new age of material prosperity which mass industrialization had brought was being paid for by abandoning spiritual values. But, more important than his philosophical or didactic intentions, the emotional intensity and lyrical beauty of Tennyson's poetry create the Arthurian world in far greater visual detail than any medieval source.

all honour in the cathedral of St Stephen, and caused a rich and wonderful tomb to be raised over her grave with an inscription which said: 'Here lies the Fair Maid of Astolat, who died for love of Sir Lancelot.'

Then came the day on which Sir Mador de la Porte would do battle with Sir Bors to prove the guilt of the queen in the matter of Sir Patrise's death, and the king and the queen and all manner of knights drew them unto the meadow beside Camelot where the battle should be. And there the queen was put in the custody of the constable, and a great fire was built around an iron stake where, if Sir Mador de la Porte won the battle, she should be burnt. Then came in Sir Mador de la Porte and took his oath before the king, that the queen had poisoned his cousin Sir Patrise; then came Sir Bors de Ganis and swore that Queen Guinevere was not guilty of treason.

Then each of them rode to their tents and prepared themselves

BELOW: *The body of the Maid of Astolat arrives at Westminster and is met by King Arthur, Sir Gawain and others of the court. From an early 14th-century manuscript.*

for battle. And Sir Mador hurried into the field with his spear and shield, shouting out to King Arthur, 'Bid your champion come forth, if he dares!' Then Sir Bors rode into the lists.

Then he saw coming from a nearby wood a strange knight, with unknown arms riding a white horse, who cantered up to Sir Bors and said: 'Fair knight, I pray you be not displeased, but you must now withdraw, for this battle should be mine.'

Then Sir Bors rode to King Arthur and told him that a knight had come to do battle for the queen.

Then the strange knight and Sir Mador rode to the ends of the lists, and couched their spears and ran together. Sir Mador's spear broke in pieces, but the other's spear held, and he thrust Sir Mador horse and all backwards to the ground.

Then both knights alit from their horses and drew their swords. They gave one another many great strokes and were fighting there for almost an hour, for Sir Mador was a strong knight, well proved in many battles. At last the stranger knight struck Sir Mador to the ground, but as he came near to take the victory, Sir Mador sprang up suddenly and struck him in rising through the thick of the thighs so that blood gushed out. When the knight felt himself so wounded and saw his blood, he gave Sir Mador a heavy blow on the head, so that he fell down full length; and he strode to him and seized his helmet to cut off his head. Then Sir Mador prayed the knight to save his life.

'I will not grant you your life,' said the knight, 'unless you freely release the queen for ever from your accusation and promise not to write on Sir Patrise's tomb that she ever consented to that treason."' That shall be done,' said Sir Mador, 'I discharge my quarrel for ever.'

Then some other knights lifted up Sir Mador and carried him from the field and the other knight went to where King Arthur sat; and the queen joined the king, and they wept and embraced one another. When the king saw the stranger knight, he prayed him to take off his helm, to rest and take a drink of wine. And he took off his helm to drink and everyone knew him for Sir Lancelot du Lake. Then the king took the queen by the hand and went to Sir Lancelot and said, 'Sir, I thank you for your great labours that you have done today for me and for my queen.'

'My lord,' said Sir Lancelot, 'you know I ought by rights to be ever in your quarrel, and in my lady the queen's quarrel, to do battle; for you are the man that gave me the high order of knighthood. That day my lady, your queen, did me great worship, or else I had been shamed; for that same day you made me knight, through my haste I lost my sword, and my lady your queen found it, and lapped it in her train, and gave me my sword when I had need of it, or else I had been shamed before all knights. Therefore I promised her at that day ever to be her knight in right or in wrong.'

'Gramercy *,' said the king, 'for this journey; and know that I shall acquit your goodness.'

Sir Thomas Malory, Morte Darthur.

Gramercy: a contraction of the French grand merci – much thanks.

THE FAIR MAID OF ASTOLAT

THE TRAGIC STORY of the girl who died of love for Sir Lancelot is a good example of how medieval writers told different versions of the same story. Malory's treatment is quite different from that of his sources, the Vulgate *La Mort le Roi Artu* and the Middle English stanzaic *Morte Arthur*.

In *Mort Artu*, the maid tricks Sir Lancelot into wearing her sleeve by asking him to make her a promise without revealing what it is; Lancelot is annoyed to discover that he has promised to wear her favour in the tournament, because he knows that Queen Guinevere will be furious when she finds out. Later, when the maid boldly declares her love, Lancelot answers with elaborate tact that a knight whose heart was not engaged elsewhere would have to be a witless fool not to accept her love with pleasure, but his heart was. She tries once more, informing him that she will die for love if he does not relent. The letter she carried on her funeral barge accuses Lancelot of being 'the most boorish man I know'. This version of the story is wholly favourable to Lancelot – the maid is wilful and stubborn and he could not have helped her.

In *Morte Arthur* the story is slightly different. Here Lancelot perceives on his first evening at her home that the maid has fallen in love with him and, when she rushes off to her chamber to weep, he follows her to comfort her. He explains that 'In another place in my heart is set/It is not at my own will,' and agrees to wear the sleeve to the tournament as a sort of consolation prize. Despite his sensitive treatment, the maid describes Lancelot in her farewell letter as

. . . none so doughty dints to deal
So royal, nor so fair thereto
But so churlish of manners in field
*   nor hall*
Know I of none, or friend or foe.

Malory changes the emphasis completely. His Lancelot is blind to Elaine's passion (Malory is the only one to give the maid a name); he agrees to wear the sleeve only because he thinks it will enable him to fool his brothers and cousins more effectively in the tournament; when Elaine declares her love and asks him to marry her, he not only refuses bluntly, but adds insult to injury by offering to settle a thousand pounds a year on whomever she does marry. Malory's Elaine is a real, flesh and blood woman, who makes a marvellous, passionate declaration of love on her deathbed to the priest ('Why should I leave such thoughts? Am I not an earthly woman?')' and her farewell letter only asks Lancelot to pray for her, becoming the acknowledgement of an equal rather than the complaint of a victim.

And ever the queen beheld Sir Lancelot and wept so tenderly that she sank almost to the ground for sorrow that he had done to her so great goodness where she showed him great unkindness.

Then the knights of his blood drew unto him, and there each of them made great joy of the other. And so came all the knights of the Round Table that were there and welcomed him. And then Sir Mador was had to leech craft and Sir Lancelot was healed of his wound, and there was made great joy and mirth in the court.

Then the queen sent for Sir Lancelot and begged his forgiveness, because she had been angry with him for no reason.

'This is not the first time,' said Sir Lancelot, 'that you have been displeased with me for no reason but, Madam, I must always bear with you, and take no account of my own sufferings.' But they made up their quarrel, and after that they loved one another even more passionately than before, so that they forgot to be discreet and many knights in the court knew and spoke openly of their love.

THE DEATH OF KING ARTHUR

In the month of May, it befell a great anger and misfortune that stinted not till the flower of chivalry of all the world was destroyed and slain; and all was caused by two unhappy knights, Sir Agravain and Sir Mordred, who were brethren of Sir Gawain. For this Sir Agravain and Sir Mordred had ever a private hatred unto the queen and to Sir Lancelot, and ever daily and nightly they kept watch upon them.

So it mishapped, Sir Gawain and all his brothers were in King Arthur's chamber. Then Sir Agravain said thus openly that many knights might hear it: 'I marvel we are not all ashamed both to see and to know how Sir Lancelot lies daily and nightly by the queen; and it is shameful that we all should suffer so noble a king as King Arthur to be so shamed.'

Then spake Sir Gawain and said, 'Brother Sir Agravain, I pray you and charge you move no such matters no more afore me, for wit you well, I will not be of your counsel.'

'So God me help,' said Sir Gareth and Sir Gaheris, 'we will not be knowing, brother Agravain, of your deeds.'

'Then I will,' said Sir Mordred.

'I can well believe it,' said Sir Gawain, 'for you are ever ready, brother, to promote all kinds of unhappiness; and I wish that you would leave all this and not make yourself so busy, for I know what will fall of it.'

'Fall of it what may,' said Sir Agravain, 'I will disclose it to the king.'

BELOW: *Sir Lancelot and Sir Mador de la Porte in combat.*

163

'Not by my counsel,' said Sir Gawain, 'for if there is war between Sir Lancelot and us, wit you well brother, many kings and great lords will hold with Sir Lancelot. Also, brother Sir Agravain, you must remember how oft-times Sir Lancelot has rescued the king and the queen; and the best of us all had been full cold at the heart root ✣ had not Sir Lancelot been better than we, as he hath proved himself full oft. As for my part, I will never be against Sir Lancelot for one day's deed, when he rescued me from King Carados of the Dolorous Tower, and slew him, and saved my life. Also, brother Sir Agravain and Sir Mordred, in likewise Sir Lancelot rescued you both, and threescore and two more, from Sir Turquin. Methinketh, brother, such kind deeds should be remembered.'

✣ i.e. dead.

'Do as you please,' said Sir Agravain, 'for I will conceal it no longer.'

With these words came to them King Arthur.

'Now, brother, stop your noise,' said Sir Gawain.

'We will not,' said Sir Agravain and Sir Mordred.

'Will you not?' said Sir Gawain, 'then God speed you, for I will not hear your tales or be of your counsel.'

'No more will I,' said Sir Gareth and Sir Gaheris, 'for we will never say evil of that man.' . . . and therewith they departed, making great dole . . .

And then King Arthur asked them what noise they made.

'My lord,' said Sir Agravain, 'I shall tell you what I can keep silent no longer . . . this we all know, that Sir Lancelot holds your queen, and has long done so; and we are all your sister's sons, and we can suffer it no longer . . . you are the king that made Sir Lancelot knight, and therefore we will prove it, that he is a traitor to your person.'

'If it be so,' said King Arthur, 'then indeed he is no other, but I would be loth to begin such a matter unless I could have proof of it . . . therefore if it is true what you tell me, I would he were taken in the deed.'

✣ Deeming: inkling, notion.

For as the French book says, the king was reluctant that any noise should be about Sir Lancelot and his queen; for the king had a deeming ✣, but he would not hear of it, because Sir Lancelot had done so much for him and the queen so many times, and the king loved him passing well.

'My lord,' said Sir Agravain, 'you shall ride tomorrow morning hunting, and doubt not that Sir Lancelot will not go with you. Then, when it draws toward night, send word to the queen that you will stay out all night, and send for your cooks, and upon pain of death we shall take him that night with the queen, and we shall bring him to you either dead or alive.'

'Very well,' said the king, 'but take knights you can rely on.'

In the morning, King Arthur went out hunting, and then sent word to the queen that he would not return that night. Accordingly, Sir Agravain and Sir Mordred collected together twelve knights of like mind, their kinsmen or those that wished them well, and these included Sir Gawain's two sons, Sir Florence and Sir Lovel. And they hid themselves in a chamber of the castle, near to the queen's chamber. In the evening, the queen sent for Sir Lancelot.

'Sir,' said Sir Bors when he heard this, 'do not go to the queen tonight.'

'Fair nephew, why not?' said Sir Lancelot.

'Sir,' said Sir Bors, 'I am afraid that Sir Agravain is lying in wait to catch you and the queen and put you to shame.'

'Do not be afraid,' said Sir Lancelot, 'I shall go and return again quickly; but since the queen has sent for me, I will not be a coward, but I will go and see her.'

'God speed you well,' said Sir Bors, 'and send you safely back again.'

So Lancelot departed and took his sword under his arm, and so in his mantle that noble knight put himself in great jeopardy; and so he passed on till he came to the queen's chamber and went inside. And then, as the French book says, the queen and Lancelot were together. And whether they were abed or at other manner of disport, I do not wish to mention here, for love at that time was not like love nowadays. But thus as they were together, there came Sir Agravain and Sir Mordred with twelve knights of the Round Table, and they said with a crying voice, 'Traitor knight, Sir Lancelot du Lake, now you are caught!'

And thus they cried with a loud voice, that all the court could hear it; and those fourteen knights were armed as they should fight in a battle.

'Alas,' said Queen Guinevere, 'now are we both mischieved.'

'Madam,' said Sir Lancelot, 'is there any armour within your chamber, that I may cover my body withal? If there is any give it me, and I shall soon stop their malice, by the grace of God.'

'Truly,' said the queen, 'I have no armour, shield, sword, nor spear; wherefore I dread me sore our long love is come to a mischievous end, for I hear by their noise there are many knights.'

'Alas,' said Sir Lancelot, 'in all my life thus was I never bestad, that I should be thus shamefully slain for lack of my armour.' . . .

Then he took the queen in his arms and kissed her, and said, 'Most noble Christian queen, I beseech you as you have been always my special good lady, and I at all times your poor knight unto my power, and as I never failed you in right or in wrong since the first day King Arthur made me knight, that you will pray for my soul if I am here slain. For I am well

ABOVE: *A couple ride out 'maying'.*

BELOW: *Sir Agravain and Sir Mordred try to persuade Sir Gawain and King Arthur about Lancelot and Guinevere's love affair.*

assured that Sir Bors, my nephew, and all the rest of my kin, with Sir Lavaine and Sir Urry, will not fail to rescue you from the fire, and therefore my own lady, comfort yourself, for whatever becomes of me, that you go with Sir Bors and Sir Urry, and they will do you all the pleasure they can, so that you shall live like a queen upon my lands.'

'Nay, Lancelot,' said the queen, 'be sure that I will never live after you, but if you are slain I shall take my death as meekly for Jesus Christ's sake as ever did any Christian queen.'

'Well, madam,' said Sir Lancelot, 'since it is so that the day is come when our love must depart, wit you well I shall sell my life as dear as I may; and a thousandfold am I heavier for you than for myself. I had rather than be lord of all Christendom that I had sure armour upon me, so that men might speak of my deeds before I am slain . . . Jesu, be thou my shield and my armour!'

Then Sir Lancelot wrapped his mantle round his arm, and called out, 'I shall open the door and see who comes in first.'

Then he unbarred the door and held it open a little way, so that just one man could come in. *A knight called Tanaguin came forward before the others, who hated Lancelot with a mortal hatred, and Lancelot, who had raised his sword on high, struck him with his whole strength, so violently that neither helm nor mail coif could protect him from being split open down to the shoulders. Lancelot wrenched the sword out and threw him to the ground, dead. *And then Sir Lancelot drew that dead knight within the chamber door; and he with the help of the queen and her ladies was quickly armed in his armour. And ever stood Sir Agravain and Sir Mordred crying, 'Traitor knight, come out of the queen's chamber!'

'Leave your noise, and go away,' said Sir Lancelot, 'and tomorrow before the king if you dare to accuse me of treason I shall make it good on you with my hands.'

'Fie on thee, traitor!' shouted Sir Agravain and Sir Mordred, 'we can slay you if we please, because King Arthur told us we could take you dead or alive.'

'Oh sweet Jesu,' said Sir Lancelot, 'is there no other grace from the king? Then defend yourselves.' *

So then Sir Lancelot set the chamber door wide open and mightily and knightly he strode in among them; and soon at the first blow he slew Sir Agravain, and eleven of his companions within a little while after he laid cold to the earth . . . and Sir Lancelot wounded Sir Mordred, and he fled with all his might. And then Sir Lancelot returned again unto the queen, and said, 'Madam, now all our true love is brought to an end, for now will King Arthur ever be my foe; and therefore Madam, if it please you that I may have you with me, I shall save you from all manner of dangerous adventures.'

'That is not best,' said the queen, 'I think you have now done so much harm, it will be best if you stop at this. And if you see tomorrow that they will put me to death, then may you rescue me as you think best.' *

*Anon, *Mort Artu.*

*Sir Thomas Malory, *Morte Darthur.*

*Sir Lancelot assumes that he can have due process of law and defend himself in a trial by combat; but they reply that they have the king's permission to cut him down without a trial as if he were an outlaw.

*Guinevere thinks that there is still a chance of reconciliation with the king.

'I will well,' said Sir Lancelot, 'for have no doubt, while I am living, I shall rescue you.' And then he kissed her, and each gave the other a ring; and there he left the queen and went to his lodging. There he met with Sir Bors, and Sir Ector and Sir Lionel and others of his kin, and he told them what had happened outside the queen's chamber. He asked them to go that same night and speak to all the other knights of the Round Table to find out who, if it came to open war, would hold with him and who would hold with the king. This they did; and at the end of the night they had the pledges of fourscore knights who for love of Sir Lancelot would never hold against him. Then Sir Lancelot planned how, if the king should judge the queen to be burnt, he could rescue her and take her away by main force, and keep her with him in his castle of Joyous Gard.

Meanwhile, Sir Mordred rode as hard as he could to King Arthur, and came before him all wounded and bleeding, and told him how all the fourteen knights were slain except himself. 'How did this happen?' asked King Arthur. 'Did you take him in the queen's chamber?'

'Yes, my lord,' said Sir Mordred, 'and we found him unarmed, but he slew Sir Tanaguin and armed himself in his armour, and then he came out among the rest of us and laid about him until all but me were slain.'

'He is a marvellous knight of prowess,' said King Arthur, 'and I sorely repent that ever he should be against me. Alas, the Fellowship of the Round Table will be broken for ever, for many of the knights will hold with him. But as things have fallen out thus, I can do no other for my worship but put the queen to death.'

In the morning, a great council was held and almost all the knights were in agreement that the queen was guilty of treason and must be given up to be burnt. But Sir Gawain said: 'My lord Arthur, it is not wise to be over-hasty in this judgement, but leave a little while to consider it. Even though Sir Lancelot was found in the queen's chamber, yet he may have gone there for quite innocent reasons. I dare say that the queen is true to you; and as for Sir Lancelot, he will make it good upon any knight who dares to say otherwise.'

'I am sure he will,' said King Arthur, 'but he shall not have that chance. For Sir Lancelot trusts to his great might and prowess so much that he fears no man and will make good any cause in combat, be it right or wrong. He shall not fight for the queen again, for she shall have the law. And if I could lay hands on Sir Lancelot, he should have it too.'

'God defend I should ever see that,' said Sir Gawain.

'Why do you say so?' said King Arthur. 'You have no cause to love Sir Lancelot, since last night he slew your brother Sir Agravain and your two sons Sir Florence and Sir Lovel.'

'My lord,' said Sir Gawain, 'I know all this, and I am sorry for their deaths; but I warned them what would happen, and they would

ABOVE: *Lancelot and Guinevere in bed together. From the French* Mort Artu.

not heed my counsel. Therefore I will not avenge them, for their deaths are upon their own heads.'

Then said the noble King Arthur to Sir Gawain, 'Dear nephew, I pray you make ready in your best armour, with your brethren, Sir Gaheris and Sir Gareth, to bring my queen to the fire, there to have her judgement and receive her death.'

'Nay, my most noble lord,' said Sir Gawain, 'that will I never do; for wit you well I will never be in that place where so noble a queen as is my lady, Dame Guinevere, shall take a shameful end . . . My heart will never serve to see her die; and it shall never be said that ever I was of your counsel of her death.'

Then said the king to Sir Gawain, 'Suffer your brothers Sir Gaheris and Sir Gareth to be there.'

'My lord,' said Sir Gawain, 'wit you well they will be loth to be there present . . . but they are young and full unable to say you nay.'

168

Then spake Sir Gaheris and the good knight Sir Gareth unto King Arthur: 'Sir, you may well command us to be there, but it shall be sore against our will; and unless we are there by your straight commandment, you must hold us excused. We will be there in peaceable wise and bear no harness of war upon us.'

'In the name of God,' said the king, 'then make you ready, for she shall soon have her judgement.'

'Alas,' said Sir Gawain, 'that ever I should endure to see this woeful day.' So Sir Gawain turned him and wept heartily, and went into his chamber.

And then the queen was led forth, and there she was stripped to her smock. And then her ghostly father was brought to her, to be shriven of her misdeeds. Then was there weeping, and wailing, and wringing of hands, of many lords and ladies.

Then was there one that Sir Lancelot had sent there to espy what time the queen should go unto her death; and as soon as he saw the queen despoiled into her smock and shriven, he gave Sir Lancelot warning. Then was there spurring and plucking up of horses, and at once they rode to the fire. And there might none withstand Sir Lancelot, so all that bore arms and stood against him were slain, full many a noble knight . . . And so in this rashing and hurling, and Sir Lancelot thrust here and there, it mishapped him to slay Gaheris and Gareth, the noble knights, for they were unarmed and unware.

Then when Sir Lancelot had thus done and slain and put to flight all that would withstand him, he rode straight unto Dame Guinevere, and made a kirtle and a gown to be cast upon her; and then he made her to be set behind him and prayed her to be of good cheer. Wit you well the queen was glad that she was escaped from the fire and she thanked God and Sir Lancelot; and so he rode with the queen unto Joyous Gard, and there he kept her as a noble knight should do; and many great lords and some kings sent Sir Lancelot many good knights, and many noble knights drew unto Sir Lancelot.

So turn we again unto King Arthur, that when it was told him how and in what manner the queen was taken away from the fire, and when he heard of the death of his noble knights, and in especial of Sir Gaheris's and Sir Gareth's death, then the king swooned for pure sorrow.

And when he was awoke of his swoon, he said: 'Alas, that ever I bore the crown

BELOW: *Sir Mordred tells King Arthur that Lancelot has escaped from the ambush set for him outside the queen's chamber.*

upon my head! For now I have lost the fairest fellowship of noble knights that ever held with a Christian king . . . within two days I have lost forty knights, and also the noble fellowship of Sir Lancelot and his kin, for now I will never be able to hold them with me again. Alas that ever this war began!' And he added: 'Now I charge you, fair fellows, that no man tell Sir Gawain of the death of his two brothers, for I am sure that when Sir Gawain hears that Sir Gareth is dead he will go nigh out of his mind. Mercy Jesu,' said the king, 'why slew he Sir Gareth and Sir Gaheris? For I dare say that Sir Gareth loved Sir Lancelot above all earthly men.'

'That is true,' said some knights, 'but they were slain in the confusion as Sir Lancelot thrust in the thick of the crowd; and because they were not wearing armour he smote them and knew not whom he smote, and so unhappily they were slain.'

'Their deaths,' said King Arthur, 'will cause the greatest mortal war that ever was; I am sure that if Sir Gawain knew that Sir Gareth is slain, he would give me no rest till I destroy Sir Lancelot's kin and himself, or he me. And therefore,' said the king, 'know you well that my heart was never so heavy as it is now, and much more am I sorrier for the loss of my good knights than for the loss of my fair queen; for queens I might have enough, but such a fellowship of good knights shall never be gathered together again in any place . . .' And ever among these complaints the king wept and swooned.

Then came there one unto Sir Gawain, and told him how the queen was led away with Sir Lancelot, and twenty-four knights slain.

'O Jesu defend my brothers,' said Sir Gawain, 'for full well I knew that Sir Lancelot would rescue her, or else he would die in that field; and to say truth he would not have been a man of worship if he had not rescued the queen that day, inasmuch as she would have been burned for his sake. And in that he hath done but knightly and as I would have done myself, if I had stood in like case. But where are my brothers?' said Sir Gawain, 'I marvel that I hear not of them.'

'Truly,' said that man, 'Sir Gareth and Sir Gaheris are slain.'

'Jesu defend!' said Sir Gawain. 'For all the world I would not that they were slain, and in especial my good brother Sir Gareth.'

'Sir,' said the man, 'he is slain, and that is great pity.'

'Who slew him?' said Sir Gawain.

'Sir,' said the man, 'Sir Lancelot slew them both.'

Gawain leapt like a madman to the chamber where they lay dead; the chamber floor ran with blood, but cloths of gold were drawn over them. Then he lifted the cloths up high—what wonder though his heart was sore to see his brothers so pitifully slain that had been such strong knights before. When he saw his brothers thus, he was not able to speak a word; the strength drained away from his limbs, and he fell across the bodies in a swoon. When he had recovered from his swoon, the bold Sir Gawain then swore by God, and spoke out loud like a great and powerful knight:

This singularly uncourtly speech was added by Malory and really sums up his feelings about the whole tragedy. Malory is not really interested in love; it is the ruination of the fellowship which moves him.

Anon, *Morte Arthur.* This scene of Sir Gawain discovering the dead bodies of his brothers was not used by Malory, but is nevertheless one of the most powerful in Middle English romance and helps to explain the change in Gawain.

170

'Between me and Sir Lancelot du Lake
No man on earth, the truth to say,
Shall truce set or peace make,
Ere either of us the other slay.'

Then Sir Gawain went to King Arthur and they mourned together. And when they had wept and swooned, Sir Gawain said to the king: *'My king, my lord and my uncle, wit you well that I shall now make you a promise that I shall hold by my knighthood, that from this day I shall never fail Sir Lancelot until one of us has slain the other. And therefore I require you, my lord and king, to prepare for war, for I will be revenged...'*

Sir Thomas Malory, *Morte Darthur.*

'I hear that Sir Lancelot awaits us both in Joyous Gard and many people draw to him,' replied the king.

'I can well believe it,' said Sir Gawain, 'but, my lord, try your friends, and I will try mine.'

So King Arthur summoned all his earls, barons and knights and their soldiers throughout his kingdom, to assemble equipped for war, and many came until he had a great host. And Sir Lancelot likewise gathered to him all those that would support him. But King Arthur's army was so great that Sir Lancelot could not meet him in battle, but withdrew into his castle of Joyous Gard. And King Arthur and his army laid siege to Joyous Gard for fifteen weeks, during which time Sir Lancelot would not permit his men to ride out against the king.

Then one day in harvest time Sir Lancelot appeared on the castle walls and spoke with King Arthur, and many harsh words passed between them, but ever Sir Lancelot refused to meet the king in battle, for he would not lift his sword against the man who had made him knight. And Sir Lancelot defended the queen against all charges of treason, and reminded King Arthur of the time when he had been right glad to have Sir Lancelot as his knight.

Then spoke Sir Gawain: *'Fie on thy proud words! As for my lady the queen, I will never say of her shame. But you, false and recreant knight,'* said Sir Gawain, *'what cause had you to slay my good brother Sir Gareth, that loved you more than all his own kin? Alas, you made him knight with your own hands; why slew you him that loved you so well?'...*

'By the faith that I owe to the high order of knighthood,' said Sir Lancelot, *'I would as soon have slain my own nephew, Sir Bors. Alas that I was so unhappy; for I did not see Sir Gareth and Sir Gaheris.'*

'You lie, recreant knight,' said Sir Gawain, *'you slew him in despite of me, wherefore take care, for I shall revenge his death.'*

At this time, King Arthur would have been reconciled with Sir Lancelot and would have taken back Queen Guinevere and forgiven all charges against her; but Sir Gawain would not allow him to do so, and ever he worked to make King Arthur and all his knights angry against Sir Lancelot and his knights. At length Sir Lancelot was persuaded to come out of the castle and fight. And Sir Gawain instructed many knights to lie in wait for Sir Lancelot to slay him; but Sir Lancelot charged all his knights that by any means they could they were to save King Arthur and Sir Gawain.

So battle was joined, with much slaughter on both sides; and ever King Arthur tried to get near Sir Lancelot to slay him, and Sir Lancelot suffered him, but would not strike against him. And in the battle, *Sir Bors encountered with King Arthur, and there with a spear Sir Bors smote him down; and so he alit and drew his sword, and said to Sir Lancelot, 'Shall I make an end of this war?' and by that he meant to have slain King Arthur.*

'Do not touch him,' said Sir Lancelot, 'on pain of your head, for I will never see that noble king that made me knight either slain or shamed.'

And there Sir Lancelot alit from his horse and took up the king and horsed him again, and said: 'My lord Arthur, for God's love stop this strife, for it does you no worship.'

Then when King Arthur was on horseback, he looked at Sir Lancelot, and the tears burst out of his eyes, thinking on the great courtesy that was in Sir Lancelot more than any other man; and the king rode away, and could not look at him, and said, 'Alas, that ever this war began.'

But the battle continued on the next day, and out came Sir Gawain, as fierce as a wild boar, and encountered with Sir Bors, and each gave the other terrible wounds. Fighting was fierce, but neither side could gain the upper hand, so at the day's end the armies parted to tend their wounded and bury their dead.

Then the Pope himself came to hear of the great strife that tore the land apart and he sent a papal bull to King Arthur, instructing him and commanding him to be reconciled with Sir Lancelot, and to take Queen Guinevere back again in all honour as his queen. And King Arthur was very ready to do so. And Sir Lancelot delivered up the queen to King Arthur before all the court and was reconciled with him, saying openly before everyone that there had been no evil or treason done between him and the queen, and that he would make it good on the body of any man who dared deny him.

But Sir Gawain would not be reconciled with Sir Lancelot, but ever gave him cursed and warlike words, and promised to have his revenge for the deaths of his innocent brothers, despite the peace made between Sir Lancelot and the king. So, because of Sir Gawain's enmity, Sir Lancelot was forced to return into his own country, though the

Lancelot's chivalrous forbearance is constantly at odds with Gawain's ferocity and his unknightly determination to be revenged at all costs.

BELOW: *Sir Gawain and his followers advise King Arthur to attack Sir Lancelot.*

172

king would have been glad to have him in the Fellowship of the Round Table again. But soon after Queen Guinevere was reconciled with King Arthur, Sir Gawain persuaded the king to make war upon Sir Lancelot once again.

So another great host was gathered and King Arthur made Sir Mordred his regent to rule over England in his absence, placing Queen Guinevere under his protection. King Arthur did this because Sir Mordred was his own son, though illegitimate. Then King Arthur and Sir Gawain and the host went over the sea and laid siege to the city of Benwick. For months they lay encamped before the castle, for Sir Lancelot still refused to fight against his king or against Sir Gawain. At last, *Sir Gawain came forth well armed upon a strong steed, and he came before the chief gate, with his spear in his hand, crying, 'Sir Lancelot, where are you? Is there none of you proud knights dare break a spear with me?'*

ABOVE: *King Arthur and his army lay siege to Lancelot's castle, Joyous Gard.*

Then Sir Bors made him ready and came out of the town, and there Sir Gawain encountered with Sir Bors and smote him down from his horse and had almost slain him, but Sir Bors was rescued and borne back into the town.

Then came forth Sir Lionel, brother to Sir Bors, thinking to revenge him; and each of them fewtered ✾ *their spears and ran together, and there they met spitefully, but Sir Gawain had such grace that he smote Sir Lionel down and wounded him passing sore; and then Sir Lionel was rescued and borne into the town.*

✾ Fewter: to place the spear in rest before charging.

And this Sir Gawain did every day, and he failed not but he smote down some knight or other . . . then it befell upon a day, Sir Gawain came before the gate all armed on a noble horse, with a great spear in his hand, and he cried with a loud voice, 'Where are you, you false traitor, Sir Lancelot? Why do you hide yourself in holes and walls like a coward? Look out now, false traitor knight, and here I shall revenge the deaths of my brothers.'

All this language heard Sir Lancelot, and his kin and his knights drew about him, and they all said to him, 'Sir Lancelot, now you must defend yourself like a knight, or be shamed for ever; for now you are openly accused of treason, it is time for you to stir, for you have slept overlong and suffered overmuch.'

'So God me help,' said Sir Lancelot, '. . . I know it as well as you. I must defend myself or be a recreant.'

And Sir Lancelot armed him and made him ready, and said to

RIGHT: *Hand-to-hand combat during a battle.*

King Arthur from the gate tower, 'My most noble lord and king, I much regret that I must bear arms against one of your blood, but now I must defend myself, for Sir Gawain has accused me of treason, so I am driven to fight like a beast at bay.'

And Sir Gawain shouted up to him, 'Leave off this babbling, Sir Lancelot, and come out and fight me—if you dare.'

Then Sir Lancelot and his supporters came out of the gates, and Sir Gawain and Sir Lancelot made ready to do battle in a combat to the death. And they ran together with all their strength, and each struck the other in the shield, so that their horses could not endure the shock and fell to the ground with broken backs. Then they drew their swords and each gave the other many sad strokes so that the blood burst out on all sides.

Now Sir Gawain had a special grace and gift, that from nine in the morning until noon his strength increased threefold, and so he always fought in the morning to have the advantage of this triple strength. Then as they fought Sir Lancelot felt Sir Gawain's strength increase, and was afraid that he would have the worst of it and be shamed, but he defended himself grimly under his shield and took all the blows that Sir Gawain could give, for three long hours. And at noon, Sir Gawain's strength returned to normal; and Sir Lancelot redoubled his strokes. At length he gave Sir Gawain a great blow on the helm, that sank through into the skull beneath, and Sir Gawain fell to the ground; but Sir Lancelot withdrew from him.

'Why do you withdraw from me?' said Sir Gawain, 'turn again, false traitor knight, and slay me, for if you leave me thus, when I am whole I shall do battle with you again.'

'I shall endure you, Sir, by God's grace, but you know well, Sir Gawain, that I will never strike a fallen knight.' And he withdrew into the town.

Then Sir Gawain was carried to his tent and doctors were sent for to heal his wounds. The wound in his head was deep and dangerous, and he lay sick in his bed for three weeks. But as soon as he could ride his horse, he armed and challenged Sir Lancelot to come out and finish the battle they had begun. And Sir Lancelot came out to him and, as before, had the worst until noon, while Sir Gawain's strength increased threefold and it was as much as Sir Lancelot could do to stand up under the rain of his blows; but at noon Sir Lancelot lay on his strokes thick and fast, until at length Sir Lancelot struck Sir Gawain on the old wound in his head and it broke open again, and Sir Gawain sank bleeding to the ground. And Sir Lancelot turned back into the town, and Sir Gawain was carried away to the camp. This time he lay sick for a month; but when he was ready to fight again, there came tidings from England that put every thought of it out of his head.

For Sir Mordred had usurped his father's throne. He had pretended that King Arthur and Sir Gawain had been slain in battle against Sir Lancelot, and had called a parliament, and had made the lords and barons of England choose him as their king. Then he withdrew to Camelot and announced that he would marry Queen Guinevere, his uncle's and his father's wife. Queen Guinevere was heavy to hear this, but she pretended to agree, and she asked leave to go to London to buy all manner of things for the wedding. As soon as she got to London she took men and provisions and shut herself into the Tower of London and held it against Sir Mordred. Sir Mordred wrote letters to her praying her in fair language to be reconciled with him, but she answered that she would rather slay herself than be his wife.

Then Sir Mordred heard tell that King Arthur had raised the siege of Benwick and was coming back to England with his army in order to be avenged on him. And Sir Mordred gathered to him a great army, for many of the people were tired of Arthur's wars against Sir Lancelot, and wanted a new king. So Sir Mordred and his army marched to Dover, to meet the army of King Arthur even as it tried to land.

Then there was launching of great boats and small, full of noble men of arms; and there was much slaughter of gentle knights, and many a bold baron was laid full low, on both parties. But King Arthur was so courageous that no number of knights could prevent him from landing, and his knights

BELOW: *Arthur's army besieging the city of Benwick.*

ABOVE: *Sir Gawain and Sir Lancelot in mortal combat, surrounded by their supporters.*

fiercely followed him; and so they landed in spite of Sir Mordred and all his power, and they put him and his people to flight.

When this battle was done, King Arthur had buried all his people that were killed. And then was noble Sir Gawain found in a great boat, lying more than half dead. And there the king made sorrow out of all measure, and took Sir Gawain into his arms and swooned. And when he awakened, he said, 'Alas, Sir Gawain, my sister's son, here now you lie, the man in the world that I loved most; for, Sir Gawain, I will discover my thoughts to you: in Sir Lancelot and you I most had my joy, and now I have lost you both, wherefore all my earthly joy is gone from me.'

'My uncle, King Arthur,' said Gawain, 'I know well my death day has come, and all is through my own hastiness and wilfulness, for I am smitten upon the old wound which Sir Lancelot gave me, and I feel well that I must die; and had Sir Lancelot been with you as he was, this unhappy war had never begun; and of all this I am the cause, for Sir Lancelot and his blood, through their prowess, held all your cankered enemies in subjection

and danger. And now,' said Sir Gawain, 'you will miss Sir Lancelot. But alas, I would not accord with him, and therefore I pray you, fair uncle, that I may have paper, pen and ink, that I may write to Sir Lancelot a letter with my own hand.'

And then when paper and ink were brought, Sir Gawain was sat up weakly by King Arthur, for he was shriven a little before, and then he wrote thus, as the French book makes mention:

> Unto Sir Lancelot, flower of all noble knights that ever I heard of or saw by my days, I, Sir Gawain, King Lot's son of Orkney, sister's son unto the noble King Arthur, send you greeting, and let you know that the tenth day of May I was smitten upon the old wound that you gave me before the city of Benwick, and through the same wound that you gave me I am come to my death day. And I will that all the world knows that I, Sir Gawain, knight of the Round Table, sought my death, and not through your deserving, but it was my own seeking; wherefore I beseech you, Sir Lancelot, to return again unto this realm, and see my tomb, and pray some prayer for my soul . . . Also, Sir Lancelot, for all the love that ever was betwixt us, make no tarrying, but come over the sea in all haste, that you may with your noble knights rescue that noble king who made you knight, that is my lord King Arthur, for he is full sorely bestad with a foul traitor, that is my half-brother Sir Mordred . . . And at the date of this letter was written, with my own hand, and subscribed with part of my heart's blood.

And then Sir Gawain wept, and King Arthur wept . . . and so at the hour of noon Sir Gawain yielded up the spirit. The King had him interred in a chapel within Dover Castle; and there yet all men may see the skull of him, and the same wound is seen that Sir Lancelot gave him in battle.

Then it was told the king that Sir Mordred had pitched a new field upon Barham Down. And upon the morn the king rode thither to him, and there was a great battle between them, and many people slain on both parties; but, at the last, King Arthur's party stood best, and Sir Mordred and his party fled to Canterbury. Then many people joined King Arthur's cause, for they said that Sir Mordred was wrong to make war upon the king. And King Arthur drew westward with his host, and a day was assigned between King Arthur and Sir Mordred, that they should meet beside Salisbury, the Monday after Trinity Sunday. ❧

Upon Trinity Sunday at night, King Arthur dreamed a wonderful dream, and

❧ Trinity Sunday is the Sunday after Whit Sunday and before the feast of Corpus Christi. It usually falls towards the end of May or the beginning of June, depending on the date of Easter.

BELOW: *Sir Mordred usurps his father's throne.*

that was this: that it seemed he sat upon a platform in a chair, and the chair was fast to a wheel, and thereon sat King Arthur in the richest cloth of gold that might be made; and the king thought there was under him, far from him, an hideous deep black water, and therein were all manner of serpents, and worms, and wild beasts, foul and horrible. Suddenly the king thought the wheel turned up-side-down, and he fell among the serpents, and every beast took him by a limb; and the king cried as he lay in his bed and slept, 'Help!'

Knights awakened the king, and then he was so amazed that he knew not where he was, and he fell on slumbering again, not sleeping nor thoroughly waking. So the king thought that there came Sir Gawain unto him. . . 'Sir,' said Sir Gawain, '. . . thus much hath God given me leave, for to warn you of your death; for if you fight tomorrow morning with Sir Mordred, as you have both assigned, doubt not you must be slain, and the most part of your people on both parties. For the great grace and goodness that Almighty Jesus has unto you, and for pity of you and many other good men that there shall be slain, God has sent me to give you warning that you do not do battle tomorrow, but make a treaty for a month from that day; for within a month shall come Sir Lancelot and all his noble knights and rescue you worshipfully and slay Sir Mordred and all that hold with him.'

Then Sir Gawain vanished away, and King Arthur woke up, summoned his knights and lords and bishops, and told them of this vision; he instructed Sir Lucan the Butler and Sir Bedivere to make a treaty with Sir Mordred, to delay the battle for one month, and to offer him whatever he would ask for to make that good.

So they went unto Sir Mordred where he lay with his great host, and they treated with him a long time; at length he agreed to delay battle for one month, in exchange for Cornwall and Kent now, and the promise of the whole realm after Arthur's death. To make final agreement, they arranged for King Arthur and Sir Mordred to meet together in between their two armies, each with a following of fourteen knights. Then privately King Arthur warned his host that if they should see any man draw his sword during that meeting to attack at once, for it would mean treachery. And Sir Mordred warned his army likewise, 'for I do not trust this treaty, since I know well my father wishes to be avenged on me'.

So they met together between the two armies and agreed on the terms that had been negotiated, and then they drank a little wine. But then an adder crept out of a little heath bush and stung a knight on the foot. And when he felt himself stung, he looked down and saw the adder and, without thinking, he drew his sword to kill it. But when the hosts of both sides saw the sun glint on the blade of the sword, each side thought the other had committed treachery, and they blew their trumpets and rushed together with a great roar.

And King Arthur took his horse, and said, 'Alas, this unhappy day!' And so rode to his party. And Sir Mordred in like wise. And never was

MORT ARTU, MORTE ARTHUR, MORTE DARTHUR

LA MORT LE ROI ARTU, the final part of the Vulgate Cycle, is one of the finest French medieval romances. Written in prose in about 1230-35, its anonymous author was very familiar with the preceding parts of the cycle, *Merlin, Lancelot* and *La Queste del Saint Graal*, but did not write them himself. The tale shows the downfall of the high chivalrous ideal of the Round Table in a beautifully structured, precisely delineated sequence which appears truly inevitable.

The Middle English *Morte Arthur*, a fourteenth-century verse romance in rhyming stanzas, is a vigorous adaptation of the French tale. It incorporates some superb touches, notably the scenes in which Gawain discovers the dead bodies of his brothers Gareth and Gaheris slain by Lancelot, the beginning of the battle of Camlann when a knight draws his sword to strike at an adder in the grass, and the final interview between Lancelot and Guinevere after she has taken the veil.

Malory drew heavily on both these sources. He disliked the French narrative technique of *entrelacement*, and disentangled the interlaced narratives of the Maid of Astolat and Sir Mador de la Porte; however he put the treason story first, so spoiling the·sequence. In this version, the original order of the episodes has been restored, but Malory is used for quoted passages, because this is quite simply his masterpiece, a heart-breaking tragedy recounted with real grief, all the stronger for its restricted vocabulary and the simple dignity of the style. Worlds away from the polished brilliance of the French *Mort Artu*, this style owes much to the ballad-like simplicity and economy of the *Morte Arthur*, but most to Malory's intense involvement in the tragedy. A man who had lived through the power politics and personal betrayals of the Wars of the Roses, he was moved most by the conflict of loyalties which underlies the actions of the central characters, Lancelot, Guinevere, Arthur and Gawain.

there seen a more doleful battle in any Christian land; for there was but rushing and riding, foining and striking, and many a grim word was there spoken, and many a deadly stroke . . . And thus they fought all the long day, and never stopped till it was near night, and by that time there was an hundred thousand laid dead upon the down. Then was Arthur wood wrath out of measure, when he saw his people so slain from him. Then the king looked about him, and then was he ware, of all his host and of all his good knights, were left no more alive but two knights; one was Sir Lucan the Butler, and his brother Sir Bedivere, and they were full sore wounded.

'Jesu mercy,' said the king, 'where are all my noble knights? Alas that ever I should see this doleful day, for now I am come to my end. But would to God that I knew where is that traitor Sir Mordred, that has caused all this mischief.'

Then was King Arthur ware where Sir Mordred leaned upon his sword among a great heap of dead men. 'Now give me my spear,' said King Arthur to Sir Lucan, 'for yonder I have espied the traitor that all this woe has wrought . . . tide me death, betide me life, now I see him yonder alone he shall never escape my hands, for at a better avail shall I never have him.'

SIR MORDRED

Sᴉʀ Mᴏʀᴅʀᴇᴅ, the villain of later Arthurian romance, first appears in the *Annales Cambriae*, where the entry for year 93 (probably ᴀᴅ 537) reads: '*The strife of Camlann, in which Arthur and Medraut perished, and there was plague in Britain and Ireland.*' This does not say whether Arthur and Medraut (Mordred) were fighting each other or some common enemy, nor does it imply that Mordred was bad or to blame. Gildas and Nennius do not mention him, but he features in surviving Welsh stories.

Geoffrey of Monmouth makes Mordred Arthur's nephew and tells the tale which became the basis of all later romances: that Mordred was left as regent of Britain while Arthur was fighting abroad, that he abducted and tried to marry his uncle's wife Guinevere, that he usurped Arthur's kingdom, and that he and Arthur destroyed one another in the final bloody battle of Camlann.

Mordred was not always the utter villain he became in the French romance tradition. In one of the tales of *The Mabinogion*, the thirteenth-century 'Dream of Rhonabwy', Rohonabwy's guide to his dream vision, Iddawg Embroiler of Britain, explains that he got his nickname for provoking the Battle of Camlann by changing Arthur's messages of peace into insults so that Mordred had no choice but to attack. Here Mordred is said to be Arthur's foster-son as well as his nephew. This may reflect the story which appeared in *Mort Artu* and later in Malory, that he was Arthur's illegitimate son by an incestuous liaison with his half-sister Morgause.

In the fourteenth-century alliterative *Morte Arthur*, Mordred is a noble character who plays an unwilling part in an inescapable tragedy. He accepts the regency with reluctance and utters a moving lament over the dead body of his brother, Sir Gawain, full of remorse for the destruction he has caused.

From the very earliest reference, Mordred's death at the battle of Camlann is standard. Later romances claimed that Mordred and Arthur killed one another; this culminates in Malory's horrid description of Mordred painfully heaving his impaled body up the shaft of Arthur's lance in order to strike him a mortal blow before falling dead to the ground.

'God speed you well,' said Sir Bedivere.

Then the king got his spear in both his hands and ran towards Sir Mordred, crying, 'Traitor, now is thy death day come!'

And when Sir Mordred heard King Arthur, he ran towards him with his sword drawn in his hand. And there King Arthur smote Sir Mordred under the shield, with a thrust of his spear more than a fathom through the body. And when Sir Mordred felt that he had his death wound, he thrust himself with the might that he had up to the bur of King Arthur's spear. And right so he smote his father Arthur, with his sword held in both his hands, on the side of the head, that the sword pierced the helmet and the brain pan. Therewith Sir Mordred fell stark dead to the earth; and the noble Arthur fell in a swoon to the earth and there he swooned many times . . . .

Then Sir Lucan took up the king on the one side and Sir Bedivere on the other, and in the lifting the king swooned; and Sir Lucan fell in a swoon with the lift, that part of his guts fell out of his body, and therewith the noble knight's heart burst. When the king awoke, he beheld Sir Lucan, how he lay foaming at the mouth, and part of his guts lay at his feet.

'Alas,' said the king, 'this is to me a full heavy sight, to see this noble duke so die for my sake, for he would have helped me, that had more need of help than I. Alas, he would not complain him, his heart was so set to help me; and now Jesu have mercy upon his soul!'

Then Sir Bedivere wept for the death of his brother. . . .

'My time hieth fast,' said the king. 'Therefore, take thou Excalibur, my good sword, and go with it to yonder water side and, when you come there, I charge you throw my sword into that water, and come again and tell me what you see there.'

'My lord,' said Bedivere, 'your commandment shall be done.'

So Sir Bedivere departed, and by the way he beheld that noble sword, that the pommel and the haft was all of precious stones; and then he said to himself, 'If I throw this rich sword in the water, thereof shall never come good, but harm and loss.' And then Sir Bedivere hid Excalibur under a tree.

And so, as soon as he might, he came again unto the king, and said he had been at the water, and had thrown the sword into the water.

'What saw you there?' said the king.

'Sir,' he said, 'I saw nothing but waves and winds.'

'That is untruly said,' said the king, 'therefore go thou lightly again, and do my commandment; as thou art to me lief and dear, spare not, but throw it in.'

ABOVE: *King Arthur's dream of the Wheel of Fortune.*

181

ABOVE: *'How by misadventure of an adder the battle began, whereby Mordred was slain, and King Arthur wounded to death.'*

Then Sir Bedivere returned again and took the sword in his hand; and then he thought sin and shame to throw away that noble sword, and so again he hid the sword and returned, and told the king that he had been at the water and done his commandment.

'What saw you there?' said the king.

'Sir,' he said, 'I saw nothing but the waters lap and the waves darken.'

'Ah, traitor untrue!' said King Arthur. 'Now hast thou betrayed me twice. Who would have thought that thou, that hast been to me so lief and dear, and thou art named a noble knight, would betray me for the riches of the sword? But now go again lightly, for thy long tarrying puts me in great jeopardy of my life, for I have taken cold. And unless thou do now as I bid thee, if ever I may see thee, I shall slay thee with my own hands; for thou wouldst for my rich sword see me dead.'

Then Sir Bedivere departed, and went to the sword, and lightly took it up, and went to the water side; and there he bound the girdle about the hilt and threw the sword so far into the water as he might; and there came an arm and a hand above the water and met it, and caught it, and so shook it thrice and brandished, and then vanished away the sword with the hand into the water. So Sir Bedivere came again to the king, and told him what he saw.

'Alas,' said the king, 'help me hence, for I have tarried overlong.'

Then Sir Bedivere took the king upon his back, and so went with him to that water side. And when they were at the water side, even fast by the bank hoved a little barge with many fair ladies in it, and among them all was a queen, and all had black hoods, and all they wept and shrieked when they saw King Arthur.

'Now put me into the barge,' said the king.

And so he did softly; and there received him three queens with great mourning; and so they set him down, and in one of their laps King Arthur laid his head. And then that queen said, 'Ah, dear brother, why have you tarried so long from me? Alas, this wound on your head has caught over-much cold.'

And so they rowed from the land, and Sir Bedivere beheld all those ladies go from him. Then Sir Bedivere cried out, 'Ah my lord Arthur, what shall become of me, now you go from me and leave me here alone among my enemies?'

'Comfort thyself,' said the king, 'and do as well as thou mayest, for in me is no trust for to trust in; for I will into the vale of Avalon to heal me of my grievous wound. And if thou never hear of me more, pray for my soul.'

But ever the queens and ladies wept and shrieked, that it was pity to hear. And as soon as Sir Bedivere had lost sight of the barge, he wept and wailed, and took to the forest; and so he went all that night, and in the morning he was ware between two grey woods of a chapel and a hermitage.

182

CAMLANN

CAMLANN, the name of Arthur's final battle, is one of the very earliest Arthurian references to survive, in the *Annales Cambriae*. It is often referred to in Welsh literature, from the *Triads*, where it is spoken of as one of the 'three futile battles', to 'Culhwch and Olwen', where in the list of Arthur's men we find the three who were the only men to escape alive from Camlann. The evidence shows a powerful tradition of this battle as a horrifyingly destructive conflict in which almost all the combatants died, including Mordred, and in which Arthur received a fatal wound. This tradition is so strong that it has led scholars to try to identify the site.

There are several plausible alternatives. 'Camlann' is probably a contraction of the British word *Camboglanna*, meaning a crooked river bank. Some sources refer to the battle taking place on the bank of a river. A real Camlan exists in Wales − in a valley containing a small river. Geoffrey of Monmouth, however, said that the battle took place on the banks of the river Camel in Cornwall; and a battle did take place there, giving rise to plentiful local legends, but it happened in AD 823 between the Cornish and the Saxons, too late to be Arthur and Mordred. The *Triads* too, asserted that the site was in Cornwall and Mordred or Modred is the Cornish form of the name (Medraut in Welsh). Alternatively, in Somerset there is the River Cam, not far from the refortified Iron-Age hill fort of Cadbury, which some people have tried to identify as Camelot. Or there was a fort on Hadrian's Wall called Camboglanna, possibly modern Birdoswald.

So Sir Bedivere went to this chapel, and there he saw a hermit kneeling beside a new-made tomb. And this hermit had once been the Bishop of Canterbury, whom Sir Mordred had deprived of his office for supporting King Arthur.

'Sir,' said Sir Bedivere, 'who is buried here?'

'Fair son,' said the hermit, 'truly I know not, but by guessing. Last night at midnight there came a number of ladies and brought hither a dead man, and prayed me to bury him, with offerings of a hundred candles and a hundred gold bezants ❧.'

❧ Bezant: a valuable gold coin, originally minted in Byzantium.

'Alas,' said Sir Bedivere, 'that was my lord King Arthur.'

Then Sir Bedivere swooned, and when he awoke he asked the hermit if he might stay with him and join in his holy life, never to go forth, but spend his days praying for the soul of his lord King Arthur. And the hermit welcomed him gladly, for he knew him of old.

Thus of Arthur I find no more written in books that are authorized, nor more of the very certainty of his death I never heard tell, but thus he was led away in a ship wherein were three queens; that one was King Arthur's sister, Queen Morgan le Fay; another was the Queen of Northgales; the third was the Queen of the Waste Lands. More of the death of King Arthur could I never find, but those ladies brought him to his burials; and such a one was buried there, the hermit bore witness . . . but yet the

183

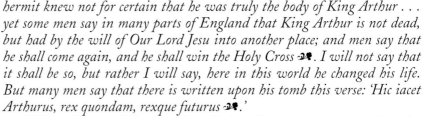

hermit knew not for certain that he was truly the body of King Arthur . . . yet some men say in many parts of England that King Arthur is not dead, but had by the will of Our Lord Jesu into another place; and men say that he shall come again, and he shall win the Holy Cross ✥. *I will not say that it shall be so, but rather I will say, here in this world he changed his life. But many men say that there is written upon his tomb this verse: 'Hic iacet Arthurus, rex quondam, rexque futurus* ✥*.'*

When Queen Guinevere heard that King Arthur was slain, she took five of her ladies and came quietly to the convent of Amesbury, and there she took the veil.

Meanwhile, when Sir Lancelot heard how Sir Mordred had usurped the throne and when he received the letter that Sir Gawain had written to him, he was almost out of his mind for grief and anger. And he gathered his host together and crossed the sea in ships and landed at Dover, where he visited the grave of Sir Gawain and wept for his old friend. Then the people of Dover told him how King Arthur and all his knights were slain, and Sir Mordred and all his knights. Then Sir Lancelot wept again, and called all his hosts together and said, 'My fair lords, I thank you all for coming with me into this country, but alas, we have come too late. Since it is so,' said Sir Lancelot, 'I will ride and seek my lady Queen Guinevere; if I do not return in fifteen days, sail back to your own lands.'

So Sir Lancelot departed from them all and rode in search of Queen Guinevere. And at last he came to the convent at Amesbury, and the queen saw him as he walked there in the cloister. She swooned so that all her gentlewomen had work enough to hold her up. When she could speak, she asked her ladies to call him to her.

When Sir Lancelot was brought to her, then she said to all the ladies, 'Through this man and me hath all this war been wrought, and the death of the noblest knights of the world; for through our love . . . is my most noble lord slain. Therefore, Sir Lancelot, know that I am set to get my soul's health . . . and therefore I require thee and beseech thee heartily, for all the love that ever was between us, that thou never see me more in the flesh. And I command thee, on God's behalf, that thou forsake my company . . . for through thee and me is the flower of kings and knights destroyed; therefore, Sir Lancelot, go to thy realm, and there take thee a wife, and live with her in joy and bliss; and I pray thee heartily, pray for me to Our Lord, that I may amend my misliving.'

'Now, sweet madam,' said Sir Lancelot, 'would you that I should turn

✥Malory probably means to go on crusade and win back Jerusalem, something that had faded into a very distant dream by the time he was writing, almost four hundred years since Jerusalem had been taken in the First Crusade, and almost three hundred since it had been lost again.

✥These words ('Here lies Arthur, the once and future king.') were inscribed on the lead cross said to have been found on the tomb of King Arthur by the monks of Glastonbury Abbey in 1191.

BELOW: *Sir Bedivere returns the sword Excalibur after the final battle. Painting by John Mulcaster Carrick.*

again to my country and there wed a lady? No, Madam, that shall I never do, for I shall never be so false to you of that I have promised; but the same destiny that you have taken you to, I will take unto me, for to please Jesu . . . For I take record of God, in you I have had my earthly joy. But since I find you thus disposed, I ensure you faithfully, I will ever take me to penance, and pray while my life lasts.'

❧ *They began with that to part asunder, but no earthly man could tell the sorrow that they began to feel; wringing their hands they wept aloud, as if they could never stop, and both of them fell down swooning for very sorrow. The ladies then with sorrowing faces carried the queen into a chamber, and made themselves busy about her to recover her. And those that were with Sir Lancelot comforted him as best they could; when he was restored he took his arms and went from them without more ado. His heart was heavy as any lead, he would almost rather have lost his life . . . away he went, as if fleeing, to a forest that was before him. He tore his clothes that were rich and rare, and gladly would have left his life. All that night he wept and wrung his hands, and wandered about as if he were insane. But early in the morning, as the day broke, he saw where a little chapel stood; he heard the bell chime slowly, and he went in to the chapel, where a priest was ready to sing mass, and he listened to it in his heart's sorrow.* This was the same chapel where Sir Bedivere had joined the hermit; and Sir Lancelot and Sir Bedivere recognized one another and spoke together after the mass. Sir Bedivere told Sir Lancelot everything that had happened in the battle and after it; and Sir Lancelot's heart almost burst for sorrow. Then he begged the hermit to allow him to join

❧ Anon, *Morte Arthur.*

LEFT: *Dozmary Pool on Bodmin Moor. 'Take thou Excalibur, my good sword, and go with it to yonder water side.'*

them as their brother, and the hermit welcomed him gladly.

After the fifteen days were up, most of the host that Sir Lancelot had brought with him took ship back to France; but Sir Bors and Sir Blamor and Sir Lionel and other knights that were close to Sir Lancelot did not return but rode about the country searching for their lord until they found him at the little hermitage in the forest. And Sir Bors took the habit and joined his lord in the penitential life. For six years they lived together in fasting and penance and prayer, until Sir Lancelot had grown lean with abstinence. Then one night he dreamed that Queen Guinevere was dead; and he was to take her body and bury it in the chapel next to her lord King Arthur. So Sir Lancelot journeyed with eight of his fellows on foot from Glastonbury to Amesbury, where they found that Queen Guinevere had died only half an hour before. Then they took the queen, with a hundred torches burning and with incense burning, and with many prayers and chants they brought her body back to Glastonbury. There they wrapped her in cloth of gold, then put her into a lead coffin, then a marble coffin, and placed her in the tomb next to King Arthur.

ABOVE: *Reconciled at last, Morgan le Fay tends her dying brother King Arthur*

❧ Sir Thomas Malory, *Morte Darthur.*

❧And on the morn the hermit that sometime was Bishop of Canterbury sang the mass of requiem with great devotion. And Sir Lancelot was the first that offered, and then all his eight fellows . . . and then Sir Lancelot swooned, and lay long still, while the hermit came and waked him, and said, 'You are to blame, for you displease God with such manner of sorrow.'

'Truly,' said Sir Lancelot, 'I trust I do not displease God, for He knows my intent. My sorrow was not, nor is not, for any rejoicing of sin, but my sorrow may never have end. For when I remember her beauty and her nobleness, that was both with her king and her, so when I saw his corpse and her corpse so lie together, truly my heart would not serve to sustain my sorrowful body. Also when I remember me how by my default, my vanity and my pride, they were both laid full low, wit you well, this remembered, their kindness and my unkindness, sank so to my heart that I might not sustain myself.'

After that Sir Lancelot would eat nothing, nor drink, till he was dead. Night and day he lay on the tomb, and he sickened and sank. Within six weeks he was dead; and he prayed to the bishop to have his body borne to Joyous Gard ❧. And so it was done. And at Joyous Gard they laid his body in the chapel, with the tomb open, so that the people could see his face; and they sang psalms and prayed about him and, as they were doing so, there came Sir Lancelot's brother Sir Ector, who had been seeking him for seven years.

❧ Malory notes here that some men say Joyous Gard was Alnwick, some Bamburgh, but declines to give his own opinion.

Then went Sir Bors unto Sir Ector and told him how there lay his brother, Sir Lancelot, dead; and then Sir Ector threw his shield, sword and helm from him. And when he beheld Sir Lancelot's face, he fell down in a

AVALON

THE FINAL RESTING PLACE of King Arthur (known as the 'Isle of Avalon' in medieval literature) gave rise to two separate traditions. In the first, Avalon is a mysterious and magical island, situated no one knows where, and seemingly derived from a Celtic legend. In the second, Avalon is Glastonbury in Somerset.

Geoffrey of Monmouth favours the Celtic legend, He mentions Avalon only twice in his *History of the Kings of Britain*, first saying that Arthur's sword was forged there and, afterwards, rather curtly remarking that Arthur was taken there after his final battle 'so that his wounds might be attended to'. In his later *Life of Merlin*, he gives a much more elaborate account, in which the bard Taliesin recounts how he accompanied Arthur to Avalon by boat, where he was received by Morgan, the chief of nine sister enchantresses who live there. Morgan examined Arthur's wound and said that she could heal him if he promised to stay on the island for a very long time.

Glimpses of much older Celtic traditions underlie this account. The first-century Roman writer, Pomponius Mela, recorded that nine priestesses lived together on the Isle of Sein off the coast of Britanny. In the Welsh poem 'The Spoils of Annwfn', the magic cauldron which the heroes are after is kept by nine maidens on a magical otherwordly island.

The root of the name, 'aval', means apple, and Geoffrey calls it *insula pomorum*, the Isle of Apples. It is possible that Geoffrey was using a lost source referring to the fifth-century exploits of Riothamus and is thinking of the real Avalon, a small town in Burgundy. Many later poets and chroniclers, however, felt at liberty to locate Avalon anywhere, and it turns up in some surprising places, ranging from Sicily to India.

The connection between Avalon and Glastonbury post-dates Geoffrey of Monmouth and probably post-dates the alleged discovery of King Arthur's tomb by the monks in 1191. Gerald of Wales, writing about the discovery of the grave, remarks:

What is now called Glastonbury was in former times called the Isle of Avallon, for it is almost an island, being entirely surrounded by marshes, whence it is named in British 'Inis Avalon', that is the apple-bearing island, because apples used to abound there. Morgan, a noblewoman of that region, and closely related to Arthur, after the Battle of Camlann carried him away to the island now called Glastonbury to be healed of his wounds. It also used to be called in British 'Inis Gutrin', that is, the Isle of Glass, and hence the Saxons called it Glastonbury.

Subsequently, this connection was strengthened by Robert de Boron and other romance authors, who wrote that the keepers of the Grail brought it west to the 'vales of Avalon', and clearly believe that this is a reference to Glastonbury. A later addition to the work of William of Malmesbury describes how Joseph of Arimathea arrived in Britain in AD 63 and founded the Old Church at Glastonbury.

But there was another and older connection between Arthur and Glastonbury, recorded by Carodoc of Llancarfan in his *Life of St Gildas*. Archaeological excavations in Glastonbury in the 1960s showed that there had been thriving Celtic communities in pre-Roman times, centring on two lake-villages built on artificial islands in the marshes below the Tor. The Christian community which later developed into the abbey was indubitably very ancient, and it almost certainly contained a tradition the Celts had already begun by associating Glastonbury, and especially the Tor, with religious worship.

swoon. And when he waked it were hard for any tongue to tell the doleful complaints that he made for his brother.

'Ah Lancelot,' he said, 'you were head of all Christian knights, and now I dare say . . . that you were never matched of any earthly knight's hand. And you were the most courteous knight that ever bore shield. And you were the truest friend to your lover that ever bestrode horse, and you were the truest lover, of sinful man, that ever loved woman, and you were the kindest man that ever struck with sword. And you were the goodliest person that ever came among press of knights; and you were the sternest knight to your mortal foe that ever put spear in rest.' Then was there weeping and sorrow out of measure. Thus they kept Sir Lancelot's corpse aloft fifteen days, and then they buried it with great devotion. Then at leisure they went all with the Bishop of Canterbury to his hermitage, and there they were together more than a month.

Then Sir Constantine, that was Sir Cador's son of Cornwall, was chosen king of England: he was a full noble knight and worshipfully he ruled his realm. And then this King Constantine sent for the Bishop of Canterbury, for he heard say where he was, and so he was restored unto his bishopric, and left that hermitage; and Sir Bedivere was there ever still a hermit to his life's end.

OPPOSITE: *King Arthur in Avalon. Painting by Burne-Jones.*

LIST OF PRINCIPAL CHARACTERS

Accolon of Gaul, Sir
Lover of Morgan le Fay, employed by her in a plot to kill King Arthur; killed in single combat by Arthur.

Agravain, Sir
Knight of the Round Table; younger brother of Sir Gawain; joined with Sir Mordred to expose Lancelot's and Guinevere's adultery to King Arthur; killed by Sir Lancelot.

Arthur, King
King of Logres (England) and High King over a large number of other countries; crowned Roman Emperor according to some sources. Son of Uther Pendragon and Igraine of Cornwall, husband of Queen Guinevere. Founder of the Round Table.

Balan, Sir
Knight of the Round Table, brother of Sir Balin; killed by Balin in single combat.

Balin le Savage, Sir
Knight of the Round Table, from Northumberland, who struck the Dolorous Stroke; killed and was killed by his brother Sir Balan. Also known as the Knight with the Two Swords.

Bedivere, Sir
Knight of the Round Table, supporter of Arthur from the beginning of his reign; the only knight to survive the Battle of Camlann.

Bernard of Astolat, Sir
Father of Elaine of Astolat, Sir Lavaine and Sir Tirry.

Bertilak de Hautdesert, Sir
Lord of the castle of Hautdesert, where Sir Gawain stayed during his quest for the Green Chapel; identical with the Green Knight.

Bors, Sir
Knight of the Round Table, son of King Bors, brother of Sir Lionel; the only knight to achieve the Quest of the Holy Grail, and to survive and return to Arthur's court.

Brangane, Lady
Cousin and confidante of Isolde the Fair, who accidentally allowed Tristan and Isolde to drink the love potion.

Ector, Sir
Foster father of King Arthur and father of Sir Kay the Seneschal.

Elaine of Astolat
Daughter of Sir Bernard of Astolat; died for unrequited love of Sir Lancelot.

Elaine of Corbenic
Daughter of King Pelles, mother of Sir Galahad.

Gaheris, Sir
Knight of the Round Table, younger brother of Sir Gawain; killed by Sir Lancelot.

Galahad, Sir
Son of Sir Lancelot and Elaine of Corbenic. The best knight in the world, who achieves the Quest of the Holy Grail most perfectly.

Gareth, Sir
Knight of the Round Table, younger brother of Sir Gawain; killed by Sir Lancelot.

Gawain, Sir
Knight of the Round Table, son of King Lot of Orkney and Queen Morgause, nephew of King Arthur; hero of many romances; killed in battle against his half-brother Sir Mordred.

Guinevere, Queen
Daughter of King Leodegraunce of Cameliard, wife of King Arthur, lover of Sir Lancelot.

Igraine
Duchess of Cornwall, wife of Gorlois of Cornwall, and subsequently of Uther Pendragon. Mother of Morgan le Fay and Morgause by Gorlois, and of Arthur by Uther.

Isolde the Fair
Daughter of King Anguish and Queen Isolde of Ireland, wife of King Mark

of Cornwall, lover of Sir Tristan.

Isolde of the White Hands
Daughter of Duke Hoel of Brittany, wife of Sir Tristan.

Kay the Seneschal, Sir
Knight of the Round Table, son of Sir Ector and foster-brother and seneschal of King Arthur.

Lady of the Lake
Mysterious faery lady who gave Excalibur to Arthur, subsequently killed by Sir Balin; also brought up Sir Lancelot du Lake from infancy.

Lancelot, Sir
Knight of the Round Table, son of King Ban of Benwick, lover of Queen Guinevere, hero of many romances and best knight after Sir Galahad.

Lot of Orkney, King
King of Orkney, Lothian and (in Geoffrey of Monmouth) Norway. Husband of Arthur's half-sister Morgause/Anna, father of Gawain, Gaheris, Gareth and Agravain; killed by King Pellinore.

Mark, King of Cornwall
Uncle of Sir Tristan and husband of Isolde the Fair.

Meleagant, Sir
Son of King Bagdemagus of Gorre, abducted Queen Guinevere; killed by Sir Lancelot.

Merlin
Prophet and magician, adviser to King Uther Pendragon and subsequently to King Arthur, whose early life he guided.

Mordred, Sir
Knight of the Round Table, illegitimate son of King Arthur's incestuous liason with his half-sister Morgause. Usurped throne; killed by King Arthur at the Battle of Camlann.

Morgan le Fay, Queen
Daughter of Gorlois and Igraine of Cornwall, half-sister and enemy of King

Arthur, enchantress, wife of King Urien of Gore.

Morgause, Queen
Daughter of Gorlois and Igraine of Cornwall, half-sister of King Arthur, by whom she conceived Sir Mordred. Wife of King Lot of Orkney, and mother of Sir Gawain, Sir Gareth, Sir Gaheris and Sir Agravain.

Nimue/Niniane/ Viviane
A damsel of the lake, who learned magic from Merlin and then imprisoned him in a stone tomb.

Pelles, King
The Maimed King of Castle Corbenic. Descended from Joseph of Arimathea and guardian of the Holy Grail; father of Elaine and grandfather of the Grail knight, Sir Galahad. Maimed by Sir Balin (the Dolorous Stroke), healed by Sir Galahad.

Pellinore, King
Knight of the Round Table, ally of King Arthur, father of Sir Perceval, Sir Tor, Sir Lamorak and Sir Aglovale; killed King Lot of Orkney and was killed by Sir Gawain in revenge.

Perceval, Sir
Knight of the Round Table, son of King Pellinore according to Malory; original hero of the Grail quest, relegated to second best by author of the *Queste del Saint Graal*.

Tristan, Sir
Son of Rivalin and Blanchefleur, nephew of King Mark of Cornwall, lover of Isolde the Fair, husband of Isolde of the White Hands.

Uriens of Gore, King
King of Gore, husband of King Arthur's half-sister Morgan le Fay, father of Ywain.

Uther Pendragon, King
King of England; father of Arthur.

GLOSSARY

assay   make an attempt

avoid   dismount from or get clear of a horse

bascinet   a light steel helmet

beaver   lower face guard of helmet

beguile   deceive

bezant   a valuable gold coin, originally minted in Byzantium

brachet   hunting dog

Candlemas   the feast of the Purification of the Virgin Mary and the presentation of Christ in the Temple, so-called because candles were blessed on that day—2 February

careful   sorrowful

charger   a very large, powerful horse, capable of carrying a knight in armour, and trained for cavalry use

cob   a sturdy, short-legged riding horse

coif   either a chain mail hood or close-fitting metal cap to protect a knight's head

despite   malicious injury

dole   sorrow

dolorous   sorrowful, painful

fealty   the obligation of loyalty and service which a tenant or vassal must swear to his overlord

fewter   to place the spear in rest before charging

fountain   sometimes means a well, but more usually in romance is a natural spring with either a stream or a pool attached

ghostly   spiritual

hart   male deer at least five years old; white harts are frequently hunted through the pages of medieval romance

hauberk   coat of mail, particularly the part which covered the upper body

kirtle   long lady's overgarment

leech   healer, physician

Logres   kingdom over which Arthur rules, roughly corresponding to England and South Wales

malady   sickness

mêlée   the part of a tournament in which teams of knights attack one another all at once, rather than the individual jousts

nasal   a metal bar on a helmet to protect the nose

orgule   pride

palfrey   a standard riding horse, especially for ladies; not big enough to carry a knight in full armour

paramour   lover, sweetheart

passing   one of Malory's favourite qualifying adjectives; a cross between 'very' and 'really'

pavilion   an ornate and splendid tent

prowess   a knight's ability to fight well; a combination of great courage and outstanding skill at handling weapons

recreant   coward, disgraced person

saddle-bow   the raised, reinforced rear of a knight's saddle, which helped him to keep his seat under the impact of striking a target with his lance

samite   a rich silk fabric, sometimes interwoven with gold

Saracen   properly an Arab or Muslim from Syria/Arabia; but popularly in romances any heathen.

seneschal   the steward of a great lord or king, in charge of his household and with all other household officers under him

serf   an unfree labourer permanently attached to the land he works, and therefore to the lord who holds the land

shriven   the state of grace one is in after a priest has heard one's confession and given absolution from sin on condition of completed penance

siege   chair; Siege Perilous = dangerous chair

surplice   loose white over-garment worn by priests

swoon   faint, lose consciousness

tierce   the third hour of the monastic daily round; about nine a.m.

trespass   sin, offence

truncheon   the broken-off shaft of a spear or lance

venery   the art of hunting

wax   grow

ween   think, judge

yeoman   a freeman whose land is worth at least forty shillings a year; often an independent farmer, but sometimes a servant in a noble household

PICTURE CREDITS